P.S.

A MEMOIR

P.S.

A MEMOIR

PIERRE SALINGER

St. Martin's Press ❦ *New York*

Grateful acknowledgment is made for permission to reprint excerpts from articles published in the *San Francisco Chronicle*.

Library of Congress Cataloging-in-Publication Data

Salinger, Pierre.
    P.S., a memoir / Pierre Salinger.
      p.   cm.
    "A Thomas Dunne book."
    ISBN 0-312-13578-5 (hardcover)
    1. Salinger, Pierre.   2. Politicians—United States—Biography.   3. Journalists—United States—Biography.
I. Title.
E840.8.S255A3 1995
070'.92—dc20
[B]   95-30777
                                       CIP

First Edition: October 1995

10 9 8 7 6 5 4 3 2 1

To Justin, Joshua, and Sasha Salinger,
my grandchildren,
and to Juliette de Menthon, my stepgrandchild.

ACKNOWLEDGMENTS

I AM DEEPLY indebted to a number of people for their help in the preparation of these memoirs, which I am pleased to present.

Obviously, the key person who helped me write this book was John Greenya. I have known John since 1983, when I brought him to France, where I was living at the time, to help meet a tough deadline for a series of articles on the twentieth anniversary of the assassination of President Kennedy. John was recommended to me and Leonard Gross (with whom I later wrote two novels) as an excellent writer with expertise in archival research. John did a survey for us in the United States, and then I brought him to Paris to help us finish the articles, which were for *Stern*, a major German magazine.

In 1993, when I'd moved back to the United States after twenty-five years in Europe, I ran into John at a reception in Washington for David Frost. I mentioned that in addition to having retired from ABC and gone to work for Burson-Marsteller, I had started to write my memoirs. That must have sounded like a very full plate, for several days later I got a note from John in which he offered to help. I called him that same day, and we quickly came to an accord that John would help me on the book. The first thing I did was to hand over to him—to have *trucked* over to him—close to a hundred boxes of files, notes, letters, articles, and other information I had kept for years (almost all of which will end up in the John F. Kennedy Library). He went through all of these papers and found fascinating things, many of which I would have forgotten had he not found them. For a year and a half, John worked around the clock helping me on the memoirs, and although (at his request) his name is not on the jacket or title page, he deserves high praise for the wonderful work he did for me and with me.

A number of my family members contributed to this book. All of them were interviewed, by phone or in person, by John Greenya. At the top of the list is my mother, Jehanne Salinger Carlson, who has played such an important role in my life, and who, although now ninety-eight years old, still has a wonderfully detailed memory of my past. The interviews also included my children, Suzanne, Stephen, and Gregory, my brothers, Herbert and George, and my half-sister, Anne. My wife, Poppy (Nicole), also did a tremendous job of helping us on the book. In addition, because she is French, her help was particularly useful in relation to the French edition, which is being published in France at the same time as this version is being published in the United States. Lots of friends, some of whom go back to, and even beyond, the days of the Kennedy administration, were also interviewed by John. The short list includes Barbara Gamarekian, Sue Vogelsinger, Tom Mathews, Bill Wilson, Art Hoppe, Bonnie Mathews, Barbara Coleman, Les Whitten, Al Bayer, Betty Duffy, Sir David Frost, John Florescu, Donald Rinkler, and Jim McManus, among others.

I also want to thank Tracey Thornton, my assistant at Burson-Marsteller, who became involved not just with my work for the company, but also with the book. I want to thank my literary agent, Ed Victor, whom I met in London, and who arranged my contract with St. Martin's Press. Finally, I salute my editors at St. Martin's—Thomas Dunne, publisher of Thomas Dunne Books, and Jeremy Katz—to whom I give my great thanks. Their advice, especially as to what should be in the book, is greatly appreciated.

INTRODUCTION

EARLY IN 1991, with the Gulf War coming to an end, I was seized by a sudden mad desire to run for President of the United States. True, my governmental career—investigator for the Senate Labor Rackets Committee, press secretary to Presidents John F. Kennedy and Lyndon Johnson, and (for five days short of five months) United States senator from California—had been rather brief. But my global views had been expanding for thirty years and I could see that there were many elements of American policy, both foreign and domestic, that needed fixing.

As I studied the prospect of running, however, it became increasingly obvious there were dramatic new views concerning the media's coverage of American presidential candidates. Back in 1960, when John Kennedy ran for office, the media were not interested in his private life. But now a candidate's private life is of paramount interest to the media. The more I thought about this, the more I realized that there probably wasn't anyone interested in running for the presidency who did not have *some* dirty little secret, or secrets, that he (or she) would rather keep from the media.

Certainly, I reflected, that would be a central problem for my candidacy.

Over the decades of my life—that is until 1983, when I met Poppy, my current wife—I'd had scores of mistresses. What's more, my first three wives had all had affairs with other gentlemen. I didn't much like that, but it certainly made it easier for me to have mistresses.

So, as far as my race for the presidency went, I definitely had a problem. What to do?

Finally, I had an idea. I would buy a half hour of time on all three major networks (well, maybe Fox, too) and announce my candidacy in a unique fashion. Here's the draft of what I planned to say:

> Ladies and gentlemen, I have decided to become a candidate for President of the United States. I will soon be giving you important details on what I will do if elected, how I would restructure America so as to improve your daily lives and straighten out our foreign policy.
>
> However, ladies and gentlemen, as you are all well aware, we live in a new era of presidential politics. As a result, the minute I announce my candidacy the media will leap upon my past and ferret out whatever they can about my private life.
>
> Well, I have decided to save them the considerable amount of time they would have spent on this issue.
>
> Here's the truth. From the early 1950s until 1983, I had dozens—no, *scores*—of mistresses.
>
> While campaigning for United States senator from California in 1964, I made love practically every night with the wife of a famous American actor.
>
> While in the White House, on several occasions President Kennedy encouraged me to take a lover, an obvious sign he also had some himself.
>
> In France, a country where the majority of men have mistresses, I happily embraced the French mentality. There is no need to identify these women, but there is the possibility some may emerge to verify the truth of what I am claiming.
>
> I am now, as I said, living very happily with my fourth wife. Her name is Nicole (or at least it was; she has changed it to Poppy). Since meeting her in 1983, I have abandoned mistresses because of my great love for her.
>
> So, ladies and gentlemen, I know what I've just said will shock some of you, and may cause you to decide not to vote for me. But for those of you who understand that private life is private life, I want to go forward with my views on how to improve the future of America. . . .

Obviously, the rest of the speech I drafted dealt with the serious issues of America's foreign and domestic policy. I polished it for months, and then it came to me: I didn't really want to be President of the United States (not to mention the unlikelihood of actually getting elected).

But, thanks to my career in government, which began when I was thirty-two and ended six years later, I became a global person. I was launched on a lifetime of covering, and conversing with, most of the major world leaders of my day.

Looking back, it's clear that in addition to all the good times, I've had my share of tragedy. I lost two of the greatest men I've ever known to assassination—and a son to suicide. But like the 120-year-old French woman just designated the oldest living human by the *Guinness Book of World Records,* whenever anything truly bad happens, "I just turn another page." That ability has served us both well.

On the positive side, which is where I choose to dwell, I have enjoyed a life that has been, for the most part, filled to the brim with the finer things— music, poetry, Bordeaux wine, cigars, *amour,* chess, children, and work worth doing.

It's been quite a life, and, take it from an old newspaperman, quite a story. I hope you'll enjoy reading about it as much as I have living it.

Pierre Salinger
Washington, D.C.
March 1995

P.S.

A MEMOIR

CHAPTER ONE

I FLEXED MY fingers, squirmed slightly on the piano bench, and tried to sneak a glance out at the audience. Even though I'd been practicing the piece for months, it was all I could do to remember the opening bars of Joseph Haydn's Piano Sonata No. 2 without being distracted by the presence of my parents, my brother Herbert, and various friends and relatives. But then, I had reason to be nervous—it was June 21, 1931, and I had just turned six.

More than sixty years later, as I was gathering material for these memoirs, I ran across an old blue copybook, covered in oilcloth. Inside the front cover, in my mother's distinctive handwriting, it says: "Pierre's homework when six years old, at 3965 Sacramento Street, San Francisco." It is dated January 27, 1932.

On the first page, in *my* handwriting, which was distinct, if not as yet distinctive, is a poem for St. Valentine's Day. ". . . The paper is lacy, The rose is Red, I made the words up in my head. I love you."

The next page has only four words: "*deux inventions par Bach.*"

Those juxtapositions—from English to French in language and from verse to music in form—quite accurately reflect the main concerns of my early life.

The first of four sons born to an American Jewish father and a French Catholic mother, I was a child prodigy (that really is the only word for it) on the piano, and as a result my early life was rather unusual.

The rest of the little copybook contains more verse—some in English, some in French—and page after page of multiplication exercises, plus a few letters in both languages. The pages of arithmetic are in the book because, like most children who display a gift for a musical instrument at an absurdly early age, I was tutored at home.

In fact, I did not have what some might call a "normal" childhood until I was almost twelve years old. But that's getting ahead of the story.

It's pretty much of a toss-up as to which of my parents had the more interesting background. My father, Herbert Salinger, was born in New York City to a Jewish family that had come over from Germany in the mid-1800s. Part of the original Salinger clan went south, where, I'm told, they set up a dry-goods company that helped supply uniforms for the Confederate army during the Civil War, while the other half stayed in New York and got heavily into real estate. Unfortunately for the southern Salingers, they were paid in Confederate money, and as a result they went bust when the war was over, while their northern cousins did very well indeed.

It has long been my recollection, based on discussions with various family members, that when my father was still in his twenties, he turned his back on Judaism to join a Christian sect, as a result of which, by the time my brothers and I arrived on the scene, there really was no Jewish influence to speak of. I am now told, by other family members, that this is not so; they say that while he did display an interest in the Ethical Culture movement, he never became a Christian, formally or otherwise. In fact, he was buried in a Jewish cemetery in San Francisco, with a rabbi performing the ceremony.

My father was a mining engineer—that was the interest that drove him west—but he loved music deeply. Along with his brother, Edgar, an excellent cellist, he founded a symphony orchestra in Salt Lake City, where, for a time, he was also an impresario, staging concerts for the likes of pianist Harold Bauer and the soprano Madame Schumann-Heink. From Salt Lake City, my father moved to San Francisco, where he married and had a daughter, my half sister, Anne (who, along with my brothers Herb and George, recently set me straight as to the extent of my father's Judaism).

The route that brought Jehanne Bietry, my mother, to California was even more unusual. Born on March 29, 1897, in an area of eastern France known as the Territoire de Belfort (in the city of Feche l'Eglise), she was the first of two daughters of Pierre Bietry, a figure of some controversy in French history. The founder of the Syndicat des Jaunes, or the Yellow Labor Union, an anti-Communist group that replaced striking workers, he moved to Brittany in 1906 to start a newspaper. The real purpose of the paper, however, was to drum up support for my grandfather's candidacy for the Assemblée Nationale, the French parliament. The ploy worked. Elected to that august body by eighty-six votes, he served from 1906 to 1910, when he declined to seek reelection.

The highlight of my grandfather's public service was his vigorous defense of Capt. Alfred Dreyfus, who had been convicted of treason (the betrayal of military secrets) in 1894. He had been sent to the infamous Devils Island, to be imprisoned for life. After it came to light that evidence proving Dreyfus's innocence (and a Major Esterhazy's guilt) had been suppressed by the military, Dreyfus became, to many Frenchmen of the day, but especially to liberal intellectuals, a symbol of injustice and right-wing repression.

At one point in 1906, my grandfather's remarks on behalf of Dreyfus became so heated that the Assemblée was shut down for the day and my grandfather ejected. Several years later, in 1914, at the outbreak of World War I, having fallen for another woman, he moved to Indochina, where he again set up a newspaper, this time in Saigon.

In 1918, while my mother and her sister, Irene, were still in school in Paris, they received word that Pierre Bietry, their father, had died suddenly at the age of thirty-nine. With that, the two young women—*Maman* was twenty-one and Irene eighteen—set off for Indochina, to protect the family's interests. My mother (who, as I write this, just celebrated her ninety-eighth birthday) has always been one to meet life's problems head-on. She managed to find a writing assignment (while her sister scandalized the family by falling madly, and unrequitedly, in love with the handsome young chauffeur).

While in the Far East, my mother traveled to China and Cambodia, met a number of people, and, as a result of her own diligence, her intelligence, and her personality, made such a favorable impression that the governor-general of Indochina asked her to cover the first Pan-Pacific conference, in Honolulu, as a journalist. After the conference, she decided to visit the United States, so she and Irene then set sail for California. The year was 1921.

Two weeks into their visit, my mother went to a party in San Francisco, and it was there that she met my father. They fell very much in love. She stayed on in the States, and one year later, in 1922, his divorce newly granted, they were married.

At the time, there was an important French community in San Francisco, and my mother became editor in chief of *Courrier du Pacifique,* a daily French newspaper that had a circulation of ten thousand. At the same time, she was special editor for art and music for the *San Francisco Examiner.* My father continued his work as a mining engineer, and from the beginning their home was a haven for writers, musicians, and other interesting folks.

My parents had been married for more than two years when I appeared on the scene, the first of four Salinger boys. I was born on June 14, 1925, my brother Herbert in 1926, followed by George in 1929 and Richard in 1931.

With the Wall Street crash signaling the start of the Great Depression, my father, like so many other Americans, lost his job. Fortunately, he was offered a position in Canada, and in 1929 we moved to Toronto. The next few years, while tough, were far easier for us than for many of my parents' friends and neighbors back in San Francisco.

It was in Canada (where my mother continued her art and music criticism) that my musical bent was taken seriously by my parents. The following, taken from an oral family history, is my mother's account of how she and my father originally came to see that my interest in and aptitude for music was different from and deeper than that of other precocious youngsters.

"When Pierre was a little fellow, we had a baby grand piano in the house. Even before he could get up on the stool, Pierre would not hit on the keys as most children do, but would put his finger and his ear to the key, just one key, to see how it sounded.

"I had a friend who was often at the house in those days, a very extraordinary man. One day when he was there, he was watching Pierre, who was only four years old, and he said, 'Do you know what's going on with your little boy? It's very interesting. He is listening to *sound*. He is not just putting his fingers on the piano; he is listening to what it is like. He is a born musician, and you should watch him.'

"When we moved to Toronto the next year, we met some wonderful people who were musicians and teachers, and my husband said, 'We have this friend who thinks that our little fellow has an ear for music.' I asked Pierre if he wanted to play the piano, and we sat him on the stool and let him loose, and the same thing occurred, except this time he was playing on a black note. So we said, 'See what you can do with him,' and that's how it happened."

Not long thereafter, my parents enrolled me in the Toronto Conservatory of Music, where my teacher was the brilliant Clement Hambourg, and my life as a student took on a regimen well known to any very young music student. Each weekday, a tutor came to the house for three hours of academic instruction, and when she left, I was "free" to practice the piano for four or five hours.

I had the same basic instruction given to any beginning student of the piano, except that there was more concentration on the ability to move the fingers and hands around the keyboard properly. There was even a separate book for that, because it was the most important basic skill for a very young player who was being groomed for a career as a concert pianist.

My "classroom" education, while only a half-time operation compared with that of my friends back in San Francisco, was also fast-paced and rather demanding. The teaching was in French, but that presented no real problem, as I had always been bilingual. In fact, I made my first trip to Paris when I was only six months old. We'd gone over to get my mother's mother, who was to live with us in the United States for the rest of her life. As my grand-mère would never learn English, I was exposed to French, in amounts at least equal to English, from the very beginning of my speaking days.

As the blue copybook indicates, I was very interested in verse, my own as well as that of others. For example, an early page contains this one:

New year's
    day
Janury 1st
last night while we
were fast asleep,
the old year went
away. It can't come
back again because
A new one's come to stay.

Another entry was in French.

    Copie de la Dictée.
La table est ronde. Il ya six tasses sur la table. J'aime la musique.
J'aime le piano. Je joue le petit berger par Debussy et aussi La
Fille aux Cheveux de Lin et deux inventions par Bach

What this means, in its baby French, is simply that this was a dictation exercise. In English it reads: "The table is round. There are six cups on the table. I love music. I love the piano. I play 'The Little Shepherd' by Debussy and also 'The Girl with the Flaxen Hair' and two inventions by Bach."

I did indeed love music and the piano. During that time, in addition to Bach and Debussy, I was falling in love with Beethoven and, a somewhat unlikely addition to the list, the American George Gershwin. (Just a few years later, when we were again living in San Francisco, I was taken back-stage by my mother, by then the art and music critic of the *Examiner,* to meet and shake the hand of Gershwin himself.)

In 1932, after a year of home tutoring, and with my family now back in the States, I was placed in an actual school for the first time in my life. I can still recall how very nervous it had made me to be surrounded, sud-denly, by so many other youngsters. Within a year, I went from a parochial school (where the nuns did not believe in sparing the rod) to a public school and then to a private secular school with the unlikely name of the Presidio Open Air School.

The Presidio was everything that the other schools were not. It was totally free-form, no structure whatsoever. My class had all of six students, and the school's total enrollment was probably twenty. Classroom instruc-tion as it is normally known did not exist at the Presidio School. We sat around "discussing" topics, writing poems, and drawing whatever we felt like drawing. No one *ever* got hit. (That would have been unthinkable.) By that point, I had two more brothers, George and Richard having been born in Toronto, and if memory serves, eventually all four Salinger boys graduated from the Presidio School.

Art Hoppe, the distinguished columnist for the *San Francisco Chron-icle*, was one of my classmates. Years later, I asked Art if he knew why it was called the Presidio Open Air School.

"Perhaps," he said, "because there was an open field next to it where we grew vegetables that ended up in the school lunch program. That was the only thing that was open-air about it. The school, which was founded in 1918 by two Jewish grandes dames after a visit by Madame Montessori, offered a progressive education. But you progressed *individually.* They just let you sit there, if that's what you wanted to do, and in some subjects I did. And so I got passed in math by a little nerd named Pierre Salinger."

My memories are much the same as Art's, and equally fond. Like him, I too remember in particular one of the founders, Flora Arnstein, an extraordinary teacher. But *all* the teachers there truly inspired us to seek higher education. That was a very happy period in my young life.

San Francisco, a wonderfully open society in those days, was filled with great characters. You never knew where you'd run into them, or what impact they might have on your life. For example, in the summer of 1937, the year I graduated from the Presidio School, my mother sent me for a month to a camp run by the ILWU, the International Longshoremen's and Warehousemen's Union. The camp, which was absolutely wonderful, and which gave me my first opportunity to play with both black and white kids, was totally nonpolitical. Yet years later, I would be criticized for attending, and my mother for sending me.

Our crime? The head of the ILWU had been Harry Bridges, the Australian-born trade unionist, and, allegedly, a hard-line Communist who was later the object of numerous (unsuccessful) deportation proceedings. Neither my mother nor I had ever had any truck with Communists, but for some people, especially in my home state of California, guilt by association was guilt period.

While it was my father's new job that brought us back to "that city by the Bay," it didn't take my mother long to land a wonderful position on her own: director of the music project of the San Francisco section of the WPA, the Works Progress Administration, created by President Roosevelt. Her section aided writers, artists, and musicians. If our house had been a refuge for such people prior to our sojourn in Canada, after our return it became a haven.

Every night, it seemed, there were grand figures at our dinner table— musicians and writers, poets and photographers. They all came, and, for the most part, they all held forth, and the effect on me and my brothers was enormously beneficial. At the time, I was increasingly interested in becoming a composer rather than a performer, and I was much influenced by the stream of musicians, several of whom were composers, that flowed through my parents' house. Among the people I recall most vividly are Edgar Varèse, the French-born composer; Yehudi Menuhin; Pierre Monteux; Ernst Bacon; Henry Cowell; and Ernest Bloch. It was at about this same time that I met and concertized with a young Russian who had just moved to San Francisco. His name was Isaac Stern, and we became grand friends.

I remember the look of intense concentration my father would get when listening to Ernest Bloch play his cello, especially if he was playing one of his own works, such as "Schelomo." Perhaps the fact that Bloch based a lot of his themes on traditional Jewish modes and melodies accounted for that faraway look on the faces of my father and his brother. As for Henry Cowell, I can still recall my shock and dismay at seeing him, for the first time, smashing the piano keys with his *elbows.* That technique would hardly have met with the approval of my piano teachers.

As for my own piano career, after moving back to California, I continued to play concerts, often with other young students. My teacher was Lev Shorr, the famous Russian who shaped the careers of so many fine pianists who went on to musical fame.

In 1937, I left the Presidio School to enter Lowell High. I was all of twelve, and thus a full two years younger than my classmates. In those days, twelve was about the age at which American boys who were training to become classical musicians began to show signs of restlessness. They wanted to go outside with their friends and play ball, go to parties and picnics (sometimes even with girls!). But not me.

I was quite happy in my pursuit of a professional career in music. It was my *parents* who were not! This is how my mother described (in the oral family history mentioned earlier) the enforced turn of events.

"When we came back to California, he had a teacher of Russian origin by the name of Lev Shorr, who was a great pianist, so we put Pierre in his hands. He was completely taken by the musical ability of Pierre, who by then was older. He came to us and said, 'You have to take this boy out of school because he should have full time to practice, and you should have a tutor for him. You should not allow him to waste his time in school. He can progress just as well in his education with a tutor, but the major part of his time should be spent on the piano.'

"His father and I talked it over and we both came to the same conclusion: We do not want our son to be a concert pianist. He will not be able to have a family because he will be traveling everywhere and will never be home."

When that interview took place, in either 1986 or 1987, my mother was not unaware of the irony of her earlier statement. She then amended, "This could not have been destiny, because of the life Pierre has been [living] as a journalist with the *Chronicle,* and later when he moved in a more busy circle. He has been traveling more than he's been at home, as is still the case today." When the interviewer commented that, seeing as how I ended up traveling extensively anyway, apparently I *should* have become a concert pianist, my mother said only, "When I look back, I think what he is doing is fascinating."

One should not quarrel with one's own mother, but I do remember that time and that decision somewhat differently. It's true that I had gotten into music very heavily. Not only was I studying the piano assiduously but I was also studying composition and conducting, *and* I'd recently taken up the violin. It is, however, also true that I was becoming less and less pleased with the life I was leading. I'm afraid Art Hoppe was right—I *was* a nerd. I had no friends my own age, and I had rarely swung a bat or thrown a ball. My only nonmusical, nonschool activity was chess (which I'd learned from the French composer LaViolette, with whom I was studying conducting); and with my usual level of intensity, it took me only one year, until I was twelve, to become a junior champion. So the decision to de-emphasize music and to attend Lowell High School just like all the other students (well, almost just like them) was my decision, as well.

Looking back, it's clear this was one of the major decisions of my life. In effect, it ended my career as a concert pianist. A few years later, I'd make a stab at it again by studying music composition with the composer Ray Green and by doing more conducting work with LaViolette, but it would never be the same.

Many years later, I would play for friends and do family musicales with my children, and twice I would even play the piano in the White House for two musical greats, Igor Stravinsky (who got up and left before I had finished) and Van Cliburn (who did not). But never again would I define myself as a musician.

In 1940, when I was fifteen, my world turned upside down. The date was November 18, and my brother Herb and I were at a concert, listening intently to a performance of Sibelius's First Symphony, when I felt someone tap me on the shoulder.

"Are you Pierre Salinger?"

"Yes," I replied.

"You should go home right away. Your father has had a serious auto accident."

Two days later, in a hospital in British Columbia, where he'd been traveling on a business trip, my father died. I can still remember the contretemps I had with my mother over my refusal to go to the funeral home and view his body, which was laid out in an open casket. Even in the face of my mother's insistence, I was adamant. He had been a wonderful father, and I preferred to remember him as he'd been when he was alive.

As might be expected, my father's death had a major impact on our family and its circumstances. At fifteen, I was the eldest. My brothers were fourteen, eleven, and nine, and our grandmother, who still lived with us, was quite elderly. My mother's job, while a very responsible one, paid very little; thus, our total family income was drastically reduced. I learned one of my first lessons in the importance of families, and how they stick together in times of trouble, when my mother told us that our uncle, my father's brother, was sending us a check every month. Still, things were tough, and, as a family, we had to hunker down.

I may have been only fifteen when my father died, but I was already a high school junior. I cannot say that those high school years, even the two while my father was still living, were particularly memorable. Being so much younger than my classmates made it hard to make friends or to compete athletically, and, to tell the truth, there were many times when I realized I missed the life I'd led, different as it was, and also the dream of concertizing. As for any kind of fun, even the most innocent, with girls, forget about it. I had my first and only date in high school on the very last day, for the senior graduation dance.

One very good thing did happen to me in high school. It was there that I discovered my love for journalism. Up to that time, most of my writing had been poetry, which is not usually thought of as a training ground for reporters. However, I learned that in addition to enjoying words for the way they could evoke emotion, I also loved them for their usefulness in conveying the kind of information that made news stories.

I became so interested in journalism that in my last year at Lowell High School I decided to try and become the editor of *The Lowell,* the school newspaper. But Lowell was a most democratic place, which meant that you had to be elected to the editorship. So I screwed up my courage and ran—on a platform of eliminating Lowell's sororities and fraternities. I lost big. The victor was a young man with brains enough to know that the Greek societies were the most popular groups in school.

Quite a few years later, when I was John F. Kennedy's press secretary, a most interesting thing happened. We were in dire need of a communications director in Saigon, and I was asked to find one. I turned to Edward R. Murrow, then the head of the United States Information Agency (USIA), and asked him to suggest some candidates. Murrow soon sent me a list of six names, along with their résumés, and, lo and behold, there on the list was Charles Davis—the same man who'd defeated me in the race for editor of the Lowell High School paper!

What else could I do but send him to Vietnam? I did not, however, send him there as retribution for having beaten me out of the editor's job; I did so because I admired and respected him highly. He did a great job in Saigon.

My social life would probably have improved in college (even though I was still handicapped by the fact that I was barely sixteen when I started at San Francisco State) had circumstances definitely beyond my control not intervened. I matriculated in the fall of 1941, just a few short months before the Japanese attack on Pearl Harbor.

The night of the attack on Pearl was one I'll never forget. We were at home when someone noticed that people were streaming up and down the streets, carrying newspapers that announced the Japanese attack on Pearl Harbor, incredible news that had not yet been on the radio. We turned on the radio and heard an alert telling people of the attack *and* of the possibility that the Japanese navy had a whole armada just off the coast of San Francisco readying an attack on our city.

We were told to turn off our lights immediately and to spread the word to others. So my brother Herb and I ran through the streets of San Francisco getting people to turn out their lights. Had we not been so frightened, it might have been fun, but everywhere we went we heard the same rumor: The Japanese were going to bomb America, starting with San Francisco!

When Herb and I got back home that night, we were greeted by the news that our Japanese cook, who had been with the family for three years, had disappeared. Months later, we learned that his work at our house had been merely a cover—he was, in fact, a Japanese intelligence agent.

When I went to bed that night, I had difficulty getting to sleep, as did millions of other Americans. We were going to war; there was no longer any doubt about it. Suddenly, for the first time in my life, I felt older than my years.

CHAPTER TWO

I MAY HAVE been one of the youngest males in my class, but I was as anxious to go to war as anyone else, and maybe even more so. Certainly the Nazi invasion of France was a lot more real to me, being half French by birth and living with my French mother and *her* French mother, than to most, if not all, of my classmates. The worried talk around my family's dinner table was not of places they'd read about or seen in the newsreels, but of places they'd been. In addition, the fact that I was younger meant I would have to wait longer to enlist.

I *finally* turned seventeen, on June 14, 1942, and enlisted in the navy that same day. It would be an entire year, however, before I would be called up. In the interim, I kept myself busy with school and looked for a job. To my amazement, instead of a job, I found my life's work.

I'd had just enough experience working on my high school paper that I thought maybe I could get some kind of low-level job on a real newspaper. So I went to the *San Francisco Chronicle,* and they hired me! My official title was desk assistant, which meant copyboy, but almost from the beginning I was sent out to cover stories. This happy (for me) outcome was the result of the fact that so many journalists had joined the military or been drafted. Within a few months, I even had my own beat covering Bay Area companies that were building ships or making arms for the war effort. I was learning how to put together a story, and I loved it.

In June 1943, a few days shy of my eighteenth birthday, I was officially sworn in as a seaman, second class, in the United States Navy. I was ready, willing, and able to fight for my country, but I must confess I didn't expect to do so in North Dakota, which is where the navy sent me one month later.

Dickinson, North Dakota, happens to be (not surprisingly) the home of Dickinson State Teachers College, one of the places where the navy was conducting what it called a V-12 school. The purpose of the V-12 program was to give college students the military education necessary for them to become officers while, at the same time, they continued their normal college studies. That was fine with me. What wasn't fine was the climate. The marvelous weather in San Francisco, which I was used to, can be changeable, but in North Dakota, the changes ran from one end of the thermometer to the other. When I arrived in midsummer, the temperature was in the nineties, but by the dead of winter it fell as low as thirty below, a range of 120 degrees.

Dickinson, a Norman Rockwell kind of place, was as caught up in the war effort as any other town in the United States, and it took us young sailors to its heart. Soon, in addition to our classes, many of us were involved in the local community. In my case, I was recruited to teach history in a local high school. At first, I did not fare too well, with my age again a deterrent factor (some of the seniors were actually older than I), but as I gained confidence, the students came to accept me, and the experiment ended up quite well. Also, when it was learned that I had a journalism background, I soon found myself editing the college paper and doing a column for the local weekly.

The people of Dickinson could not have been more friendly. On the rare nights we could get off campus and into the local taverns, we found it impossible to pay for our own food or drinks. The best fun, however, was the music. I may have abandoned my career as a concert pianist by that point, but I could certainly still play. There were some talented musicians in my V-12 class, and we soon formed a dance band that was so good we were invited to play all over the state.

A crucial part of my ongoing education that also took place in North Dakota happened to be extracurricular. As I said earlier, prior to joining the navy, I'd had but one actual date, at my high school's graduation gala. Throughout high school, my female classmates were all several years older than I. Comparatively speaking, I was a kid, and no high school junior or senior, female variety, wants to date a kid. In Dickinson, however, all that changed. To my great delight, I learned that a uniform did, as rumored, attract women. I can still remember the glorious night in a park in front of the state capitol in Bismarck, North Dakota, where I made love for the first time in my life.

While I was still in Dickinson, there was another woman in my young life. I was convinced I was in love with her. I have vague but nonetheless wonderful memories of making weekend train trips to the tiny town one hundred miles from Dickinson where her parents owned a bar. As the bar was closed on Sundays, we'd spend the entire day there, drinking beer, dancing to the jukebox, and generally mooning and moping over each other. It was grand.

By early 1944, the navy, perhaps frustrated by the fact it took four whole years to produce an officer at the Naval Academy in Annapolis, had opened a school (in Plattsburgh, New York) where it could be done in four *months.* In February, a number of us were selected for the new school, and I said an emotional good-bye to Dickinson. In many ways, I had come of age there. As the train pulled out of the picturesque station, I knew instinctively, in the way the young sometimes do, that I would not be back. I was right.

The program at Plattsburgh was rigorous and highly competitive. Working under brutal deadlines, we learned everything from navigating with sextants to how to make a two-second identification of approaching aircraft. Even though I missed two weeks of classes because of pneumonia, I passed, and on June 27, 1944, I was commissioned as an ensign in the United States Navy, which wasted no time whatsoever in assigning me to subchaser training school in Miami.

In Florida, our training in methods of attack and maneuvering was both exacting and exciting, but I grew increasingly frustrated. We were winning the war, and I wanted to see action before it was all over. So when an officer came into our class one day and asked whether anyone wanted to leave school right away and take up a post, I immediately volunteered. Three days later, I had my orders—I was the new third officer of SC (for subchaser) *1368,* which was "somewhere in the Pacific."

On my way to that assignment, I had the great pleasure of visiting my family in San Francisco (where my mother was the director of the French section of OWI, the Office of War Information; over the radio, she broadcast the propaganda messages to Indochina).

En route, I also had a terrible experience, which involved something very much in the news in recent years, navy officers and sexual harassment. On layover in Honolulu, a group of us, all officers, went out for dinner, after which one of the men invited me to his room for a drink, where he attacked me sexually! He started to pull off my clothes, clearly intent on rape. I fought him off and got out of there. I was so stunned that I never reported his actions. At nineteen, it was too much of a shock to me that an officer in the United States Navy would attempt the homosexual rape of another officer.

Our top secret destination after leaving Honolulu was the Mariana Islands, and my job as the ship's communications officer was to make sure that news did not leak out in letters home. (There I was, a *reporter* in charge of censorship.) However, I figured out that the sailors knew where we were going when I read the twentieth letter stating, "When I get home, I'm going to marry Anna." I was relieved to be relieved of that duty once we docked.

Several days later, we were on another ship, this one headed for the island of Eniwetok, an eight-day voyage. Once there, a small boat picked me up and took me to my new home, *SC-1368,* which was anchored in the harbor. A small but very fast California-built ship, the *SC-1368* was 110 feet long and built entirely of wood. It had what were, for that era, high-tech engines, twin diesels that gave it speeds up to twenty-five knots. (By comparison, the PTs, like the eventually famous *PT-109,* could do forty knots.)

On the ship were twenty-five sailors and three officers. I was coming aboard as the third officer. The commanding officer, a lieutenant, had his own cabin, and the second officer and I shared one. Our job, for months at a time, was to accompany slow-moving tankers from Pearl Harbor to the Mariana Islands, ever alert for Japanese submarines. If we spotted any, we were to attack. At sea, each of the officers was on duty for four hours and off duty for eight. Conditions were not difficult, but we were restricted in our use of water, with the result that whenever we arrived at a port, we all were bearded.

Once aboard the *SC-1368,* I had a serious bout of seasickness. It caused me to write the Navy Department and request a transfer to public relations work on land. The answer that came back was positive; I could do so—"after you've spent two years on a ship."

That negative experience was countered by my learning to play poker. I'd never played before, but many of the crew were excited about the game and urged me to learn (probably thinking they'd found another "fish"). Each month, when the crew and the officers would be paid their meager salary—in cash—the games would begin. There were seven of us who'd agreed to play uninterruptedly (except for when it was time to go on duty) until one of us had won all the money on the table.

It was a tough game, and it took me some months to adjust to it, but fairly soon I became, to my immense delight, the person who walked away with all the cash. In fact, I got so good at poker that I eventually saved over ten thousand dollars, part of which I later used to buy my first car.

After months of escort duty, we were finally assigned to a base in the southern part of Palau, the northern half of which was occupied by the

Japanese. Upon our arrival in Palau, we learned that our commanding officer had been transferred, and a new third officer was assigned. That meant I was now the second officer. My young chest swelled with pride, but I had little idea what was soon to come.

As drinking was not allowed on the ship, about once a month we disembarked on an empty island—and every single man on the ship was given his own case of beer. Because they wouldn't see any more beer for another month, almost every sailor would proceed to drink the entire case during our eight-hour stay on the island. That's three bottles of beer an hour, which doesn't sound too bad—at first.

On one occasion, our brand-new commanding officer was one of the men who drank his entire case. When he came back on board, instead of shoving off for our home port, he ran the ship aground. He was summoned to the flagship and fired, which made me commanding officer—at age nineteen.

One of my first actions as commanding officer was to take a step that was against navy regulations. Upset over what had happened to our commanding officer, and believing that the case-in-one-day policy was as dangerous as it was foolish, I told the crew that the next time we went to the island for our beer day, they would have the right to bring back on board the beer they had not finished drinking. *And,* while under sail, they would have the right to drink one bottle a day. Great joy followed this announcement. The next time we visited the island, no one drank more than four beers, and thereafter the new policy worked perfectly (even if it was against navy rules).

Taking command of the ship caused me some apprehension about my age. Everybody on board, the twenty-five sailors and the two other officers, was older than I. So I decided I should do something to "toughen up" my image. But what? I thought and I thought, and finally it came to me—cigars! I would take up the smoking of cigars. I did so, and instantly I *felt* older and tougher. Little did I know that I had embarked on what would be a lifelong love affair (or what one former wife referred to as an "obsession") with *le cigare.*

Just a few weeks later, I was on duty when I heard shouts and looked up to see a kamikaze *swimmer* stroking toward us. He had but one goal—to plant a bomb on our hull. Fortunately, one of the sailors on deck fired a pistol at him, and, his mission frustrated, he began to swim away. Just then, the bomb exploded. He was killed, our ship was spared, and I had witnessed my first death in wartime.

We were on the island of Guam, in early August of 1945, when we learned that the United States had dropped the first atomic bomb on Hiroshima. About a week later, we got the word the Japanese had surrendered. The war was over.

Our party that night was a classic, and it proved that desperation can also be the mother of invention. We had absolutely no alcohol on board, at least not any legal alcohol, but, as American servicemen were doing throughout Europe and the South Pacific, we improvised. We drained the plain alcohol from the ship's compass and added it to grape juice, which we all consumed until we were quite drunk.

Our happiness at the news of the war's end was short-lived, for we soon learned that SC-1368 was to be converted to a minesweeper and would eventually be sent to the southern seas of Japan. The irony of the fact that we could be killed after the war was over was not lost on any of us.

In October 1945, by which point we had been in Okinawa for a month, I was promoted to lieutenant (junior grade), but I lost my job, anyway. A new commanding officer, who had more experience than I did with minesweeping, was put on the SC-1368. Once again, I became second officer.

One day not long after his arrival, we were about eight hours out of Naha when the red alert sounded. An enormous typhoon was heading for the island. Our return cruise was tough, as we had to go through the typhoon's northern end, but we made it back to the harbor. There, chaos reigned. The parking chains on a number of ships had broken, and the ships were careening about, smashing into one another, causing one or more of them to sink. That day and night, more than one thousand sailors were killed.

The new commanding officer seemed unsure as to which course of action was best. Finally, I told him I thought the only way to save the ship was to run it aground on a sandy beach. I'd found a map that showed the whole bay and where the sandy beaches were located. I laid out the map in front of him and, pointing, said, "Here's where you run the ship aground."

He did so, and just in time, for the winds had reached 180 miles an hour. The situation was becoming more and more desperate.

When the center of the typhoon passed over the island, providing a respite from the storm's fury, I saw that six men were trapped on a reef in the harbor. It was clear to me that they would never survive the second half of the typhoon, now but minutes away.

With ropes looped over our shoulders, two crew members and I plunged into the churning sea for what turned out to be one of the most intense physical and emotional experiences of my life.

Shortly after my active duty ended, I received this communication, signed by Secretary of the Navy James Forrestal:

The President of the United States takes pleasure in presenting the Navy and Marine Corps Medal to Lieutenant, Junior Grade, Pierre Emil George Salinger, for service as set forth in the following. For heroic conduct during a rescue while attached to the USS SC 1368 in Buckner Bay, Okinawa, Ryukyu Islands, October 9, 1945.

Volunteering to lead a rescue party to the aid of six men stranded on a reef after their vessel had been wrecked during a typhoon, Lieutenant Junior Grade Salinger swam through the high surf for approximately one hundred and fifty yards, and with the aid of the other two members of his party, succeeded in rescuing the survivors. By his courage and initiative, he contributed materially to the success of the rescue attempt and upheld the highest traditions of the United States Naval Service.

One next-to-last anecdote. Given the disaster that had occurred in Buckner Bay, the navy decided to demote my new superior, making me commanding officer once again, and to retire *SC-1368* from the minesweeping business. Three days before Christmas, 1945, we arrived on tiny Johnston Island, west of Hawaii. As it had been months and months since anyone on the ship had received any mail, I figured there had to be a lot of it back in naval headquarters at Pearl Harbor. I talked the naval authorities on Johnston Island into putting me on one of the three navy planes that flew to Pearl each day, and when I got to the naval post office, I found an enormous sack of mail for the crew. I flew back to Johnston Island, and on Christmas Eve I played Santa by distributing the oh-so-welcome mail from home. It was a very sentimental party, and it cemented my good relations with the crew, many of whom I kept in touch with for years and years.

We remained on Johnston Island for the rest of the year, and in early January 1946, we headed for Honolulu. From there, we sailed for San Francisco and home, arriving in mid-February. We docked at Angel Island, the very same island in the middle of San Francisco Bay where the Golden Gate International Exposition had been held in 1939.

Now it was time for another memorable party, this one at my house in San Francisco, where my aging French grandmother made an extraordinary meal for the entire crew and my fellow officers. Everyone loved it—and her and the rest of my family—but at one point a crew member made the mistake of asking for catsup! My grand-mère hit the roof. She was justifiably proud of her cooking, and the idea that it needed "improvement" from a lowly catsup bottle was most upsetting.

After dinner, we repaired to a nearby bar, where we continued the celebration until four in the morning. My mother, worried that we were out so very late, kept looking out the window. Finally, she saw the crew members of *SC-1368* carrying me on their shoulders up the hilly street to my house. From then on, my mother understood that from time to time I drank alcohol.

While the ship and I may have been back in San Francisco, my navy career was not quite over. Navy regulations specified that you could not leave the service until you had attained a certain number of points, and I was missing a few. So off I went on a series of train trips, accompanying navy personnel to various cities in the United States as they completed their military service. Over the next four months, I made six round-trip rail journeys—to New Orleans, New York City, Chicago, and Minneapolis, among other cities.

I soon discovered that sailors loved to jump off the train and get a drink on short stops, so, in a stroke of genius, I invented a navy regulation: Anyone who missed his final destination would have to serve another entire year in service. I did not lose a single person.

In June of 1946, I was discharged from the navy, a far more open and confident young man than I had been four years earlier. Of course I had no way of knowing it then, but we would be the last returning American servicemen to be treated as heroes.

CHAPTER THREE

IN *THE BEST YEARS,* Joseph C. Goulden's excellent and aptly named book on the United States in the period immediately after World War II, he writes, "Peace. The return of more than 15,000,000 men and women from war. The strong probability of continuing economic plenty. National confidence. A high degree of unity, born of the shared adventure and triumph of war. An acceptably popular President. . . . Americans truly had reasons to anticipate the best years of their lives."

I must have shared that attitude, for in my first six months back home I took three very positive steps: I managed to get rehired by the *Chronicle,* reenrolled in college, and married—all of this by January 1, 1947, six months before I would turn twenty-two.

I was discharged from the navy on July 3, 1946, and after a day of independence—*on* Independence Day—I was rehired by the *Chronicle* as a reporter, but this time I had a more interesting assignment. Starting that summer, I covered the San Francisco Police Department, and I continued to do so when classes began in the fall. I worked the night shift, four to midnight, so I had to make sure all my classes were over by 3:00 P.M.

Before the war, I'd gone to San Francisco State, mainly because its tuition was low to nonexistent for Californians, but after my discharge, and armed with the purchasing power of the GI bill, one of the many ways Uncle Sam thanked us returning vets, I enrolled in the University of San Francisco, better known locally as USF. As a Catholic growing up in San

Francisco, I'd always been impressed by USF, a Jesuit school, and now that I could afford to go there, I was downright excited.

At San Francisco State before the war, my major had been education (which was why I got involved in teaching in Dickinson, North Dakota), but at USF I majored in history. In addition, I'd always leaned toward journalism. I'd had an excellent four-month course in that subject in my last year at Lowell High School and it had been very helpful when I first went to work for the *Chronicle.* I continued to manifest that interest at the University of San Francisco by becoming managing editor of the school newspaper, *The Foghorn,* which still exists.

USF was everything I'd thought it would be, but, in truth, I was in such a hurry to get on with life that, with only about a year's worth of courses to go, my main goal was the diploma. I'd done pretty well at San Francisco State before the war, but after it I really became a good student. The University of San Francisco and I have now been fast friends for almost fifty years. I'd admired the school greatly before I ever got there, loved it when I was a student there, and have loved and admired it ever since. Five years ago, USF returned the compliment by awarding me an honorary doctorate.

The other half of my life was work. Not every night on the police beat is a big night. There are many nights when nothing happens, and reporters have a lot of time on their hands. Some of them passed it playing poker, but I didn't, despite my newfound love of the game. I had noticed that the investigative reporters I most admired, and whose ranks I hoped to join, spent their downtime trying to come up with a feature story. They'd dig through records or work on new sources. I emulated them.

The records I chose to plow through were the old court and arrest files, especially those having to do with bail bond money, and after a while I began to smell the faint odor of corruption.

It always sounds impressive to people when they read that Judge so-and-so set bond in a murder case at $500,000 (or whatever it might be in such serious cases), but in real life very few people ever put up that amount in full, nor do they do so out of their own pockets. That's where the bail bondsman comes in. For a fee, 10 percent being the usual amount, the bondsman puts up *his* money for the bail, and when the defendant shows up in court, the bondsman gets the money back. The amounts can range from a high of ten thousand dollars for a felony to as low as fifty dollars for a misdemeanor. If the defendant fails to show up, then the court keeps the money, and, in theory, it is deposited in the city's coffers.

I say "in theory" because what I was seeing in the old records was that certain judges were returning the bond money to certain bail bondsmen even though the defendants had not showed up. As a result, the city of San Francisco was being shorted a considerable amount. I went to my editor and got his okay to check it out.

I learned that a number of judges were involved and that they were justifying their actions by reliance on a legal technicality. The more I looked into it, the more it became obvious that it was a racket. What they were doing, quite simply, was robbing the city treasury.

On Friday, October 3, 1947, the *Chronicle* ran a *huge* headline across the top of the front page: JUDGES' "REFUNDING" OF BAIL ON FUGITIVES REVEALED—CITY PAYS! The story, which carried the sole credit "By Pierre Salinger," began:

> The wholesale return of bail to bail bond brokers by San Francisco judges—while the defendants are still fugitives from justice—was uncovered here yesterday. This refunding of bail has cost the City Treasury thousands in the past 19 months and an untold amount of money over the years.
>
> Every single manipulation involved in returning bail is legal. But District Attorney Edmund G. Brown said the cases were "abuses of judicial privilege."

My story put the practice in simple terms. Men were jailed and then released on bail; they failed to appear in court and their bail was forfeited; then, while they were still being hunted by the police, the bail was returned to the bail bond broker who had put it up. The story went on to give further examples, and, citing the reactions of a number of judges and other officials, it ended with a Q and A: "How long has this kind of thing been going on in San Francisco? It is hard to say—but a member of the staff of the District Attorney's offices said, 'This type of bail manipulation has been going on for a long time—and it is perfectly legal too. Nobody took the trouble to dig out the facts before,' he said."

On each of the next four days, to the tune of growing public indignation, I reported on further aspects of the bail bond story. Months later, on October 23, the *Chronicle* ran my final take on the story. In type even larger than the first story, the headline announced, CURBS ON BAIL JUGGLING URGED BY THE GRAND JURY. Then, in smaller type, it said, "Proposals Adopted, Brown Told to Draw Up New Regulations."

To be honest about it, I was thrilled with my success. The story had turned out to be of a size and importance that any reporter, of any age and degree of experience, would have been proud to have broken. That I had done it, and all alone, at twenty-two made me proud and happy—and convinced I had done exactly the right thing in returning to journalism.

* * *

I had also done something else of far greater import that same year. Unfortunately, it would not turn out as well as did my return to the paper. I realize that is a very negative way to introduce the subject of marriage, but the first of what would eventually be four trips down the aisle (before I finally got it right in 1989) had a happy beginning and a disastrous end.

There is no way to sugarcoat it. On the plus side, the union produced three of my four children (my only daughter and two of my three sons), but before it was over ten years later, we'd all have been buffeted about so badly that the court agreed to award me custody of the children. Obviously, I must proceed very carefully with this aspect of my story, but these memoirs would be incomplete, and less than honest, without it. And while two of those three children, my daughter, Suzanne, and my son Stephen, are going to read this, neither their mother nor her firstborn, their brother Marc, will, because they are both dead. In a way, that makes it easier to tell.

In the summer of 1946, on a visit to San Francisco State College, my prewar school, I ran into a charming French-Canadian girl with whom I was immediately smitten. Renee Labouré had dark eyes and dark hair, which she wore pulled back, revealing classical facial features. She loved to laugh, and, clearly, she was intelligent. As beautiful and fun-loving as Renee was, there was also about her a certain air of sadness. As it turned out, while she had a father with whom she had a fairly good relationship, she had never known her mother, not even who she was. I found myself wanting not just to love her but also to protect her and to bring some sunshine into her life.

Our love blossomed quickly, and on New Year's Eve, December 31, 1946, instead of going to a party, as I'd told my mother we were doing, Renee and I flew to Reno, Nevada, and got married in the very first hours of 1947. When we got back to San Francisco, my mother went, in a word, berserk. Never before had I taken a step even remotely as important as this without asking or telling her. Fortunately, she liked Renee and after she'd calmed down from the initial shock, we managed to appease her by agreeing to a second, more proper, ceremony. So, ten days after the first nuptials, we were wed in a Catholic church, with many of our friends and relatives present.

Twenty-one months later, on the last day of September 1948, Renee gave birth to our son Marc, who was followed by his sister, Suzanne (September 6, 1951) and their brother, Stephen (September 3, 1952). Clearly, we celebrated our wedding anniversaries each New Year's Eve with amorous abandon. In no time at all, it seemed, we were no longer a young couple, but a young family, settling into a series of rented houses, and the weeks and months flew by.

The first few years of our marriage were, indeed, the best, as we were still very much in love, and San Francisco was as great a city to live in as the *Chronicle* was a great place to work. But after about four or five years into the marriage, I had to face the unpleasant fact that Renee had what we then called "a drinking problem." I was certainly no teetotaler, but I began to realize that if Renee had her way, we would be the first couple to show up at a party and the last to leave. I had the sinking feeling that before things got better, they would only get worse. And I was right, except that they never got better. So I did what I would continue to do when things were not running smoothly at home: I lost myself in my work.

I've spent so much of my life in journalism that at times I forget I ever thought about doing something else. But in going over old papers and documents for this book, I was struck by the sudden memory of my interest in world affairs. I had realized early on that my interests were different from those of most other West Coast kids. They all looked to the Pacific when they thought of foreign countries, whereas I, mainly because of my French background, always looked east, to the Atlantic and Europe. In fact, "Join the Navy and see the world" was one of the reasons I raced to the recruiting office on the day I turned seventeen.

At one point during my last year in college—probably *before* I got married—I thought seriously of applying to Georgetown University (another good Jebbie school) to get a master's degree in diplomacy in order to qualify for a career in the foreign service, and possibly even, should fortune deign to smile on me, as an ambassador. I went so far as to write to Georgetown and ask how to apply, but when I began to do well in journalism, I thought, Oh well, this is really what I should be doing in life.

During the late 1940s and early 1950s, as I was learning my craft of reporting, with a growing interest in investigative assignments, I wrote about a variety of subjects. The jumbled congeries of clippings that constitute my "scrapbook" remind me of how diverse some of them were. For example, the *Chronicle* of July 1, 1948, carried my story about a big fight that broke out at the International Labor Conference (SQUABBLE IN THE ILO, "Communists Protest Seating of French Delegate") and later that same month I wrote three more stories based on the same conference.

I was given this assignment partly because I spoke French, and while the ILO delegates came from all over the world, almost all of them spoke French. An interesting aspect of the conference was that each country sent three representatives, one from the government, one from industry, and the third from a union. I found the meetings fascinating, though not entirely for journalistic reasons. For example, I met and got on well with the business delegate from Czechoslovakia. He had just lost, to the new Communist regime, ownership of the company that made Pilsner Urquel beer, then as now my choice as the best beer in the world. Proud of his product, he had brought twenty-five to thirty cases of it to the conference, and every night, after I'd written my story, I'd join him at his hotel for a couple of bottles.

In October, I had something in *Picture News*, the Sunday magazine section of the *New York Star* (probably a reprint of a *Chronicle* article), but the folder that once contained a copy of it is as empty as my memory of the story itself. Later that same month, my final story on the bail bonds scandal ran on the front page, and in November I wrote a front-page piece that any San Franciscan of that period would recognize as a typical *Chronicle* story. Its bold headline read, BALES AWAY! THE MARS (A TRUNK LINE) FEEDS ELEPHANTS. It told the tall, but still true, tale of how the U.S. Navy's "gigantic flying boat," the *Swarthmore Victory*, dropped food for a group of starving animals. (". . . Twelve bales of hay went over the side as the flying boat made a series of passes over the freighter—choice red-oat hay, desperately needed to ease the hunger pangs of eight baby elephants that the freighter is bringing to assorted zoos on the mainland.")

In the early 1950s, I broke a story about an FBI inquiry into attempts to influence a federal grand jury. My story resulted in an exposé of the Internal Revenue Service, and the firing of four top IRS aides. Not long after that, I did a story on the government's breakup of the Waxey Gordon heroin syndicate. An earlier version of the French Connection, the caper featured heroin smuggled into this country from Italy by seamen paid by Lucky Luciano's organization. Luciano was a name we would all hear more of as the years passed.

The clipping of one particular story is undated, but its faded condition indicates it is definitely from the same period. It is about, of all things, sports—namely, football. Apparently, while still in school, not only did I cover some of USF's sporting events for the *Chronicle* but also went on the road to do so.

The faded article in question is datelined "Detroit Stadium, Oct. 7," and below a smaller head ("A 38–14 Surprise") it screams, DON'S AIR ATTACK BAFFLES DETROIT. Please note my firm grasp of the journalistic essentials of who, what, when, and, where (if not also why): "USF's star quarterback, Jim Ryan, turned in the greatest performance of his college career as he threw four touchdown passes and led an aroused Don eleven to a surprising 38–14 victory over the University of Detroit here tonight before 16,648 spectators."

There's a coda to this story. The reason I got to make this out-of-town boondoggle was that the USF athletic director, only slightly older than I, had become a friend, and he'd set it up so that I could go along and cover the game for the *Chronicle*. A loyal alumnus had also done some setting up—he'd arranged for two young ladies to meet us right after the game for a night on the town. We were told their names and exactly where they'd be waiting. The AD and I had been traveling all day, and by the time the game was over and I'd written and filed my story, it was really late. But, lo and behold, when we finally walked out of the stadium, there were the two girls, as described, waiting patiently. My friend and I were so tired by this point that we just kept on walking.

For the record, that young USF athletic director was Pete Rozelle, who later became the highly respected commissioner of the National Football League, as well as my friend for lo these many years.

> Writing a story for a daily newspaper is creation, and all creation is formed of fragile ideas and feelings. The reporter can at times be lightly guided but he cannot be directed. Rigid memos about how things will be done can be posted on the bulletin board in the city room, and constant flagellation of the reportorial mind and psyche can create a corporate style of writing. But the results will not be creative. The stories will be acceptable—safe at first base. None will ever clear the fence for a beautiful, easy home run.
>
> In the uncertainties of journalism there is one certainty; the reporter is the single, indispensable ingredient of a good newspaper. Many a paper—God knows—is duller and less perceptive than its staff. But no paper can rise very far beyond the competence of its reporters.

That lovely quote is from Abe Mellinkoff, former city editor of the *Chronicle,* in the introduction to *The San Francisco Chronicle Reader,* a collection of memorable articles from the paper compiled by two of its editors, Bill German (who is *still* on the paper) and Bill Hogan. I'm proud to say that two of my pieces are included. One of them is very serious and the other is about cigars. Wait—*both* of them are very serious. Even just dipping into this 1962 volume gives a very good feel for just how special the *San Francisco Chronicle* was in those heady days.

Speaking of cigars and the *Chronicle*'s specialness reminds me that in the fifties we had *a* woman reporter. Her name was Carolyn Anspacher. One day she came up to my desk, bearing an envelope filled with cash, some thirty dollars in all.

"Here," she said, grinning, "we took up a collection."

"What for?" I replied.

"We think it's time you moved up to a higher degree of cigars."

I get the impression that nowadays the news and city rooms of big metropolitan dailies are hotbeds of competition, thanks in part to people like my friend Ben Bradlee, who championed the concept of "creative tension," which certainly worked on young *Washington Post* reporters Bob Woodward and Carl Bernstein. Their award-winning unraveling of what turned out to be the Watergate scandal all but single-handedly led to an upsurge in journalism school enrollments.

This has not been, however, an unmixed blessing. In fact, I'm not entirely sure it's been a blessing at all, in that the current state of journalism is characterized by no-holds-barred, highly intrusive reporting about anyone's—as long as they are in the public eye—professional and personal lives, and it is usually based on unnamed sources, when sources are cited at all. Suffice it to say that we are not living in a golden age of journalism.

There are two reasons for this, in my opinion. The first is that after Watergate an entire generation of young journalists viewed bringing down someone famous and powerful as the way to make their *own* name and career. That started the breakdown in responsible journalism. The second reason is that this new generation of journalists comes to us in almost all cases straight out of journalism school. When I think back on the *Chronicle* newsroom, I can't recall a single person whose degree—if he had one—was in journalism. We learned the trade by working as journalists. I think this lack of a broader education results in an unfortunately narrow focus.

Also, while I'm sure there are exceptions, I find it hard to believe that in this intensely competitive atmosphere you find many older reporters giving away story ideas to their younger and oh-so-hungry colleagues. In my day, however, the reverse was true. There was a great deal of collegiality in the *Chronicle* newsroom, in large part because we had a group of very talented journalists with enough confidence in their own ability so as not to feel threatened by Young Turks, and not at all above helping them.

It should be remembered that during the time period I'm writing about, the desks of the *Chronicle* were graced by the likes of such fine reporter-writers as Herb Caen, Vance Bourjaily, Stanton Delaplane, Art Hoppe, Tom Mathews, and the one and only "Count Marco." It was a lineup heavy with talent. I've never changed the opinion that I formed after my first week there: I had a dream job.

If I had a favorite among my older colleagues, it was probably Robert DeRoos. At one point in those days, Bob had the unenviable task of taking over Herb Caen's daily column when Caen defected, for a brief period, to the *San Francisco Examiner.* Caen would become so popular that in 1962 the editors of *The San Francisco Chronicle Reader* described him in the following manner, "In the wonderful world of San Francisco journalism Herb Caen is the champion. It's no contest. Caen outdraws anything in the paper. You must read Caen to be in the know. You find out what's doing, who's who, how it is, and where it happened."

Obviously, his was a tough act to follow. But Bob DeRoos made a manful, and largely successful, effort, and I am proud to say that for a while I helped him. He hired me to be his "street man," which meant I had the tough duty of spending frequent nights in fancy restaurants, night-clubs, and other in places, gathering information on the social lives of San Francisco's VIPs. Some years later, after I'd become well known, thanks to John F. Kennedy, DeRoos wrote a column about me.

I was writing a daily column then, and Pierre Salinger was my assistant. He was a great help. He knew everyone in town, and had some kind of built-in sonar or radar gear which homed in on small talk or gossip. A great asset for an assistant columnist and man of politics, which Pierre was. I never knew anyone to get as many calls as Pierre, mostly from his family. He was the eldest son and the acknowledged genius of the tribe and was called upon to make judgments. I can still hear him shouting, "That's riddickeless, that's riddickeless," to someone near and dear to him.

After one of those phone calls, Pierre would swear and blow out smoke and brood, useless for the next 15 minutes. He was already on to cigars . . . and we both took to smoking cigars that came in little aluminum tubes, the brashest kind of newly rich, and very happy about ourselves.

Later in the piece, Bob mentioned that I was also his assistant on his local television show. Each Friday, I got to announce the name of the elderly lady who would get that week's "Roses from DeRoos," which I would then deliver in a new Nash from our sponsor, James Motors. Bob wrote, "Off he'd go to deliver the roses. Then it became the task of the people at James Motors to get their car away from Pierre. They would lie in wait for him, attempt to intercept him at intersections, and they phoned frequently, 'Where is that car?' Some weeks they did not catch Pierre until the following Tuesday." (That's a gross exaggeration; it was Monday.)

My two biggest stories of that period, however, and the two of which I am most proud, were investigative pieces that won me prizes and solidified my reputation as an investigative reporter. The first had to do with George Holman, an indigent black man whom I came to believe had been unfairly convicted of murder; the other involved the appalling conditions in many of California's jails, a situation that I exposed after having myself thrown into a number of them.

In addition to being humorous, Bob DeRoos was a very able reporter with a great deal of hard-news experience. One day after I had finished my series on the collusion between the judges and their favorite bail bondsmen, Bob called me over to his desk and told me he'd been working on a case that might interest me. The story had to do with a fire that had occurred in the city in 1944, while I was still in the navy.

"It's in the morgue," Bob said, "under 'New Amsterdam Hotel' or 'George Holman.' Read the clips, especially about the evidence. I always thought there was something funny about this one. Why don't you take it and run with it?"

I found the file easily enough, and it made for intriguing reading. The fire, apparently an arson, had taken the lives of twenty-two denizens of skid row, and there had been a great hue and cry for the arrest of the arsonist-murderer. Finally, the police arrested George Holman, and on the word of an eyewitness, he was swiftly convicted, given twenty-two consecutive life sentences, and hauled off to San Quentin.

DeRoos was right. There was something peculiar about this case. It concerned the evidence, which gave new meaning to the word *flimsy*. The key prosecution witness was a drug dealer who had been George Holman's rival for the affections of a prostitute who lived in the New Amsterdam. This "unbiased" witness testified that he had seen Holman run out the rear door of the hotel seconds before the conflagration erupted—and that he was carrying a gas can!

Now this sounded pretty doubtful to me for a couple of reasons. One, the witness clearly had an ax to grind; and, two, wouldn't any arsonist in his right mind toss the can away *before* running out where he could be seen? In addition, the witness said Holman set the fire because he wanted to murder the prostitute, but it turned out that she lived on the first floor, which meant that all she had to do to escape was to open her window and leap to safety from the dizzying height of three feet, which was exactly what she had done.

My first stop was San Quentin, where I interviewed Holman and his warden. I found George Holman, who by this time had been in prison for almost five years, mild-mannered and direct, and hard to picture as a lying arsonist.

Warden Clinton Duffy surprised me by saying, "Every man in San

Quentin claims to be innocent, but if there *is* an innocent man here, it's George Holman." From other interviews, I learned that prior to his arrest and conviction Holman had had a perfectly clean record, not so much as a traffic ticket. He was considered one of the hardest workers in the prison and one of the most popular inmates.

With Bob DeRoos's blessing, I put together a string of leads, which at first proved rather frustrating. I learned the Los Angeles whereabouts of the drug dealer, only to find out he had died two weeks earlier. As for the prostitute, I tracked her to the tiny town of Hazelhurst, Mississippi. When I got off the plane, the editor of the Copiah County *News* met me, and before he'd even said hello, he asked, "Why would a white man come two thousand miles to get a nigger out of jail?" I interviewed the prostitute, but, clearly fearful that if she said anything even potentially helpful to Holman she would have to return to California, she chose to say nothing.

DeRoos and I went back to work. We interviewed everyone involved in the trial—judges, defense lawyer, prosecutor, and jurors. We dug up two witnesses who said they had seen George Holman running out of the hotel, but *without* a gas can. Next, we came up with evidence that the fire was not caused by arson but by spontaneous combustion. For years, the owners of this fleabag hotel had sprayed the walls with kerosene to discourage the cockroaches. One day, the place simply went *poof.*

I got all this information into the paper in a series of articles that received a big play. I thought that because we had uncovered brand-new information clearly pointing to Holman's innocence, Governor Earl Warren (later the chief justice of the United States Supreme Court) would free George Holman. Not so.

I'm no longer sure if our next step was my suggestion or DeRoos's, but the idea was a beaut. We went to the famous mystery writer Erle Stanley Gardner, whose "Court of Last Resort" (a feature of the very popular national magazine *Argosy*) had been set up to be just that, a last resort. Gardner assigned a young investigator named Robert Rhay to work with us, and he caught the fever wonderfully. Eventually, Rhay wrote not one but a series of articles for *Argosy*. They helped immensely in swelling the volume of the public outcry to free Holman.

In 1956, almost a decade after we had started working on the case, what failed to move Earl Warren did move his successor, Governor Goodwin Knight, and he paroled George Holman.

As the forties cruised into the fifties, I began to develop a strong interest in politics. Up until then, my only personal foray had been my vainglorious attempt to become, by election, the editor of my high school paper. Because I did not cover politics, I was able to make an agreement with the *Chronicle* that allowed me to work, initially as a volunteer, for a number of candidates.

In 1946, I worked on Frank Havenner's campaign for mayor of San Francisco, and for John F. Shelley, the following year, when he ran for the U.S. Congress. In 1948, I worked for Harry Truman in his successful bid for the presidency, and two years after that I did a stint on behalf of Richard Graves when he ran for governor of California.

A great deal of what I did was some form of campaign PR (I didn't do much work as a speechwriter until the 1952 Stevenson campaign), such as planning and finding sites for rallies. I also spent a lot of time strategizing, as well as nose counting and other nitty-gritty aspects of electoral politics. Apparently, my "ascent" was noticeable, because in 1952 I was asked to be one of the directors of communications in California for Adlai Stevenson's run for the highest office in the land.

I should confess I was not one of those loyal campaign aides so totally devoted to the cause of the candidate that he could never imagine himself in the limelight. Beginning as early as 1946, when I came back to the paper, I began to think about the possibilities of a political career for myself. By 1952, I had become so fascinated by politics and public service that I gave serious thought to seeking the Democratic nomination for the U.S. House of Representatives. My opponent would have been Caspar Weinberger, then known as a liberal Republican. At the last minute, I changed my mind and dropped out. My personal political ambitions had to remain on the shelf for a decade.

(At one political rally for Adlai in 1952 that I had labored mightily to help organize, I was thrilled to meet and shake hands with a Hollywood star who was a big Stevenson backer. His name was Ronald Reagan.)

I realize this may sound like revisionist personal history, but it is true nonetheless. During this same period, I began to develop a rather unusual ambition—I wanted, someday, to become a press secretary to the President of the United States. It seemed to me that with my journalism background and my growing involvement with politics I could perform that job and actually make a contribution. I swear it.

Until I wrote the Holman stories, I had known little about prison life, and, in fact, had not learned a great deal about the subject while doing the legwork for the series. Like most Californians (like most Americans, probably) the day-to-day life of incarcerated men and women was not something I thought about very often. However, in April of 1953, I was given an assignment that led me to think about it a great deal. That routine

assignment—to cover a meeting of the American Friends Service Committee—also led to my last exposé for the *San Francisco Chronicle.*

The meeting had been called to voice the committee's demands for
more humane treatment of prisoners in county jails throughout the state.
The chair of the meeting was the then attorney general of the state of
California, Pat Brown. I went, not quite sure what I'd hear, but certainly
not expecting the horror stories that were told. I was appalled at what the
committee had uncovered, and I decided on the spot that what this situation called for was not a single story on the Friends' demands, but a series
on the appalling conditions they'd uncovered. And the more I thought
about it, the more I realized that the best way to do the story would be
from the *inside.* If I was to tell this ugly story accurately, I would have to
become a prisoner myself.

When the meeting was over, I went to see Pat Brown, with whom I
had developed a professional rapport based on the Holman series and other
stories. I said, "The public must become aware of this situation, but I don't
think covering this meeting and writing about it is the way to do it. I think
I ought to get myself arrested and thrown in a couple of these places, and
then if they're as bad as you say they are, I can write about it from the
inside."

Attorney General Brown gave me a funny look, then said, "Fine. I'll
set it up."

Several days later, Pat Brown called me into his office and said,
"Here's how it will work. One week from next Friday, you're going to
get arrested in Stockton at one in the morning. Five or six days before that,
stop shaving. Start looking a little weird. Then go to Stockton, and three
hours before you're to be arrested, go to a bar and start drinking beer. At
twelve-thirty-nine, walk down Main Avenue to the hotel, and you'll see a
brown four-door Hudson parked on the street. It will be unlocked. Crawl
in the backseat and go to sleep, and that's where you'll be arrested.

"Then, when you appear before the judge, be sure you insult him."

"Why?" I asked innocently.

"So that he'll be sure to throw you in jail."

As part of the plan, I got a new identity. Pierre Emil George Salinger
became Peter Emil Flick. (For what it's worth, my new last name in French,
and minus the *k,* means "cop.") Three days before D (for drunk) day, I
stopped shaving. On the appointed night, I went to a bar within walking
distance of the brown Hudson, had half a dozen beers, and smoked two
big cigars. Then I walked down the street and crawled into the backseat
of the car.

Several hours later, I heard the heavy jail door clang shut behind me as a beefy Stockton policeman led me by the arm to a battered wooden desk.

"Empty your pockets," said an unsmiling inmate trusty. I did, and out came my wallet, a small black comb, $2.32, a paperback mystery, and my watch. The bored trusty shoved all but the comb and the coins into an envelope, and had me sign a pink booking slip.

Then I was shoved, unceremoniously, into a dimly lit cell. The first thing to hit me was the smell—of dirty bodies, dirty feet, urine. There was an open toilet in one corner. In another, a man sat up, retched onto the floor, and then turned over and went back to sleep. All the other floor space was occupied by men—seventeen in all—lying on the filthy wooden floor without blankets or even mattresses. My research had begun.

In the next seven days, which I spent in two of California's county jails (after Stockton, I went to Bakersfield), I witnessed brutality, filth, and degradation. I ate inadequate meals. I paid inmate trusties for some decent food or a pack of real cigarettes. I saw men leave jail and come back the next day because they had no money, no place else to go. And I got a thorough education in several criminal activities.

A passer of bad checks who was on his way to San Quentin told me how to beat the banks on bum checks. A narcotics addict told me the joys of a first marijuana cigarette. A twenty-two-year-old youth told me how to get high on Nembutal. And a five-time loser told me how to write a writ of habeas corpus and beat the law.

The conditions I encountered were not as bad as I had expected— they were worse.

Some weeks later, on January 26, 1953, the seventeen-part series began. I'd thought the headlines used for my Holman stories had been large, but the size of the type used by the *Chronicle* to announce the first story in my series on prison conditions was the biggest the paper had used since the end of the war! Even the *third* subhead was larger than my Holman headlines.

Across the entire top of the page was slashed, in *red*: EXCLUSIVE: INSIDE CALIFORNIA'S JAILS. Below that, in even larger type, it blared: COUNTY JAILS EXPOSED—STORY OF CRUELTY, FILTH.

Above the story itself, which took up a quarter of the front page in width, were two headlines, the first in bold type: BRUTALITY... CROWDED CELLS... "Chronicle Reporter Does Time: Shocking Account." Then, still well above my byline, the editors included this amplification.

Last year more than 600,000 Californians were locked up in city or county jails.

One might be a teenager in until his parents can raise the money to pay his fine for a traffic violation. Another, a professional killer waiting two months for his trial to begin. Or another, a bookmaker serving a year. Often they serve their time together—in filthy tank cells, ruled by con bosses.

A Chronicle staff writer, under an assumed name and unknown to his jailers as a reporter, did time in two of these jails and studied many more up and down California.

This is his documented report of a scandalous and dangerous condition too long ignored.

The beginning of the series ran under a larger byline than I'd seen for any story in my entire eight years on the paper. In the remainder of the very lengthy series—some thirty thousand words in all—I gave example after example of what Attorney General Brown meant when he said, "These county jails are just the breeding grounds of crime. They set the feet of petty first offenders on the road to serious offenses against society."

The response by the reading public was electric. Circulation jumped almost 20 percent, and the cry went up for hearings and new legislation.

Governor Earl Warren, who had failed to move on behalf of George Holman, acted this time. He took personal charge of the probe into the situation, and the result was real reform. One of its direct results was the construction of new prisons in both Stockton and Bakersfield ("my" prisons), but of even greater importance was that the state of California took a new and enlightened approach to penology—rehabilitation, not just punishment.

When I turned thirty, in June 1955, it must have appeared to outsiders that I had, as the song goes, "the world on a string." And I did, professionally. In my private life, at home with Renee and the children, things were not good at all. Her alcoholism was becoming more and more evident. Not the type of drinking where a housewife might, as it was put in those days, "tipple" all day long yet still run the house, it was getting to be the ugly kind, where she would disappear for several days at a time and I would have to ask my family members for help with the kids while I searched for her.

At work, I was ecstatic; at home, I was scared to death.

CHAPTER FOUR

IN LATE 1954, there was a big blowup on the staff of the *San Francisco Chronicle*, and Larry Fanning, about as good a managing editor as any paper could wish for, and a man for whom I had the greatest trust and respect, was fired. On the day of his firing, I walked into his office and said, "I quit."

"Okay," said Larry, "but before I accept your resignation, I'm sending you to Guatemala. There's just been a coup there, so cover it and file a story. Then"—he smiled at me—"come back by way of New York City."

"New York City . . . why?"

"So you can stop in and see Smitty at *Collier's*. I'll call him and tell him to expect you."

Smitty was Paul Smith, until recently the editor of the *Chronicle*, and, like Larry Fanning, also one of nature's noblemen.

I accepted the assignment and flew to Guatemala, where I managed to stay out of harm's way long enough to get and file a story. I returned via New York, a city I hardly knew at the time, but one that I would come to know quite well over the coming years, and had an excellent meeting with Paul Smith, at the end of which he offered me a job as one of the two contributing editors in the West Coast office of *Collier's*, the other being Bob DeRoos. (Clearly, Larry Fanning had been his usual effective self behind the scenes.) This general-circulation magazine is no longer with us, like so many others over the years, but in the fifties it had *5 million* readers each and every week.

While I would be doing mainly investigative pieces for *Collier's,* the magazine also wanted me to report on the other love of my life, politics. One of my first assignments was to cover the 1956 Democratic National Convention, which was to be held in Chicago that summer. (Earlier in 1956, I'd received a call from the nominee himself, Adlai Stevenson, asking me to write speech drafts for him. I agreed immediately but said that in order to avoid any possible conflict of interest I would do so gratis.)

I was pleased that *Collier's* thought enough of my background in politics to give me such a coveted assignment as the Democratic convention, because it meant that a lifelong personal interest had been transformed into a professional asset. I was even more pleased that they assigned me to work alongside a man who was then best known as an excellent reporter *and* an excellent writer, the two skills not always being present in the same individual. The name of this war correspondent turned political writer was Theodore H. ("Teddy") White.

Three years later, just after John Kennedy had become the Democratic candidate, Teddy White, by then my good friend, came to me and asked for my help. He had an idea for a book on the campaign, but he needed the cooperation of the candidates. I went to Kennedy and told him of White's plan, which involved a great deal of access. The senator, himself a student of history, liked it immediately and said, "Tell him that's fine." Armed with our cooperation, White then went to the Nixon camp, which also agreed. The result, of course, was *The Making of the President, 1960,* a runaway national best-seller. The first of what became a series, it was the book that won him the Pulitzer Prize in 1962. Teddy White and I remained close friends until his death in 1986.

It was around this same time that I helped another writer, but the circumstances were as different as the two men. By 1959, Teddy White, a Harvard graduate, had written four books, including *Thunder Out of China* and *Fire in the Ashes.* The other writer, a young black officer in the U.S. Coast Guard, was just getting started. For some months, he'd been sending me material "over the transom," which I'd put off reading. But one day, I got around to it, and to my surprise, I found it to be very good. I recommended him to *Collier's,* and he got several assignments that made it into the magazine. After that, he began to pick up work with other places, as well. The young man, who would go on to considerable fame and fortune, was Alex Haley, and, among other things, he wrote the monumental book *Roots.*

Years later, when Alex was the toast of the globe, I interviewed him for a French magazine. He said a number of wonderful things, including this fascinating tale of how he had become a writer:

> When I went into the Coast Guard, it was at a time that if you were Black and went into any of the naval services you automatically went into what was called the "steward's department." You waited on tables, made beds, shined shoes, the menial things. If you did them sufficiently well, you eventually would become a cook. I did become a cook on an ammunition ship on the Southwest Pacific. On that ship our biggest problem was boredom. I began to try to solve mine by, each evening after I had finished cooking, I would go down to the hole of the ship and just write letters to everybody I could think of. All my ex-schoolmates, friends, even teachers. Anybody. I would just write letters, and they would be taken ashore by other ships. Sometimes ships would come out to us and bring mail. Mail call was a very epochal event for us, and when I got things going well I would get maybe thirty, forty letters every mail call. I quickly got the image of being the ship's most prolific correspondent. Concurrently, we would be at sea maybe two months at a time. When we would get ashore somewhere, maybe Australia, New Zealand, our topmost priority was to find anything that looked like a girl and run her to the ground. This was the whole crew. We would go back out to sea and there would be all these guys smitten with some girl whom they'd left ashore— and girls get all the more lithesome in your mind the longer you are at sea. Some of my friends who were awfully articulate on the ship were not that way on paper, and they began to come around to me in covert ways and suggest it might be nice if I would help them write a letter to a girl, since I wrote so many letters. I began to do this simply because they were my buddies and I wanted to try to be helpful.
>
> They would, literally, in the evenings on ship, line up while I sat at a mess table with a stack of index cards. As they got to me—one by one—I would interview them about the girl: what she looked like, hair, eyes, mouth, nose, what not—Where did you go with her? What did you say? Anything special? And whatever they told me I reduced into notes on a card. Later, as I got the chance, I would take each of these cards which had his or her name on it for each case, and I would use the information he told me about that girl and try to tailor a kind of love letter, for him to write in his own handwriting.

If a guy told me, as many of my "clients" did, that a girl's hair was blond—many of my clients were white—I would get a fit of creativity and write something like, "Your hair is like the moonlight reflected on the rippling waves," and then these letters would go out to the girls.

I will never forget one time we went to Brisbane, Australia, after about three months at sea. My clients came back the following morning almost as if a script had been written—each one of them, before an increasing large and awestruck audience, would describe, in the graphic way that only young sailors can, how when he met that girl in person behind those letters that I had written for him that he just met incredible results—practically on the *spot,* some of them swore! I became heroic that day on the ship.

I can tell you the truth, Pierre, that was literally how I stumbled into doing nothing but writing. From that day until the end of the war, at least until the end of my time at sea, I didn't do anything on that ship but write love letters. My clients did my work for me. And I discovered I really liked doing nothing but writing. That was how I stumbled into trying to write stories for magazines.

I began writing women's confession stories. They would always come back right away. I would make out I was a girl and this *lout* had done this, that, and the other thing to me, and I was trying to solve my problem. When I look back that was how I stumbled into trying to write for publication.

From there it went to the men's adventure magazines, like the old *Coronet.* That's where I began to sell and then ultimately I came out to San Francisco and that was the background against which, as you know, by then I was writing for some of the larger magazines. It was the way I kept writing [while I was still] in the service. I should say here that I had gone from a mess boy to become a cook, but once my stuff started selling in national magazines the Coast Guard changed my rating to the first "journalist" in the Coast Guard. Finally, I retired as Chief Journalist when I was 37 in San Francisco. I then went straight to New York and into full-time freelance writing.

Of course no one at that time had so much as an inkling of all the tumult that would ensue during the next decade. Here is the way longtime Kennedy aide Ted Sorensen would look back, thirteen years later, at that time.

Jack overcame his disappointment over the Vice Presidency in 1956 by immediately starting his campaign for the Presidency.

It was not an announced decision on his part or even an inner commitment. He simply recognized that his sudden new national status had opened a door that until then had seemed unlikely to open for some years. Without knowing how far he would be able to go beyond that door, where it would lead him, or who else would be there when a final commitment had to be made, he started through it. Had his subsequent travels and organizational efforts across the country proved unrewarding, he would have stayed out of the 1960 race and waited for another year. Had his religion and age proved to be insuperable obstacles, he might have reluctantly accepted the Vice Presidential nomination. But his goal from 1956 on was the Presidential nomination in 1960. . . .

In the balloting for vice president, Stevenson having thrown open the choice to the full convention, Kennedy surprised many people by mounting a serious challenge to Tennessee's Senator Estes Kefauver. At first, it even appeared that Kennedy was winning, but then the senator at the podium noticed that some of the delegates were holding up one finger to signal they wanted to change their votes. With that, the voting pattern shifted dramatically to Kefauver, who eventually emerged the winner by a small margin.

Sitting there watching the results, I figured that when it came time for Kennedy to address the convention, he might be angry or bitter, but instead he was absolutely gracious in defeat. His speech was stirring, and he impressed me greatly.

Hmm, I thought, this guy Kennedy is actually lucky he didn't get the VP slot, because Stevenson is not going to win, and I'd be willing to bet that one of these days Kennedy will make a hell of a candidate—for President.

I had very mixed feelings about leaving the *Chronicle*. On the one hand, I was grateful for the new job with *Collier's*, but on the other I knew I would miss the special camaraderie of that most talented and unusual band of "ink-stained wretches." The newsrooms of today, with their ubiquitous computers and E-mail message systems, bear very little resemblance to our noisy, smoke-filled arena. Never having even heard the word *cubicle*, we had our desks jammed up against one another, and guys would be hunched over their sturdy Royal typewriters, typing away like the wind, usually with just two fingers, a telephone attached, with seeming permanence, to one ear. If a big story was breaking, everyone was aware of it, whether or not they were working on it themselves. As for those who were, they'd be banging it out on their typewriters, and often with little, if any, rewrite needed.

These men were skilled reporters and journalists, but they were also highly skilled writers. The degree to which *Chronicle* stories of that era were marked by style and grace far exceeds, in my opinion, that of the so-called New Journalists who would be lauded in New York in the next decade. (We were doing Tom Wolfe way before Tom Wolfe was doing Tom Wolfe.) As evidence, I submit the fact that Vance Bourjaily went on to write fine novels, and reporters such as Bernard Taper and Kevin Wallace became writers for *The New Yorker*. Not only were these people good writers; they were also good friends—much more so, I would guess, than the journalists of comparable ages today. We all palled around together in a San Francisco so magical that it already seems to have been one long and vivid dream.

The *Chronicle* was a morning paper; our chief competition, the *San Francisco Examiner,* came out in the afternoon. That meant we put the paper to bed at 1:00 A.M., after which most of the guys would head straight to Hanno's—a legendary saloon on the corner of Mission and Fifth—whose proprietor, Mel, was patron saint and father confessor to half the staff. It was not at all unusual for us to get home in time to greet the milkman and wake the kids for school.

I can recall one time at about three or four in the morning when I *knew* I'd been overserved, and rather than attempt to drive home in that condition, I wisely stopped my car and went to sleep in it. Unfortunately, I'd neglected to pull over. I had "parked" my car in the middle of the access lane to the Golden Gate Bridge. The first friendly face I saw over the next six hours was that of my colleague Tom Mathews, who'd come to bail me out of jail.

At the time I left, the *Chronicle* was in the midst of a bitter circulation war with the *Examiner* that had split the newsroom right down the middle. There were those purists, such as Larry Fanning, who wanted the *Chronicle* to become "the *New York Times* of the West." There were others, I'll simply call them the pragmatists, who felt that noble ambition took a distant second to the goal of winning the circulation battle. To that end, the pragmatists thought nothing of such stunts as the hiring and grooming of the one and only Count Marco as a columnist on the woman's page.

It wasn't just that Count Marco, a homosexual hairdresser with a loyal following in his chosen profession, wasn't really a count; it was also the fact that he had no journalistic skills and could not write. The pragmatists solved that by assigning the best rewrite men to take over his copy, much as the Count had made over madame's tresses in his earlier incarnation, and to color the prose deep purple. That worked fine for a while, and the Count, to the consternation of those who wanted us to polish our image in pursuit of all the news that was fit to print, West Coast–style, became a very popular addition to our pages.

Given the Count's success, the pragmatists looked to extend his range and thus assigned him to cover a lurid murder trial in Los Angeles. As he was incapable of writing rough copy (to say nothing of understanding what was going on in the courtroom), they assigned Tom Mathews—as Count Marco's chauffeur. Every day of the trial, Tom, one of the most gifted writers on the paper, would show up at the hotel driving the Count's famous Rolls-Royce, pick him up and drive him to court, then sit next to him, surreptitiously drinking in all the colorful details, before depositing the Count and his party at a grand restaurant for dinner, so that he could hurry back to his hotel to write and file the story.

At one point, one of the purists on the paper stopped Tom in the newsroom and told him he was "debasing journalism," whereupon Tom told him to perform an unnatural act, and several other staffers had to bring the "discussion" to a conclusion.

Did I remember to say that the *Chronicle* won the circulation war hands down?

While my professional star continued to rise, things were worsening at home. Renee's problem with alcohol was reaching crisis proportions. It was no longer the occasional lapse; it was the occasional bender. She would disappear for days on end, and more often than not she would get in a tussle with the police. Several times, these verbal battles resulted in her being jailed overnight. When I tried to talk with her and get her to seek professional help, she refused, or just took off on another lost weekend, sometimes with a male drinking buddy.

I didn't know what to do. Someone suggested I hire a private investigator to document her behavior in case I ever needed proof, but I couldn't bring myself to do that. Dealing with this problem was not the kind of thing I did particularly well. I would wait and hope things would get better, all the while fearing they would not.

The course of my life changed sharply in 1956, first because of a phone call and then because of a brief item I read in a newspaper.

"Pierre? This is Ken McArdle. How ya doin'?" said a cheery voice on the phone one morning not long after the Democratic convention.

As the editor of *Collier's*, Ken McArdle was my boss. For him to be calling me personally from the home office in New York City was not rare, but it was not exactly a common occurrence, either.

"What's up, Ken?"

"I've got something that I think will interest you. Adlai has asked John Martin to come and work for him again on the campaign, and of course I'm happy to release him. But John was working on a story that I don't think will keep—at least I don't want it to have to keep."

McArdle was referring to John Bartlow Martin, arguably the magazine's top writer. Martin had taken a leave of absence in 1952 to write speeches for Stevenson during the campaign, and evidently the governor had asked him to do so again. It was the kind of offer a journalist could hardly refuse, because it would put the writer in line to become White House press secretary, the dream job goal for many of us. Of course, no one seriously thought Stevenson was going to beat Eisenhower, but then anything could happen (such as another presidential heart attack) during the long course of a campaign. So I was not at all surprised that John took the job again.

"What's the story?" I asked, trying not to sound too eager. If Ken was calling me to take over a story from John Bartlow Martin, it would have to be a big story.

"The Teamsters union. John was looking into all these rumors about widespread corruption, both in Seattle with the president, Dave Beck, and in Detroit with Jimmy Hoffa, his heir apparent. It's too good a story to sit on for three or four months, so I'm offering it to you. You'd have to transfer out here to the main bureau, but you'd be spending a lot of time in Seattle and, to a lesser degree, Detroit. And I'll make you a contributing editor. What do you say?"

It took me but a few seconds to say a delighted "Yes!" For the first time in my journalistic career I would be working on a story with national, not just local or statewide, significance. I was thrilled.

I already knew the Teamsters were big-time, but I had no idea just how big. A Teamsters official soon educated me by saying, "When a woman takes a cab to the hospital to have a baby, the cab is driven by a Teamster. When the baby grows old and dies, the hearse is driven by a Teamster. And in between, we supply him with a lot of groceries." As I would also soon learn, if the Teamsters union decided to call a general strike, the entire country would be crippled. It would be far worse than a strike by, say, the steelworkers, or the miners, or the autoworkers. If there was something wrong with the leadership of this union, it could already be having a negative effect on the whole country. I could see why Ken McArdle didn't want to wait on this story.

For the next three months, I crisscrossed the country, spending most of my time in Seattle and also quite a bit in Detroit. Very soon, I began to feel as if I had taken the top off a can of worms. I couldn't decide which was worse, the corruption or the brutality. Beck was getting rich at the expense of his members, and Hoffa, whose official bailiwick was the Central States Conference of Teamsters, was putting together a goon squad of thugs and ex-cons. I ran across sweetheart contracts all over the place, not to mention the blatantly dishonest and illegal practice of awarding union charters to gangsters for *nonexistent* locals in order to make sure crooked incumbents were able to beat back the challenges of reformers.

The newspaper item that would have such a tremendous effect on my future appeared one day in mid-October 1956. I was in my office at the main bureau of *Collier's* in New York, reading the *New York Herald Tribune,* when a three-paragraph story caught my eye. It said that the United States Senate was going to be looking into the same subject I'd been working on. Senator John McClellan was about to convene the Senate Select Committee on Improper Activities in the Labor or Management Field. According to the article, the Arkansas Democrat had named Robert F. Kennedy as his new chief counsel. Kennedy was the younger brother of Senator John F. Kennedy, a member of the committee, and the same man who had so impressed me with his great speech at the Democratic convention back in June.

Even though I'd never met Bobby Kennedy, I immediately picked up the phone and called him. I told him what I had been doing and said that I would love to compare notes someday. I was particularly interested in knowing when the McClellan committee would start its public hearings, as the magazine would certainly want to time the publication of my series to coincide with them.

"What are you doing for lunch?" he asked abruptly and with that near twang that would eventually become so familiar to millions of Americans.

"Nothing," I replied, "and I can be on a plane for D.C. in half an hour."

I was, and we had an absolutely fascinating two-hour lunch, during which I asked few questions because I was so busy answering those of Mr. Kennedy, who turned out to be a most inquisitive fellow. I must say it was an odd experience for a journalist to find himself giving answers instead of getting them. I did, however, learn that the new committee's first hearing would be in February 1957, which would be perfect for *Collier's.*

I said good-bye to Bobby Kennedy, promising to keep in touch (though, in truth, thinking I'd not see him again for quite a while—if ever) and returned to New York. It was time for me to start writing.

TEAMSTERS (PART ONE)
by
Pierre Salinger

Ted Daley hunched his 190 pounds over the steering wheel of his 12 ton truck and trailer rig and highballed south eight miles from Kingston, New York. It was a late drizzly afternoon. The road was slick.

Suddenly, there was a loud report. Daley thought his drive shaft had snapped. But a moment later his driving sense told him what had really happened—the two drive wheels directly below the cab had spun off.

To the left lay a heavy line of oncoming traffic. Daley jammed the steering wheel to the right and headed the truck off the road into a grove of trees. Daley didn't have a chance to jump even if he wanted to. The 30,000 pound load of paper in the truck's trailer jackknifed and the truck crashed through the trees and shuddered to a stop in a sand embankment.

An hour later, the 28-year-old red-headed truck driver was in a hospital in Poughkeepsie. His back and legs throbbed with pain from the serious dislocation of his vertebrae. As he heard the faraway voices of the State Troopers telling him the lugs which held the wheels had come loose, Daley remembered he had been warned.

It had been a week earlier, at a meeting of Local 445 of the Teamsters Union in Yonkers, N.Y. Daley had been the leader of a group of rebels trying to throw out the local's two principal officers, who had been convicted of extorting $64,000 from New York milk dealers.

In the clamor of the meeting, Daley found himself on his feet. "What I want to know," he shouted, "is what happened to the $500,000 in the treasury?"

As he turned to leave the small meeting hall that night, one of the henchman of the two extortioners had turned to him: "You've gone too far this time Daley. One of these days we're going to get you."

Violence is not an unusual thing in the International Brotherhood of Teamsters, Chauffeurs and Warehousemen and Helpers AFL. The union's history is dotted with goon beatings, organized hoodlumism. In one year alone, during the ascent to power of the union's General President Dave Beck in the Pacific Northwest, a special investigator for the governor of Oregon cited 233 crimes of arson, assault and battery charged to 120 persons. . . .

Against this backdrop, a powerful, young, up-and-coming leader [James Riddle Hoffa] is waging an intense and bitter struggle with an aging, once all-powerful national figure for control of the Teamsters.

The battle is of keen concern to you and every family in the country. . . .

I then proceeded to illustrate the vast power of the union that had become so corrupt and to explain by a series of dramatic examples why the Teamsters were so important to the American public. For some three thousand more words, the article went on to lay out the dishonesty and deviousness of both Beck and Hoffa. And also, in Hoffa's case, the extent of his mob connections. I ended with the following example of the cynicism of Teamster officials:

It is axiomatic that members of Teamsters locals which are not racket controlled do better wagewise, condition-wise over the bargaining table with their employers than those which are run by chisellers and thugs.

The appalling lack of feeling for the union members by this type of men is demonstrated by the story of Joey Glimco, the ex-convict trustee of the Chicago taxi cab local.

Everytime he goes for a taxi ride in the Windy City he tips the driver $2.00.

"Thanks an awful lot, mister," the driver invariably says.

"Don't thank me, it's your money," says Glimco.

In modern-day America, no union has ever amassed the power which is now in the hands of the Teamsters. No union has ever presented the nation such a perplexing problem.

The second article was equally blunt. It was also equally long, approximately five thousand words. I began by introducing a young driver I'd met at a diner in the East. He said:

"Sure, I'll talk to you about the Teamsters Union, but don't go using my name. I've got enough troubles as it is."

In California, in Montana, in Pennsylvania, in Illinois, I talked to [other Teamsters and] found a great reluctance on the part of these men to talk publicly about their union. And I found those who did talk knew appallingly little about this powerful union of which they were a part. In this they are no different from the vast majority of the American People whose daily lives are intricately wound up with the activities of this union. . . .

After documenting all the things that were wrong with the Teamsters and how few of its members were aware of these problems, I ended with:

> Certainly, a way must be achieved to arouse the membership of this great union so they take a greater interest and voice in what the union is doing. Whether the very character of the union would defeat such progress is certainly problematical. The plain fact is, however, that there is very little in the present leadership of the union to arouse public confidence.
>
> A top economist told me: "Jimmy Hoffa is a benevolent dictator. He has as much power as the hydrogen bomb or the president of the United States. Like any dictator, he could cause chaos if he got up some morning on the wrong side of the bed."
>
> Jimmy Hoffa has said the Teamsters wouldn't dare tie up the country. "We're too smart for that," he told me. But in a more candid moment, Hoffa told a San Francisco newspaper reporter: "We control the United States. Everything shipped from the east to the west passes through the Central Conference. We can tie up the whole country."

The article was tough, hard-hitting, and, if I do say so myself, well written. It would have quite an impact; that is, it *would have had* quite an impact had it appeared in *Collier's*. The reason it did not was that *Collier's* itself stopped appearing.

Shortly after I'd finished the articles on the Teamsters—which were based on three months of interviews and digging all around the country—I was sent to a small town outside of Pittsburgh to do a story on a community of refugees from Hungary who had moved there after the bloody revolution in their homeland. I finished my research and flew back to New York during the first week of December 1956. Exhausted, I didn't even unpack, just slid between the sheets and went right to sleep.

I'd been asleep but a short time when the phone rang. It was Dick Trezevant, the managing editor of *Collier's*.

"Don't bother finishing the Hungarian article," he said. "If it ever gets printed, it won't be in *Collier's*."

"What?" I said groggily.

"The owners are folding the magazine. It's dead."

There was a brief flurry of activity on the part of the staff (led by Teddy White) to try and find new investors who would save the magazine, but ten days before Christmas it was all over. We were all out of work. Merry Christmas, everyone.

Within the next forty-eight hours, I received two very interesting phone calls.

One was from Smitty, who said that if I was looking for a job, he knew of one—with the Teamsters! Einar Mohn, then the executive vice president of the union, had said they wanted to hire me to run their public relations office. Apparently, the union felt that if I went to work for them, I would never dare print my article. Thanks, but no thanks, I said.

The second call was from Bobby Kennedy, who wanted to know what I was going to do with my Teamsters material. I said I would be happy to make any or all of it available to him.

"Great," he said. "I'll be in touch."

CHAPTER FIVE

IT WAS VALENTINE'S Day, 1957, and though the envelope I held in my hand contained a surprise, its delivery would not be considered a loving gesture. I was in the waiting room of Einar Mohn's grand office in the Teamsters' $5.5 million marble-covered national headquarters in Washington, D.C., waiting to see him.

I was ushered in to Einar's office within minutes, and he greeted me warmly.

"Pierre," he said, "I've been waiting to hear from you. I hope you have good news for me."

"Not exactly," I said, handing him the envelope.

As he scanned its contents, his expression changed from surprise to concern and then to something like bewilderment.

"I'll be goddamned," he said, "this is a subpoena!"

That it was, a subpoena from my new employer, the U.S. Senate Select Committee on Improper Activities in the Labor or Management Field, and it was signed by my new boss, its chief counsel, Robert F. Kennedy.

Einar Mohn shook his head and then said, laughing, "This is a hell of a way to turn down a job offer. You tell your Mr. Kennedy that I'll comply fully. I have nothing to hide."

And he didn't. Einar Mohn was one of the most honest officials in the entire union, and he had no entanglements with either Dave Beck or Jimmy Hoffa. He knew his union had serious problems, and he never held my investigative work for the magazine or the select committee against me. (In fact, seven years later when I ran for the U.S. Senate, he saw to it that the Teamsters union made a healthy contribution to my campaign.)

Quite a few things had happened in the relatively short period of time between *Collier's* folding and my going to work for Bobby Kennedy. Just a day or two after I talked with Mr. Kennedy, I got a call in New York from a man who identified himself as Carmine Bellino. He was the chief accountant for the McClellan committee, as the select committee was generally known, and he wanted to know how soon I'd be ready to make my material available to the committee. "Right away," I said. The very next day, he and Paul Tierney, one of the best investigators on the committee's staff, were knocking on the door of the New York office of *Collier's* (or what was left of it). I showed them to my files, and they rolled up their sleeves and went to work.

Several hours later, they'd finished their reading and were ready to question me. It was soon apparent that these men were thoroughly professional and very smart. When they'd finished, Bellino thanked me and said, as he left, that I would be hearing from Robert Kennedy.

My immediate problem was simple—I needed a job. When *Collier's* folded, there was no severance pay, no two-month notice. My last paycheck was my last paycheck. However, as luck would have it, I got a late Christmas present in the form of a call from the editor of a magazine called *House and Home;* he was looking for an assistant news editor. It was far less interesting work—I would be writing about such things as the mortgage market for returning servicemen—but the pay was adequate, and I was in no position to be choosy.

By this point my marriage, for all intents and purposes, had been over for several years. I had filed for divorce, but it had not yet been granted. I had met a lovely young woman by the name of Nancy Joy, and we were planning to get married as soon as my divorce from Renee was final. Nancy and I were living in a rented apartment in Manhattan, and I was, of course, supporting my children, who were living with their mother back in California (which meant another rent check each month). That situation, however, was deteriorating rapidly.

Renee's drinking had escalated, and the kids, young as they were, were beginning to notice and be discomfited by the differences between their lives, and life-style, and that of their friends. My eldest son, Marc, had already hinted that he would like to come and live with me and Nancy, but I didn't think much of the idea at that point, given my circumstances. For one thing, Nancy and I lived in a tiny apartment in the middle of New York City, and for another, we were not married (this was, after all, the

1950s). My mother kept me in touch with the realities of the home-front situation in California, and it was becoming increasingly clear to me that something was going to have to be done, and the sooner the better.

I reported for work at *House and Home* on December 29, 1956, but within weeks my gratitude was fraying around the edges because the work was so boring. Then one day during the first week of February 1957, the phone on my desk rang and I picked it up, to find Bobby Kennedy on the other end. To my great delight, it turned out he was offering me a job as an investigator on the Senate select committee.

Three years later, in *The Enemy Within,* his best-selling book on our investigation of the Teamsters, Bobby Kennedy would write, "The first investigator to join our staff after we became a Select Committee was Pierre Salinger, a former newspaperman who had written many stories on the Teamsters." Seeing as Mr. Kennedy would drive me harder than anyone else in my life, before or since, I have always been very proud that he went on in his book to describe me as "inquisitive and indefatigable." Coming from Bobby Kennedy, that was high praise indeed.

Of course I had no way of knowing, but that would turn out to be the most significant phone call of my life.

My initial meeting with Senator John L. McClellan, the conservative southern Democrat who chaired the select committee (also known as the "rackets committee") was definitely inauspicious. I didn't know it until later, but Bob Kennedy had gone out on a limb in hiring a reporter as an investigator, something that may never have been done before on Capitol Hill. When I was introduced to Sen. McClellan on my first day on the job, he was polite, but he left me with the chilling warning that if he ever heard I had been leaking, or even *speaking*, to the press, he would deal with me "in the harshest manner possible." I was determined to give him no reason to do so, and I did not.

That first day on the job ended with an invitation from Robert Kennedy to go out to his house for dinner. I accepted immediately and with pleasure. (Nancy was still in New York, and I was living in a cheap hotel until I could take the time to find a decent apartment or small house to rent. The thought of a good meal in what I'd heard was a great house was very appealing to me.)

Bob led the way down Pennsylvania Avenue, past the White House (where the Eisenhowers had been ensconced for what seemed ages), into Georgetown, and then across the Potomac and out Chain Bridge Road to Hickory Hill, their estate in the Virginia suburb of McLean. They had bought the house, a small mansion that came with tennis courts and a swimming pool, from Bob's brother Jack and his wife, Jackie, when they moved to the N Street house in Georgetown, where they lived when he was elected president.

Senator Kennedy and his wife, who'd bought Hickory Hill from the widow of Supreme Court Justice Robert Jackson, loved the place, but they'd found it was too far away for Jackie to be able to get back to the city to join Jack for dinners and other social events. For Bobby and his wife, Ethel, whom I met that night for the first time, it was ideal. Although they'd been married for less than seven years, they already had five children—and would eventually have six more, including a daughter born late in 1968, the year her father was killed.

(Mrs. Hugh D. Auchincloss, Jackie Onassis's mother, once recounted a brief history of Hickory Hill, as it related to the Kennedy's, to an interviewer. Asked if Jack and Jackie had actually lived in the house, she said, "Oh, yes. They bought it and they moved in there intending to live there always, and they did quite a lot of remodeling. I remember all the effort Jackie went to for Jack's bathroom and dressing room. The shoe shelves had to be in just the right place to reach and the drawers had to be so he wouldn't have to lean over to open them—so that it wouldn't hurt his back. I remember the endless trouble she took over that. But they only lived there about [six months] . . .

"They spent so much time remodeling Hickory Hill. I guess they must have bought it in the spring and worked all through the summer. Then when they moved into it, it was still in a state of being fixed. . . .

"It was a difficult place for Jackie to live. When you are married to a busy senator . . . She was alone very much out in the country; because Jack would not get home until very late in Georgetown, she could rush down here and have dinner with him or he could get home late. . . .

"It really had been too lonely for her there, I think, particularly because she was having Caroline that winter. . . . Everybody decided that the best thing would be for her to live in town, where he could bring people home with him and they could get home under their own power, or if he couldn't get home, she was in the city, with people around her. Then Ethel and Bobby, I think, were in very crowded quarters in town, so that worked out very well. They bought the house from Jack and Jackie."

When Bobby pulled up in the drive that night, with me right behind, he was met by a tidal wave of tiny tykes, plus an equal number of dogs. All seemed impervious to the cold night air. It was love on foot, and hoof. Norman Rockwell would have swooned.

Once inside, he led me to a large sofa in a comfortable den, where a monstrous fire blazed. Legions of Kennedys beamed out at me from silver picture frames everywhere I glanced in the room. "Want something to drink?" Bobby asked.

"Nothing until dinner, thanks," I replied, "but then I wouldn't mind a glass of wine."

Bobby made a face. "I'm afraid we don't have a bottle of wine in the house. I could send somebody for one."

"Not to worry," I said, and went out to the trunk of my car, where I kept a bottle of good California pinot noir for just such an emergency.

At first, I wondered if the small amount of wine Kennedy drank with dinner had loosened his tongue, because our conversation was quite candid. (Later, I would learn he was always very direct and to the point.) Halfway through dinner, he turned to me and said, "Pierre, I have a confession to make. I'm having some misgivings. I wonder if I made a mistake in hiring you."

"Why?" I asked, trying not to choke on my food.

"Because you're not a trained investigator. I know you've done a lot of investigative reporting, and Bellino and Tierney tell me they're both impressed with you and the work you did, but I suspect my legal standards are more stringent than those of your editors. No offense, of course."

"None taken," I said, lying adroitly and wondering if Bobby was expressing his personal concerns or those of *his* boss, Senator McClellan, "but I beg to differ. I believe that a good reporter can hold his own against any investigator you can name."

"Well," he said, flashing that magnificent grin, "in any case, I just feel it would be better if I didn't send you on the road right away. I'm going to keep you in Washington for a while. I think that would be the safer course. Now, let's have some more wine and talk about Jimmy Hoffa."

That we did, for hours, and his stories were at least as good as the ones I'd run across during my own investigation of Teamsters president Dave Beck and his heir apparent, James Riddle Hoffa. For example, he told the sad tale of a man who had made the mistake of standing up to the Teamsters. It happened on the West Coast—in San Diego, specifically.

"A union organizer from LA who'd gone to San Diego to organize jukebox distributors had been warned to stay away," Bobby said. "Unfortunately, for him, he did not, and he was bashed over the head and knocked unconscious. When he woke up the next day, he was covered with blood and had such intense stomach pains that instead of driving home, he headed for the nearest emergency room, where, following an examination, he was rushed into surgery. They removed a large cucumber from his backside."

"Oh my God," I said.

"He was warned," added Kennedy, "that if he ever came back to San Diego, next time it would be a watermelon. He never went back."

The conversation continued in that vein for quite a while, and when I left, it was almost midnight. It had been a special evening, spoiled only by the fact that Bobby Kennedy felt I needed "seasoning"—or something—before I was qualified to go out on the road for the committee.

At seven thirty the next morning, a Saturday, the phone jarred me awake.

"Pierre? This is Bob Kennedy. I've changed my mind about keeping you in Washington. There's a plane for Seattle that leaves National at two this afternoon. I'm sure you can still get a seat. Bellino's at the Olympic Hotel. You should stay there, too. He's already started digging into Dave Beck's financial records, and he can use your help finding some items that are 'conveniently' missing."

To this day I don't know why Kennedy altered his plans for me, but I've always been grateful. Perhaps it proves the importance of always having a bottle of good red wine on hand.

I received my baptism of fire in the ways and workings of the Senate select committee that very evening. It was almost midnight when I checked in to the Olympic Hotel, and seeing as the next day was Sunday, I figured I'd have a day of sight-seeing and getting settled before starting work on Monday morning. No way. There was a message waiting for me at the front desk. It said, "Welcome to Seattle. See you at eight in the morning. Bellino."

The work that began on a cold and rainy Sunday morning in Seattle would continue for two and a half years and result in a series of congressional hearings that would peel back the thin layer of respectability to expose the core of rottenness that was the Teamsters union as run by Dave Beck and then Jimmy Hoffa. As we would discover over and over again, the members themselves were almost all honest, hardworking people, but at the very top of the organization their leaders were corrupt. These leaders used trade unionism for their own ends, simply as a means to acquire power or money or both. They made a mockery of a great American—a great world-wide—movement; thus it will remain one of the proudest achievements of my life that I was able, thanks to Robert Francis Kennedy, to play a role in bringing down those corrupt labor leaders.

The modus operandi of the select committee was that the investiga-tors *and* Bob Kennedy would fan out across the country, gathering evi-dence in the form of sworn statements and a variety of documents (eventually the staff of investigators, accountants, and secretaries numbered more than one hundred). Then, back in Washington, we'd repair to our offices in the Old Senate Office Building and put together a case against one of the corrupt leaders, be it Dave Beck, Jimmy Hoffa, or a lesser official. Next, we would subpoena that person to appear before the committee at a public hearing. We would also subpoena people who were not the objects of our investigations but who might have direct (but not culpable) knowledge of illegal transactions by higher-ups in the union.

For example, in Seattle, on my "maiden voyage," my assignment was to try to find the source of a twenty-thousand-dollar "loan," the proceeds of which we believed had been used to build a bar in which Dave Beck had a financial interest. Our chief suspect was a union official in Spokane; if this man had lent Beck the money out of the union's coffers, that would definitely be an illegal act. Bellino had already sent two other investigators up to Spokane, but the man had stonewalled them. Carmine thought I might have better luck. I did.

The man simply opened up and told me what he had refused to tell the other investigators, and it was just the information we were looking for. One reason he did so was that we had a number of mutual friends who were union leaders in San Francisco, and it may also have helped that he'd heard of my newspaper work in California and the Northwest. But the clincher was that my prospective father-in-law was a most unusual and interesting man who just happened to be from, you guessed it, Spokane, Washington.

Whatever the reason, he decided to talk. But first he decided to punish me a little: I had showed up at his door at dinnertime, and he made me wait, hat in hand, while he demolished a huge steak. Then, over coffee, he said, "I might as well come clean. It's only a matter of time until you dig up the truth, anyway. The twenty grand came from my union. Let's go down to the office and I'll show you where I hid it in the books."

I phoned Bobby Kennedy from the union office to tell him of my find, and he was elated. He asked to speak with the union leader, then proceeded to convince him to fly back to Washington with me—and his records.

Several days later, I sat next to the man from Spokane while he told the committee, and the American public, how the international president of the Teamsters stole money from the rank and file of his own union.

Bob Kennedy's practice was to have the investigator who'd uncovered the evidence present it to the committee; he would appear in person before the panel of eight senators (four Republicans and four Democrats) and read his findings into the record. That established the basis for the questions to be asked when the object of the investigation came before the committee.

On the morning my man from Spokane was to appear, I was seated next to Bob at the counsel table. The senators were taking their seats, and the huge old room, the same one in which the famous Army-McCarthy hearings had been held just a few years earlier, was packed with spectators. Like those hearings, these, too, were televised, and interest was running very high. I had turned away from Kennedy to get something out of my briefcase when I felt a tap on my shoulder.

"Pierre," said Bobby, "I'd like you to meet my brother Jack."

I stood up and shook the hand of the man I would help to become the next President of the United States.

"Senator Kennedy," I said, "I really enjoyed your speech at the '56 convention."

"Thank you. My brother tells me you're doing a fine job. I'm looking forward to hearing your witness."

To this day, I've retained two clear memories of that initial meeting. The first is that he was taller than I thought he would be; the second, that his hair wasn't half as bushy as the editorial cartoonists like to portray it.

I can still remember the wonderful nervous anticipation of those days just before our hearings began. Bobby Kennedy was a whirlwind of activity, dashing here and there, making sure our exhibits and our books of deposition testimony were in order so that no tactical advantage would be lost while someone searched for the right document. The forum was not a courtroom, but that made no difference to the young chief counsel. He was as ready as a lawyer would or should have been going into the biggest case of his life.

To the public, the Teamsters union was represented by two men whom, to the extent they knew them, they probably admired. One of them, International President Dave Beck, presided over the vast affairs of the union from the palatial marble and mosaic-tile headquarters at the foot of Capitol Hill in Washington, D.C. The other, at forty-two, twenty years Beck's junior, was Jimmy Hoffa. The modesty of his headquarters building in Detroit belied his power, which was not only vast but also growing. By the time we would be finished with these men, the American public would come to know them for what they really were—crooks.

Both Hoffa and Beck had made the mistake of underestimating Robert Francis Kennedy. They didn't know what was about to hit them.

When we began our hearings, Dave Beck was the head of the Teamsters union, and though it was clear to all who followed organized labor that Hoffa was about to take his job, to the American public, Beck *was* the Teamsters. He played golf with senators, and even on occasion with President Eisenhower. He talked a very good game about ridding his union of the "bad apples," the criminal element, who had somehow taken over many of the largest locals. But it was all lip service. While not as bad as the worst of them, Dave Beck was as bad and as criminally corrupt as the men he claimed he wanted to kick out of the union.

On March 26, 1957, Beck appeared before our committee. Bobby was more than ready for him. Although Beck, aided by friendly (Republican) senators on the committee, was able to pontificate in full view of the TV cameras throughout most of the day and managed to come across as genuinely concerned for the good of his members, he had not reckoned with the zeal of our chief counsel.

Bobby later said to me, "You know, Pierre, I have to confess that when Dave Beck first took the stand, I felt sorry for him. I mean, here's a major public figure about to be utterly and completely destroyed before our eyes. But within five minutes of the start of the hearing, that feeling left me."

I knew what Bobby Kennedy meant. From my excellent seat, I watched our star witness closely. As the afternoon session wore on, Dave Beck seemed to be enjoying himself, and, in fact, as Kennedy later admitted, for most of it he completely dominated the hearing. Then, just when it appeared to be over, Bobby dropped a bombshell.

He said, "Can you tell the committee what your relationship has been with Mr. Nathan Shefferman?"

That was probably the last name Dave Beck wanted to hear at that point on that day. Nathan Shefferman was his Achilles' heel. And Bobby Kennedy went for it, but, using a trial lawyer's tactic he may have learned from his new friend, attorney Edward Bennett Williams, having mentioned the dreaded name, he then, seemingly, forgot about him.

MR. KENNEDY: Were Union funds used, Mr. Beck, to pay for gardening at your home?

MR. BECK: I must decline to answer this question because this Committee lacks jurisdiction or authority under Articles 1, 2, and 3 of the Constitution; further I decline to answer because I refuse to give testimony against myself and invoke the Fourth and Fifth Amendments; further because the question is not relevant or pertinent to the investigation.

MR. KENNEDY: Did you take some $320,000 of Union funds?

MR. BECK: [same answer.]

As Kennedy knew, Beck was not about to answer any questions of this sort. So, having demonstrated that, he called Nathan Shefferman. Chairman McClellan asked Beck to remain in the hearing room in case the testimony would "refresh your recollection."

Half an hour later, it was almost embarrassingly apparent that the air had begun to go out of the balloon that was Dave Beck. Not only did it turn out that Mr. Shefferman was a well-paid union *buster*; it was revealed he was also Dave Beck's very well-paid gofer. With a total of $85,000 (in union funds) given him by Beck over a few years, Shefferman had bought, for Beck and his family, among other things: undershirts from Sulka's in New York City, a radio; golf balls and clubs, sheets and pillowcases, football tickets; twenty-one pairs of nylons; five dozen diapers; outboard motors; shirts; chairs; love seats; rugs; a gravy boat; a biscuit box; a twenty-foot Deepfreeze; two aluminum boats; a gun; a bow tie; and six pairs of "knee drawers."

As Bobby said, "Wonder no longer who the 'I' is in the expression, 'I can get it for you wholesale.' It's Nathan W. Shefferman."

In July 1957, after I'd been with the select committee for almost six months, Bobby Kennedy sent me to Detroit to beard the lion, Jimmy Hoffa, in his own den. By this point, we'd already had several public hearings, and the negative impact on the Teamsters union in the media and the court of public opinion was considerable. If that bothered Hoffa, he gave absolutely no indication of it.

I had been sent to open a select committee office in Detroit and to get the ball rolling. So the first thing I did was to subpoena the officers of five Detroit locals. The next morning, I got a phone call from Frank Fitzsimmons, the president of Local 299, Hoffa's own (and the man who would, to Hoffa's increasing fury, succeed him after our investigation started the process by which he was eventually sent to jail).

"Jimmy wants to see you," said Fitz.

The first thing I did was call Carmine Bellino in Chicago and ask him to join me. Together, we encountered an angry Jimmy Hoffa in his office, surrounded by his five most important local officials, all presidents. I noticed that each of these men was holding his subpoena to appear before our committee along with all pertinent records. I also noticed that Hoffa's mood was quickly darkening. He was no longer just furious; he was livid.

"What are you trying to do to me?"

Carmine Bellino explained that we had an ongoing investigation into the Teamsters and that if he had nothing to hide, then he had nothing to fear.

"You tell Bobby Kennedy for me that he's not going to make his brother President over Hoffa's dead body!" (If ever a statement was fraught with irony, that one was.) He then got up from his oversized desk (which sat on a raised platform in order to give the five-foot-five-inch

Hoffa a certain advantage) and grabbed the subpoenas out of the hands of his lieutenants.

He was too smart to rip them up, but he was clearly letting us know that he was the dominant figure in the room. Bellino and I thanked him for his time, then left. We knew that the man we worked for was also a strong figure and that our day would come—and soon.

When it did, we were more than ready for him. Our ducks were all in a row. And Hoffa, try as he might—and did he *ever* try—could not joke away or ignore our evidence of his massive corruption. Bobby Kennedy presented the case against Hoffa in much the same way that he had against Beck, but not in the same manner. For Jimmy Hoffa had gotten to Bob Kennedy, had deeply offended his innate sense of honor and decency. Thus begun a blood feud.

Hoffa's appearance before the select committee was something to behold. It raised arrogance to new and dizzying heights. If Dave Beck had given the initial impression of being in control, then Jimmy Hoffa gave the impression of being in *charge*. He began by making the outrageous demand that he be given permission to edit the committee's record of his testimony, by which he meant change it in order to keep from being charged with perjury at a later date.

The first few senators to question him were relatively friendly; nonetheless, he treated them with condescension. But when the questioning from senators less favorably disposed to the huge union and its leadership began to get pointed, Hoffa bristled—and lost his memory. (As *Time* put it, Hoffa displayed "the kind of amnesia that hoods have long resorted to—before the era of the Fifth Amendment. To every implicating question there came an equivocating answer or a variety of dazzling disclaimers, e.g., 'to the best of my recollection,' 'I just don't remember,' 'I don't recall.'")

Finally, the Republican senator from New York, Irving Ives, who'd been one of the friendly ones, had had it. Glaring at Hoffa, he told the witness he had "one of the most convenient forgetteries of anybody I have ever seen. . . . By golly, you have not taken the Fifth, but you are doing a marvelous job crawling around it."

It only got worse. Yes, said Hoffa, a dishonest union boss might take advantage of business deals and loans made with employers of truck drivers; fortunately for the Teamsters, he would never do such a thing because he was "an honorable man." Nonetheless, he could not recall who'd lent him part of the twenty thousand dollars he'd invested in one company or why he had borrowed five thousand dollars from a businessman who had a Teamsters contract.

Finally, with the hearings almost over, Senator McClellan announced that he would be asking the Justice Department to check Hoffa's testimony for evidence of perjury. He said Hoffa had displayed "arrogant disrespect for members of the union, the general public, and the United States Government."

By 1960, when the McClellan committee made its final report, the Teamsters union was being run by monitors installed by a federal court and Hoffa was trying hard to regain control. The committee was scathing in its denunciation of Hoffa.

> The record before the committee very clearly establishes Hoffa's contempt for duly constituted authority. Time and time again he has evaded answering pertinent questions by referring the committee to other persons he claimed were in possession of the desired information. When these persons were summoned to testify they invoked the fifth amendment. . . .
>
> When to this conduct is added the spectacle of Hoffa raising five fingers as a signal to such witnesses to invoke the fifth amendment, no further comment on his motivation is necessary. . . . The decent elements of organized labor have hung a pariah's label on him.
>
> When the committee said a year ago that "if Hoffa is successful in combatting the combined weight of the U.S. Government and public opinion, the cause of decent unionism is lost and labor-management relations in this country will return to the jungle era," the statement was indeed prophetic. . . .

Bob Kennedy and I were relaxing at the end of a day not long after Hoffa had completed his testimony. Bobby remarked, "Hoffa is always saying how tough he is, how he destroyed employers, hated policemen, and broke men who stood in his way. But you know, Pierre, I've always felt that if a person was truly tough, actually had strength and power and the ability to excel, he wouldn't need to brag about it. When a grown man sits for an entire evening and talks continuously about his toughness [which Hoffa had done during the course of a dinner meeting between the two men just before the hearings], I can only conclude that he's a bully hiding behind a facade.

"I thought, Jimmy Hoffa has been reading his press clippings. And he is afraid I have missed them."

In mid-1957, my divorce from Renee became final. We'd had many good times, some bad, and several very bad. Most important, we'd had three wonderful children together. In the last few years of our marriage, I had been on the road a great deal, and it seemed to me best that the children were living with their mother in San Francisco, despite Renee's problem. However, it was becoming apparent that the problem was worsening, and I had to face the possibility of going to court to seek custody of the kids.

"My Pierrot"—thus began a touching and eloquent letter my mother wrote to me in early May of 1957, a letter that perfectly captured the *tristesse* of that special time in my personal life. The club in Detroit where I'd been staying during the Hoffa investigation did not have my forwarding address in Washington and so it returned to my estranged wife a letter she'd written me. Renee had phoned my mother, who also did not know of my move (because I hadn't called her), and my mother was worried.

She wrote that she'd dreamt of me that same night and that in the morning she'd had the strong sense that I was "right next to me, a sort of real presence as though you were thinking of me hard and needed me. Perhaps it was the stirrings of my subconscious mind."

Her letter continued, "When I brought Marc home yesterday, a pleasant surprise. During the weekend, when she was alone with Suzanne, Renee had really turned the house upside down—washed all the windows so they sparkled—washed the floor in the room where she has the TV and bookcase—put attractive curtains on the kitchen window. In a word, I don't remember having seen the house so attractive at any time. But it was a heartbreaking day, too—on the bookcase she had an adorable photo of yourself and of her taken by an itinerant cameraman shortly after you married and when you used to call for her at Livingston's after the Chronicle work—and all she did all day was to talk about you and the things you used to do together the first years of your marriage—and trying to rationalize your own contemplated marriage [to Nancy] while I knew all the while that the very thought hurt her so much that she could have gone out of her head right then. To break the spell, I suggested I'd like to phone her grandma and tell her how nice the house looked. But poor Grandma Laboure has been worrying herself sick. She said, 'Who cares how the house looks. This is May and in a few more weeks that divorce is final,' and she broke into tears at the other end—I had to hang up so Renee would not know! In other words, a day like a funeral..." The funeral would take quite some time to conclude.

At times, Renee was her old wonderful self (in September, she wrote me a lovely note on her thirty-first birthday, telling me that the notepaper and pen were gifts from the three children; she closed with, "A big hug and kiss to an old ex-husband"). At other times, she simply lost it.

In the fall of that year, she was arrested for threatening to jump from the roof of a house on Russian Hill. The *Chronicle,* which featured a picture of her captioned "Height-Loving Lady Snared," reported:

> Mrs. Renee Salinger who wanted somebody to talk to, found plenty of conversation yesterday—mostly with firemen, policemen and reporters. Mrs. Salinger, a willowy brunette who claims she is 22 [she was thirty] was found capering around the roof of a Russian Hill home at 1154 Filbert Street, threatening to jump off. . . . At first she refused to give a name. Later, police identified her as the divorced wife of Pierre Salinger, former San Francisco newspaperman. Still later, when booked at city prison for resisting arrest and drunkenness, she insisted that she was the wife of an unmarried assistant district attorney. Finally, she explained that she had only "borrowed" the assistant district attorney's name. . . .

The following summer, having received numerous reports from various family members (not to mention the children themselves; our son Marc had been living with me for several months at this point) that Renee was again drinking heavily, I hired a private detective. I did so with great reluctance, but in cases where one spouse asks the court to overturn the original award of custody (which was what I wanted now that Nancy and I were married and had a very nice rented house in Georgetown), California law required strong proof of parental neglect and unsuitability.

In late September 1958, I received the investigator's report. After identifying the neighbors whose statements were enclosed, it said, in part: "In my opinion, with additional trial preparation, you would have an excellent case for change of custody and it apparently would be a benefit to the children."

After mentioning the neighbors' report that a "new boy friend" had spent the weekend at the house, and that Chuck, Renee's old boyfriend, had been seen watching the house at night, he went on to write:

> According to Mrs. B. and Mrs. H. [the neighbors] Mark [sic], the boy you presently have, was late to school about 58 times and this was due to Mrs. Salinger sending him on errands just at school time when he was outside ready for school and awaiting a ride with Mrs. H. who takes 13 children to school. According to Mrs. H., the boy took the blame from the Sisters at school rather than tell them it was his mother's fault and Mrs. H. straightened them out because they thought the boy was lazy or dallying en route to school.

Another avenue that could be explored is that Mrs. Salinger apparently is well-known in the Irving Street bars and one night she took the gun out of the holster of Joe Meehan, police officer on the beat. Fortunately, she returned it without anything happening. Another possibility would be assistance from Chuck, the deposed boy friend. Everyone seems to feel that he is a nondrinking man who really loves her and has tried to help her. I believe your mother has spoken with him.

In August of 1958, Bobby Kennedy called and asked for my help in selecting a present for his father, whose seventieth birthday was to be celebrated in September with a big party in Hyannis Port. Bobby said his father's great wealth made it very hard to find something he didn't already have. I thought and thought, and then suddenly remembered a name— Jacques Lowe. Jacques was a gifted photographer with whom I'd worked on my last story for *Collier's*. I suggested to Bobby that he hire Lowe, have him come down from New York to Washington and take plenty of pictures of him and Ethel and the kids, and then assemble the best of them in a special "book," for Joe Kennedy. Bobby thought it was a great idea, so I made the arrangements (I think it cost Bobby one thousand dollars) and Lowe came down and took the pictures.

The morning before the day of the big party, I got a distress call from RFK. The book had not yet arrived. Where was it? I called Jacques Lowe in New York, who told me the book was ready and waiting to be picked up. When Bobby heard that he dispatched me to get it. "Bring it up to Hyannis, and stay for the party." I did so, and it was a grand affair.

When Joe Kennedy opened his present from Bobby, he didn't just like the pictures, he loved them. In fact, he was so impressed that even though it was eleven thirty at night, he picked up the phone and called Jacques Lowe in New York. "I just want you to know," he said, "that you are now the official photographer of the Kennedy family."

Thus began a wonderful, and mutually beneficial, relationship between Jacques and the Kennedys, a relationship that spanned the White House years and beyond. I am proud to say that I played a central role in forging that bond.

Another assignment from another Kennedy resulted in another, albeit smaller, accomplishment of which I am also proud. It was the fall of 1961, and President Kennedy was preparing to host the first White House Correspondents' Dinner. He said to me, totally out of the blue, "I think we need a singer. Can you think of one they'd like?"

Coincidentally, I'd just been hearing reports from the West Coast about a young woman who was getting rave reviews. I mentioned her name to JFK, who said, "I've never heard of her, but that doesn't mean anything. See if you can get her."

I did, and she performed spectacularly. Her White House reviews were even better than the ones from California, and gave her fledgling career a boost. Her name? Barbra Streisand.

In May 1959, after I'd been working on the select committee for over two years, I received a phone call from Paul Butler, the Democratic National chairman, with a job offer. The committee's work was winding down, so Mr. Butler's timing was excellent. I went to see him in his Washington office.

"Pierre," he said, "part of my job as national chairman is to beef up the Democratic Advisory Council, which has the task of attacking the Republican record both foreign and domestic and putting forth Democratic alternatives. We'd like you to take the job of publicity director of the council."

I was flattered, and said so, but I told Butler I had a problem.

"What's that?" he asked.

"It seems to me that in that job I'd have to give equal weight and effort to all of the Democratic candidates for the presidency, and," I said, pausing, "I couldn't do that because I've already made my own choice for President."

"And who's your choice?"

"John F. Kennedy."

A smile crept across Butler's face. "That will present no problem."

I hurried to the nearest phone and called Bobby Kennedy to tell him of the offer.

"Hold your horses," said Bobby. "Don't give them an answer for twenty-four hours. Okay?"

I agreed. The next morning, I had been at work for just a short time when the phone rang. It was Senator John F. Kennedy.

"Pierre, could you come up to my office right now?"

Of course I could, and did, and when I walked in, he came around from behind his desk and stuck his hand out.

"Pierre, I'm going to run for President next year, and I want you with me in the campaign."

He stopped right there. No mention of what the job would entail or what I would be paid or even when he wanted me to start. None of that made any difference to me.

"Senator," I said, grasping his hand, "you've got yourself a man."

CHAPTER SIX

Sixteen people attended this conclave and it is well to pause and study them, for their craftsmanship and vitality were in the next year to create a President—and with greater precision, against greater odds, across more contrary traditions, than had been shown by any group of amateur President makers since Abraham Lincoln's backers a century before, had changed the structure of nineteenth-century politics.

So wrote Teddy White, in *The Making of the President, 1960*, about a meeting that took place in the Hyannis Port, Massachusetts, home of Robert Kennedy on Wednesday, October 28, 1959. He then went on to introduce Kenny O'Donnell, Larry O'Brien, Ted Sorensen, Jack and Bobby's brother-in-law Stephen Smith, the pollster Lou Harris, among others, and me, about whom he wrote the following:

Also there, for the first time admitted to the in-group, was Pierre Salinger, then thirty-four. Salinger, a man of French descent, a man of dark, round face and broad cheeks, might, with ten or fifteen more years of age, be mayor of any Burgundian village—large in manner, full of gusto, a wine drinker and brandy bibber; his mind, in the French manner, is at once jovial and quick, shrewd, practical. In the year to come, as his cigars grew bigger and his duties more responsible, Salinger was to harden from a boy to a man. Wartime skipper of a minesweeper in the Pacific at the age of nineteen, then a newspaperman in California, then a congressional investigator, he had twin loves—the craft of the press in general and the folklore of politics. It was, and is, a marvelous combination for press secretary, and no one who followed the Kennedy campaign through 1960 remembers Salinger with anything but respect and affection.

Much as I appreciate the late Teddy White's kind words, I would have to disagree slightly with some of his adjectival excesses, but I would agree completely with his statement that this was my first important meeting as one of the inner circle. No one was more aware of that than I.

I've never lacked for self-confidence, to be blunt about it, and at thirty-four I had an enviable record of achievement. But I *was* an outsider—indeed, as White pointed out, the only outsider. I'd worked with talented, sharp people before—especially at the *Chronicle*—but the drive and intensity of these people was of a type and degree I'd never before witnessed in a group that large. And they all knew one another well, whereas the only one in the group I knew any way near as well was Bobby Kennedy. I think it's fair to say that for quite some time I walked on eggshells.

I have two least-favorite memories from the precampaign period. One has to do with a press release I put out based on information dictated to me by Bobby. When a story based on the release ran the next day, I got an angry call from JFK.

"Damn it, Pierre," he asked, "how did that story get in the paper? Where'd you get that information?"

"Ah . . . from your brother Bobby."

"Look," he said, not at all mollified by what I'd thought a perfect explanation, "you're not working for Bobby anymore; you're working for me. Don't do anything he tells you to do without checking it with me."

For the rest of the time I worked for John F. Kennedy, I did not.

The second unpleasant memory involves the premature release of a letter. Somewhere in the Senate office buildings, each senator has a room known as the robotype room; it contains the large machine used for the reproduction and preparation of mass mailings. One day in mid-December, an enterprising reporter for United Press International (UPI) noticed quite a bit of activity going on as he passed the Kennedy robotype room, so he went in and picked up a copy of a form letter that began: "I am announcing on January 2, my candidacy for the Democratic Presidential nomination." (The letter was to be sent to Kennedy supporters around the country to give them a few weeks advance notice of the senator's plans.) As JFK had yet to make a public announcement of that intention, the letter was clearly *news*, and the UPI reporter did a story to that effect. The press immediately came to me for an explanation.

"Senator Kennedy," I said, rather lamely, "has not yet made a decision as to whether or not he will seek the Democratic nomination in 1960. The unsigned draft published by the United Press International is but one of a number of drafts being prepared by his staff covering all possible eventualities concerning the senator's decision."

At that point, I should have shut my mouth, but unfortunately, I did not. I added, "I have grave doubts the senator has even seen it." That caused one newspaper to editorialize that it had "grave doubts about the future of Mr. Salinger's job."

To my immense relief, after a brief explosion, Senator Kennedy found the whole thing quite amusing. It turned into a kind of baptism of fire, and our ensuing conversations were more relaxed and confidential, and I began to feel more like a member of the team.

Several similar incidents were mentioned by Barbara Coleman, eight years later, in her oral history interview for the JFK Library. A smart young former newspaper reporter whom I'd hired only a few weeks after the meeting in Hyannis Port, she had some interesting observations to make about the insider-outsider issue. "I don't know," she recalled, "that we had any special feeling that we were one group and the Senate staff was another. I think they, the Senate staff, the people who were around there, the people like Sorensen, in most of our opinion, were the insiders. There was just no question about it; they were the ones who were writing the speeches and making a lot of the decisions. Of course, Steve Smith was the one making the major decisions in the Esso Building [our unofficial campaign headquarters at the foot of Capitol Hill], and, of course, he was an insider, too."

That's certainly the way I saw it, and the way I have remembered it ever since. O'Donnell, Sorensen, O'Brien, Powers, Smith—they were all friends or relatives, or both, of many years standing. As for the other nonfamily members at that historically important meeting in October 1959, all of them knew the candidate far better than I did. Organizationally speaking, I was the new kid on the block, and that naturally made me a little nervous.

There were other reasons for being nervous. For one, everyone wanted to be as far up the chain of command as was reasonably possible, *and* as close to the candidate. In his 1969 book, *The Kennedy Legacy*, Ted Sorensen, who had been with John Kennedy since he'd come to the U.S. Senate in 1953, described how he felt to be bumped as campaign director by someone whose ties were even closer—Robert Kennedy: "Because his joining the campaign on a full-time basis as a member of the family 'club' immediately reduced me from number-one to number-two man in the throne room, there was at first some resentment on my part as well."

In all my jobs prior to the Kennedy campaign, I had found I could get along with just about anyone, so I didn't really anticipate problems with our team. And, as Sorensen also wrote, in reference to his feeling one-upped by RFK, "But there was more than enough for everyone to do. Bob and I each recognized very quickly that the other had not only a unique devotion but also a contribution to make to JFK's success that no one else could make. And the common affection we all had for our candidate and our common determination to put him across soon swallowed up all outward signs of dissension."

On a different level of the campaign, I underwent a similar metamorphosis. Still, it is interesting to note that Sorensen said, "all *outward* signs of dissension," and not "all signs." As for me, I chafed briefly over cracks I'd overheard, especially those having to do with my California roots, my lack of an Ivy League background, or my, ah, too casual attire. (In fairness, having gone over a large number of old photos from those days in preparing these memoirs, I have to admit that some of my outfits *were* different, especially in comparison with those of, say, the candidate.)

"[I]t would have been hard to find two men less alike," wrote another author (Patrick Anderson, in *The President's Men*) in describing Ken O'Donnell and me. "Pierre Emil George Salinger, a San Franciscan of French ancestry; Patrick Kenneth O'Donnell, Boston Irish. O'Donnell, the former Harvard football captain, lean and hard, Kennedy's bodyguard, sometimes carrying a gun; Salinger, a child prodigy as a pianist, the connoisseur of good food, wine, cigars, and women, who made a national joke out of his refusal to take a fifty-mile hike . . .

"To understand Salinger's unlikely presence in the Kennedy Circle, one must first understand that, beneath the Camelot glitter, there was always a strong prep-school flavor about the New Frontier. The main promulgator of this atmosphere was Robert Kennedy (Milton Academy '43) who in his days as Attorney General liked to yank down his necktie, toss a football on the Mall, and hang out with athletes."

Ted Sorensen is absolutely correct, however, when he says that our common goal of electing John Fitzgerald Kennedy the President of the United States overshadowed and overcame all individual differences. I still recall my surprise that even though we were already solidly for JFK, he continued to do and say things that increased our respect and admiration.

For example, at that memorable October meeting, after all the preliminary chitchat was out of the way, Kennedy got up and walked quickly to the focal point of the living room, the fireplace. Standing with his back to it, he began to deliver one of the most incisive and pragmatic political seminars I've ever heard. He spoke, completely from memory, for almost three hours, and in the process he took us all over the country, back and forth, up and down, assessing his political strengths and weaknesses region by region across the entire United States. In drawing us an amazingly detailed campaign blueprint, JFK had displayed a political knowledge that was simply encyclopedic. When the meeting broke up and we were leaving, I asked Larry O'Brien "How does he *do* that?"

He laughed and said, "You're talking about a guy who can still drive down a street in Boston and remember which stores put up his campaign posters ten years ago."

That example is but one of many reasons why, in the few short months that followed this meeting, I found myself changing from a Kennedy fan to a Kennedy *disciple*.

My deepening respect for John Kennedy continued on the campaign trail, specifically in the frozen north. Well, the frozen northern part of Wisconsin that makes up the Tenth Congressional District, which is about as far north as one can get in the state of Wisconsin and pretty close to as far north as one can get in the entire country.

In this area, the month of March is very definitely still wintertime, and I retain a vivid memory of Senator Kennedy, hatless, trudging like a trooper through the icy streets of one tiny town after another, his hands plunged into the pockets of his blue cashmere topcoat during the few moments when he wasn't shaking hands and greeting the local folks, many of whom were openly startled to see the charismatic young candidate in the (reddening) flesh on their own Main Street.

St. Patrick's Day, which had begun in the Ninth District town of Eau Claire, ended in the Tenth's Hurley, with a later visit to Ashland. At one point, after a street-corner drunk had urged the senator, unsuccessfully, to have a drink from his bottle, Kennedy turned to me and said, "That might play well in certain parts of Boston, but the *New York Times* wouldn't like it."

After his predictably easy win in New Hampshire, the nation's first primary, Kennedy had entered the Wisconsin primary, slated for April 5, because the state bordered Minnesota, the home of Hubert Humphrey, his main Democratic presidential rival. If Kennedy could carry Wisconsin, it would be a serious, perhaps even fatal, defeat for Humphrey; if he could carry the Tenth, which was overwhelmingly Protestant, it would send an important message to the rest of the country as to the electability of a candidate who happened to be Catholic.

In one modest grade- or high-school auditorium after another, John Kennedy stood and spoke to the young people, and if there weren't a whole lot of variations on his main theme—"I'm here looking for votes because Wisconsin is a key primary in a key state and the presidency is of tremendous importance to all of us"—there was a consistent sincerity that impressed me deeply. I'd followed a lot of candidates into a lot of towns, and I've never seen anyone who could match John F. Kennedy's vitality and, to borrow one of his favorite words, vigor.

What he kept hammering home at every stop was the fundamental importance of the presidency. He did so with such simple yet moving rhetoric that his words lifted all of us to a higher place, thoroughly convincing me that I had made the right decision in deciding to work for him.

I can remember that as early as the fall of 1959, after I'd heard JFK give a speech in Wisconsin, I came home and said to just about anyone who would listen, "This man is going to be the next President of the United States." I was so enthralled that I proceeded to call up half a dozen friends and tell them I'd just heard the most remarkable man in American politics, to which all of them replied, basically, "What have you been smoking? You're crazy. You've been in Washington too long."

Later, in New Hampshire in February, I was having dinner with John Bailey, head of the Democratic party in Connecticut (and later national head of the DNC) and Pat Morin, a very astute political reporter who was covering Kennedy for the first time. Pat and I had known each other for years, had always been on excellent terms, and also had, I'd thought, mutual respect for each other's political judgment. Yet when I told him I believed JFK would be the next President, we ended up in a big argument.

"For Christ's sake, Pierre," he said, "I'm not even convinced he can get the nomination."

"Okay, Pat," I replied, "here's what I'll do. I'll bet you a hundred dollars even money that Kennedy will be nominated on the first ballot."

"Are you crazy?" said Morin, who was about to add something when John Bailey interrupted.

"I'll take half the action—on Pierre's side of the bet."

I realized afterward that it might have appeared we were trying to influence Morin's coverage of Kennedy, but I had made the bet impulsively—yet with confidence—and would do it again under the same circumstances. However, my gesture did have that effect, because Morin later told me that he walked away from that dinner saying to himself, If those two bastards are willing to bet one hundred dollars even money on a first-ballot nomination, they really must know what they're doing.

After Wisconsin, I was even more excited about Kennedy's chances. Again, I put my money where my mouth was.

Twelve years earlier, in California, I had placed my one and only "big" bet on a political race. It was the 1948 presidential election, and I was so put off by the conventional wisdom that Truman had no chance that I bet twenty dollars, all my spare funds at that time, on HST at twenty-to-one odds, for a four-hundred-dollar payoff, a most impressive sum at the time. I'd not bet on a presidential race since then, but I was so impressed with John F. Kennedy that I took the plunge. In fact, I took it several times. I managed to come up with two thousand dollars, all of which I bet with a bookie in Las Vegas on JFK, at three-to-one odds. My friends, including fellow Democrats, told me I was nuts, but in November I pocketed a cool six thousand dollars.

For what it's worth, while Kennedy *did* win the Wisconsin primary, six districts to four, over Humphrey, he lost the Tenth District badly. All that driving around in that frigid weather and all those heartfelt speeches to schoolkids about the importance of the presidency had not softened the hearts and minds of the good burghers in Ashland and Hurley and Ladysmith and the scores of other towns in which we had campaigned.

Mistakes are a part of every campaign, and the 1960 Kennedy presidential campaign was no exception. Two of the biggest miscues were made by our in-house pollster, Lou Harris. In Wisconsin, Harris said his polling showed there was a slim chance that JFK could win the Ninth and Tenth, the far northern districts, and no chance to win the Second, a most important one, which contained Madison, the state capital. In fact, as we later learned, just the reverse was true. JFK remained bitter about that situation for quite a while, and his mood was not improved when Harris also made a mistake in West Virginia, the next primary.

Kennedy, ever the political realist, instantly knew the significance of the result in Wisconsin: "What does it mean?" asked one of his sisters. "It means," he said softly, "that we have to do it all over again. We have to go through every one and win every one of them—West Virginia and Maryland and Indiana and Oregon, all the way to the convention."

Kennedy would later say it was a mistake to have gone up and spent all that time in the Ninth and Tenth districts, both of which he lost (figuring if he'd used that last day to campaign in and around Madison, he might have taken the Second, for a seven-to-three win), but I disagreed. I've always felt that it was in the frozen north that John Kennedy forged his will to win.

As all students of the modern American presidency know, the next stop on the road to the White House was the big one—the West Virginia primary. It was in West Virginia, in May 1960, that Jack Kennedy demonstrated the viability of the idea that a Roman Catholic could become

President of the United States. Millions and millions of words have been written about the central importance of the West Virginia primary. I am not going to swell that total by much, but there are a few points I would like to make.

First of all, I should mention two important elements of the campaign that we had introduced earlier. One was the care and feeding of the press, which we had basically mastered in Wisconsin, and the second was the idea of the instant transcript of the candidate's remarks, which we had introduced in the New Hampshire primary (I hired a professional transcription service that worked twenty-four hours a day to produce almost instantaneous copies of JFK's remarks, an innovation the media just loved). By the time the campaign reached West Virginia, we had those tools well in hand.

There was another reason in addition to the religious issue why the West Virginia primary was so important. Senator Kennedy was clearly upset over the fact that by and large the national media, especially the press, had reported his 6-4 congressional districts win over Hubert Humphrey as a squeaker. We all felt that, quite to the contrary, it was an impressive victory, coming as it did in Humphrey's virtual backyard. As things turned out, however, that misreporting had an ironic twist.

Years later, Hubert Humphrey told me he'd decided that if Kennedy won big in Wisconsin, he would immediately drop out of the race and any further primaries; but he was sufficiently buoyed by the press accounts of the result in Wisconsin that he decided to stay in the fray. That, of course, turned out to be a bad, and financially costly, decision for Hubert, one of the nicest men ever in American public life.

Humphrey's presence on the West Virginia ballot gave John Kennedy the opportunity to face the religious issue head-on, and how brilliantly he did so is now history. A notably *un*successful effort, certainly by comparison, was my attempt to enlist the help of one of America's religious icons, the Reverend Billy Graham.

We were in the process of trying to get the nation's leading *Protestant* churchmen to sign a public statement urging religious tolerance in the political process, specifically in the West Virginia primary. While the statement was still in draft form, I happened to be on a train (from Bluefield, West Virginia, to Indianapolis), having breakfast, when I recognized the Reverend Billy Graham, who was doing the same thing.

I went over and introduced myself, and told him about the statement. He said he would sign it. I was elated. But it took Ted Sorensen, to whom I'd passed that particular ball, three days to get the religious leader on the phone. When he did, Billy Graham gave him a flat-out *no.* He said he had decided it would be wrong for him to "interfere in the political process."

Later that year, however, Graham appeared at a number of political rallies for Richard Nixon. (Apparently, it would have been wrong to interfere in the political process *on behalf of a Democrat.*)

We got to West Virginia several weeks early, armed with a Harris poll that showed Kennedy running ahead of Humphrey by a whopping seventy-to-thirty margin. Unfortunately, when he ran that poll, Lou neglected to remind the West Virginia voters that Kennedy was a Catholic. Once that word had spread, the margin *reversed,* and Hubert Humphrey had the huge lead. Had we known the lay of the land earlier, we would not have had to scramble so frantically. However, the scrambling was very good for us. It gave us the toughness that we needed going into the convention.

A funny thing happened on the way to the forum (the Sports Arena in Los Angeles). With two primaries still to go, Indiana and Oregon, the voluble, eloquent John F. Kennedy lost his voice. Suddenly, the candidate was speechless. We had several speeches already scheduled, one of them that very night in early May. We just *couldn't* pass up the in-person opportunity to expand on his views, to get them across to the hometown audience.

I had an idea. Picking up a yellow pad, I said, "How about if we have a Q and A session—the audience asks you their questions and then you *write out* your answers, and I'll read them?"

Kennedy looked at me and smiled. He grabbed the paper and wrote, *"Great Idea!"* And come evening, that was exactly what we did. The audience loved it. So did the newspapers, as I soon found out when friends all across the country sent me clippings of the story and accompanying photos from their local papers.

My strongest memory of the primaries is that the mental tape goes by so fast that everything is blurred. The things that stand out are often the oddities. For example, there was the political reporter whom I lost not once but twice.

My main job during the primaries was to shepherd the press and make sure they had access to the candidate and with as little difficulty as possible. This was not always easy. I distinctly remember one poor soul by the name of Ken Frye, the political editor of the *Milwaukee Journal.* Twice, buses pulled away, leaving him behind in some obscure city in the middle of a snowstorm. It happened that Frye did not like JFK (indeed, he was downright unfriendly to him in print), but that was not why I overlooked him. I just *lost* him, though I'm sure that to this day he thinks he was marooned on purpose.

I believed that the most effective thing I could do for the candidate was to create a climate in which it was as easy as possible for the reporters to cover our campaign. I also wanted to keep them all (even Ken Frye) as happy as possible. My success in this endeavor was limited during the primaries, but when we got to the general-election campaign, I believe we did just about everything we hoped to do. (Interestingly, it would turn out that my approach to the media was the exact opposite of that employed by Richard Nixon's people.)

Another difficulty was caused by the candidate himself. As the campaign wore on, John Kennedy got better and better at extemporizing, and he would simply jettison the prepared speech we had handed out to the press (whose members, of course, were working against deadlines). In fact, if we had put out a text for the senator, 95 percent of the time he wouldn't use it. Increasingly, this infuriated the reporters. They would file a story based on the speech, and then JFK would give a *different* speech, without even mentioning the main points of the prepared text.

Finally, I developed the policy of putting out a prepared text of only one or two pages, and he would dutifully make good on those pages. *Then* he would ramble. He knew he was better extemporaneously, and it took him a while to realize that he was generating considerable ill will among the press because we were passing out speeches that he didn't give.

After a while, Kennedy became almost sophisticated about the process. He would say to me, "Go talk to the boys and find out what it is in the speech that they particularly like, and then tell them I'll be sure to say that." So I'd go and talk to the AP guy or the UP guy and say, "What's your lead on this story?" I'd communicate the answer to the senator, and that part would always be in the speech. He would make sure their lead held up.

Kennedy had an insight into and an understanding of the press that was amazing. I remember one time not that much later when Henry Luce, the creator of *Time* magazine, walked into our office; JFK said, "I see Otto Fuerbringer got well and is back at work."

Luce about fell out of his chair. Fuerbringer, who'd been out for six weeks, had gone back to work the issue before, and Kennedy, who hated Fuerbringer, could tell. He knew *Time* so well that he could tell the difference when Fuerbringer was there and when he was not.

Something happened to John F. Kennedy in West Virginia. I believe that as a result of the time he spent there, during his visits to both the coal-mining regions and the big cities, there was a real transformation in him as a person. It was the first time that he came into direct contact with poverty. Prior to that, he knew what had happened because of the technological changes in coal mining, but in West Virginia he saw the human face of poverty up close—actual people, hundreds of them, sitting around with absolutely nothing to do, just sitting there letting grains of coal run through their hands.

That experience affected him deeply, and in my opinion, it changed his whole outlook on life. This was also true, though to a lesser extent than in West Virginia, of all the primaries.

A lot of people criticize the primaries, but I think they are absolutely essential to the education of a President of the United States, because they take him from the very narrow perimeter of his own life and environment out into the country, which is *so* vast that very few people ever get to know it.

For John Kennedy, who was born and raised in wealth in Massachusetts, suddenly to see the life of West Virginia was, I believe, the thing that produced Executive Order Number One, on January 20, 1961—the order for additional food stamps for hungry people.

The fact that Kennedy *cared* came through to people in West Virginia, and it came through more clearly than in any other state in which he had campaigned. Coming from a seventy-thirty disadvantage to win the election with a sixty-forty plurality was nothing short of amazing. No one expected him to win by that much. By election day, we predicted he'd win by a margin of fifty-one to forty-nine, or even fifty-two to forty-eight, but no one had predicted a sixty-forty win.

That primary won the election for him. As far as I'm concerned, that was the key to it right there.

I was not the only one who felt that way. That very same night, John F. Kennedy himself knew that he was going to be elected President of the United States. About 9:00 P.M., Robert Kennedy called him in Washington and told him the good news. JFK flew right down, led the celebration, and turned around and returned to Washington that same night.

I flew back with him, and he was simply elated. He was as loose as I'd ever seen him, telling jokes, laughing. That night, he *knew* he had the nomination. The funny thing is that he always knew he was going to get it. I don't think he ever had the slightest doubt about it.

West Virginia was the last tough primary. Kennedy won handily in Indiana and Oregon. By late spring, we were focusing entirely on the convention, which was scheduled to begin on July 11 in Los Angeles, at the Sports Arena, where we wanted not just to win but to do so, convincingly, on the first ballot. (After all, I had *money* on it!)

In *With Kennedy,* my 1966 book, I wrote at some length about our frenzied yet well-organized preparations for the win in LA, and I recommend that book (which can still be found in libraries) to readers who may want more details. What follows is a list of the highlights.

Among our primary objectives at the 1960 Democratic National Convention for which we found innovative solutions were:

- Setting up a central command post at the Sports Arena and organizing the demonstration on the convention floor when JFK's name was put in nomination (I went out to Los Angeles *three weeks* ahead of time to get started on these tasks).
- Housing the command post in a model home left over from a home show that closed on the eve of the convention. Senator Kennedy's old Harvard classmate Robert Troutman, an attorney in Atlanta, talked the home show officials into leaving the model home, which was located right next to the Arena intact; as for the demonstration, he enlisted the covert help of a *Republican* actor friend by the name of George Murphy. (In one of life's cruel ironies, four years later that same George Murphy would defeat me in my bid to win the U.S. Senate seat to which I had been appointed in March of 1964.)
- Creating a communications network (including walkie-talkies) that enabled us to be in almost instantaneous touch with our staff and with the leaders of the various state delegations. In order to augment that system, we published our own telephone directory, which, in addition to the delegates' hotel room numbers, listed when and where their caucuses were to be held and the various spots around Los Angeles, right down to their favorite watering holes, where they might be found on short notice.
- Devising a pocket signaling device which we called a locator. It was given to all Kennedy aides so that they too could be found in a hurry.
- Compiling a master card file on each and every delegate and alternate delegate that indicated whether or not he or she favored JFK (and if so, how strongly), where the candidate had met them, and what their nicknames might be. Each card also indicated religion, profession, local Democratic party office held, and even the delegate's hobby, if applicable.

In her oral history done for the JFK Library some years later, Barbara Coleman recalled the cards: "I think the whole card system was fantastically interesting. I never knew they would do something like that. I didn't know anything to compare it with; I didn't know what other candidates did. It seemed to me then that that was very practical. Whether or not anyone else had ever done it, I wasn't aware, but I know they kept those cards with great secrecy because they were putting all kinds of stuff on them that they probably didn't want people to know they were accumulating."

Two additional objectives were:

- Keeping our press headquarters open and fully functioning twenty-four hours a day and preparing a professional press kit on the candidate (who was clearly drawing more media attention than anyone else).
- Publishing a *daily* convention newspaper to keep the delegates, whose lodgings were all over LA, informed about the senator's position on various issues, and on those of the other candidates, as well. Every night of the weeklong convention— sometime between midnight and six in the morning—the paper was slipped under each delegate's hotel room door. This feat, which had never been accomplished before, was perhaps our single best idea. (In a display of nepotism to be outdone only by the President himself, I hired my brother Herb, normally a high school principal, as one of the paper's few *paid* staffers.)

When John Kennedy learned we had a daily press run of twelve thousand copies, as well as our own city room replete with AP ticker and a darkroom, he wanted to know if we could afford it. I said we were able to put out the paper's seven issues for a grand total of six thousand dollars. Kennedy, who knew a lot about the newspaper business and harbored dreams of running a paper someday when his career in public service was over, looked pleasantly surprised—and he said no more about it.

All national party conventions have their moments of low drama, even *low-class* drama. One of the lowest and least classy moments in the 1960 Democratic convention took place without my even knowing about it. In 1964, while interviewing me for the JFK Library's oral-history program, Teddy White said, "May I stop you just for one second, because whatever we say here can be released only at your wish. . . ."

I nodded, and he went on to say, "A person who is now very high in Johnson's administration called me about five days before the Los Angeles convention and said, 'I think you should know that John Kennedy and Bobby Kennedy are fags.' I said, 'You're crazy.' He said, 'We have pictures of John Kennedy and Bobby Kennedy in women's dresses at Las

Vegas this spring at a big fag party. This should be made public.' I said, 'I'll print it if you give me the pictures.' He said, 'I'll get you the pictures in twenty-four hours.' "

No pictures were ever delivered, and Teddy White never wrote about it. Unfortunately, such tawdry stories are hardly unusual during national party conventions. In fact, as such bizarre tales go, that one, in my experience, is one of the mild ones.

All of our efforts coalesced on the night of July 13 when John Fitzgerald Kennedy won his party's nomination for President of the United States on the very first ballot. I can remember few, if any, nights that were more exciting. By the time the roll call of the states got to the W's, Wyoming knew it had an historic opportunity. Robert Kennedy and I were among the faithful huddled in front of the small television set in the model home. When we heard "Wyoming casts all fifteen votes for the next President of the United States, John F. Kennedy," we leapt to our feet and danced an impromptu French-Irish jig around the room.

Our hard work was over. Our hardest work was about to begin.

In the years since the Kennedy presidency, one of the few truly persistent questions has had to do with the circumstances of JFK's choice of Lyndon Johnson as his running mate. In my opinion, which has not changed over the years, much of the controversy and confusion over LBJ's selection resulted from a semantic misunderstanding. When Bobby Kennedy told the Johnson forces that certain labor leaders and northern politicians opposed his nomination for vice president, Bobby's main objective was to find out if LBJ would fight for it. But Johnson's people interpreted this as an effort to talk him out of the race. This was not RFK's intention, *and* he certainly wasn't acting on his own, as some writers have suggested. He would never have undertaken a mission of this kind without Jack's knowledge and direction.

The reason I so firmly believe that Bob Kennedy did *not* want to keep Lyndon Johnson off the ticket is that he was the first person who told me LBJ was *on* it. At seven in the morning following JFK's nomination—but before the vice presidential candidate had been named—Ken O'Donnell and I walked into Bobby Kennedy's hotel room. He was taking a bath, and he called out, "Do you think we can win the election with the North, the Northeast, and the South?"

Ken O'Donnell immediately said, "Are you talking about Lyndon Johnson as a vice presidential candidate?"

"Yes," said Kennedy.

As it happened, both O'Donnell and I opposed the choice. (My preference was Senator Stuart Symington of Missouri, and Ken wanted Henry "Scoop" Jackson of Washington.) But the point is that Bobby Kennedy would never have said what he did when he did unless he had agreed that LBJ was right for the ticket.

John Kennedy admired LBJ. He believed, and often said, that if he didn't win the nomination, he thought Lyndon Johnson was the best-equipped Democrat to serve as President. The wisdom of his choice was certainly vindicated by the events immediately after the assassination.

But at least one element of mystery over Johnson's selection will always remain: That is the question of whether Senator Kennedy expected Lyndon Johnson to accept second position on the ticket or whether his offer was merely a pro forma gesture. A day or two after the convention, I asked JFK for the answer to that question. He told me much of what I've just related, then suddenly stopped and said, "The whole story will never be known. And it's just as well that it won't be." I cannot explain the cryptic remark, I can only report that JFK made it.

I mentioned earlier that my respect for Senator Kennedy, which had already been high, increased as I traveled with him during the primaries and listened to him speak. As I might be considered a biased observer, let me offer the observations of a young woman who, like Barbara Coleman, came to the campaign early on. Her name is Barbara Gamarekian. (After working in the White House, she went on to write for the *New York Times*.) Her comments, from her June 1964 oral history interview for the JFK Library, refer to the immediate postconvention period.

"I worked as a volunteer with the Minnesota delegation and then came back to Washington and pounded on the door at the Kennedy headquarters and eventually got a very interesting job working at the administrative end of the campaign.

"I didn't have, I think, strong feelings about President Kennedy at that point as a candidate. I had seen him on the Hill and had known about him, of course, for years. I didn't have any great sense of personal loyalty to him. There would have been, perhaps, several candidates I could have worked for as easily as for President Kennedy, although I was a very staunch Democrat and wanted any Democrat to win over Nixon."

Asked what kinds of things she was doing on the administrative end of the campaign, Barbara Gamarekian replied, "All the campaign coordinators reported to us. We had campaign coordinators in each of the states who were Kennedy men. They went in and tried to discover the progress of the campaign on the state level and report back to us.

"Larry O'Brien headed up this organization. I worked with Dick Donohue and Ralph Dungan and we supposedly were to have our finger on the pulse of the campaign at the grass-roots level and supposedly knew how it was progressing across the country and where we needed to send shock troops and where we were in trouble. It was a fascinating place to work because you got an overall view of the campaign, and I think the one thing I discovered was that you never really do know exactly what's going on. We had as many surprises, I think, as other people. But even at this point I didn't see much of the President. He was always campaigning on the road and we were working back in Washington.

"I think, like many Democrats, the TV debates were the first thing which began to make me identify somewhat with him and feel that I knew him a bit as a personality and a person rather than as the Democratic candidate. And it was great to begin to get terribly excited about your candidate and to begin to feel some feeling of personal loyalty and devotion to him."

Fortunately for me, my personal life during this period was about as settled as it had ever been. Nancy and I were happily married, and she was taking wonderful care of all three of my children, who were then (thank the Lord) not yet teenagers. We were still renting the nice house on O Street in Georgetown, but I told Nancy that if Senator Kennedy became President Kennedy, we would move to a bigger house that would be better suited to the size and shape of our young family. I'd heard about a very pleasant community called Lake Barcroft in the northern Virginia suburb of Arlington. It was a fifteen-minute drive from what I hoped would be my new work address—1600 Pennsylvania Avenue.

Not only was my immediate family well situated but so, too, were my mother and my three younger brothers. Well, two of the three, anyway.

An interesting and somewhat unusual thing had just happened to my mother: She had remarried. Of course, there's nothing unusual about a second marriage (I should know; I've had three of them). What made hers unusual was that both she and her new husband had lied about their ages. Through a friend, my mother had met Jerry Carlson, a tall, quiet, easygoing man whose business was renovating homes in the Monterey area, south of San Francisco. The attraction was evidently mutual, because neither one wanted to chance losing the other, so they altered their ages. Jehanne Salinger told Jerry Carlson she was ten years younger than she was, and Jerry Carlson told Jehanne Salinger he was ten years *older*. Today, they are still married, and still happy. He is seventy-eight, and she is ninety-eight. The difference in age made no difference to them.

As for my brothers, Herbert, then thirty-four, and Richard, twenty-four, were fine. George, thirty, was another matter. I don't know where his alcoholism came from, because drink never affected the rest of us to anything like the degree it did George, but that was clearly his problem.

To this day, our mother will not hear of anyone's using the word *alcoholic* to refer to her third child; she prefers to say that George "had a problem with drink from time to time." As George himself phrased it back then, "I can take the booze or leave it alone, but I always prefer to take it." Luckily, as the election drew near, George was in good shape, and though he was still preferring to take it, he was doing so in relative moderation.

I realize that it sounds selfish to say this, but at the time I wanted no distractions from the task at hand—getting John F. Kennedy elected President, and thereby positioning myself for a very good shot at a job that until then I had only allowed myself to dream of having, press secretary to the President of the United States of America.

With the sole reservation that one should never underestimate the importance of the West Virginia primary, I wish to go on record—along with so many others—as saying that the television debates ensured the election of John Kennedy. In fact, the very first one did so.

Rather than try to re-create my memory one more time, let me quote my Q and A with Teddy White on this topic a year after the assassination.

P.S.: . . . about seven or eight days after our convention and the beginning of the Republican convention . . . we received a telegram from Bob Kinter [head of NBC] offering seven, eight, or nine hours of television time for a debate between Kennedy and Nixon. . . . I took the telegram to [Kennedy]. He made an immediate reaction—"Why not?" or "Let's do it." Then he said that we'd check with Leonard Reinsch [the Democrats' radio and television strategist]. I can't remember whether Leonard Reinsch was there or we called him on the phone. I talked to Ted, I believe, who was there. Within twenty minutes after we received the telegram, we had sent off a telegram to Kinter saying we wanted to do it. The feeling was that we had absolutely nothing to lose by a debate with Nixon. If we accepted right away, that would put Nixon in a position where he had to accept. Everybody just felt that the debates would be most helpful to Kennedy. . . .

T.W.: Do you, after setting up the thing, remember anything of Kennedy's reaction to it? Was he sure that he could take Nixon?

P.S.: He was always very confident, but he was going to do his homework. . . . He always did. He spent the day in Chicago with Sorensen, Feldman, and Goodwin. Then he came down to the studio. I remember when he arrived at the studio and when he had his first confrontation with Nixon. Nixon looked awful off-camera, he really did.

Kennedy went back to this dressing room and remarked how awful Nixon looked.

T.W.: Maliciously?

P.S.: No, no. He just looked awful. Not that [Kennedy] was not confident already, but it gave him an extra bit of confidence. He walked out of there knowing that he had him. . . . I think he thought Nixon was afraid.

At the end of the debate there was a lot of mixed reaction. A lot of people were saying it was a draw [especially those who had *heard* the debate on the radio, but not seen it on television]. Kennedy sent me out to talk to the press to find out what they thought had happened. Scottie [Reston] said it was a draw. The next day we hit Cleveland. The people were coming off the walls.

T.W.: I remember.

P.S.: As we drove down the street, out of the car behind me we heard guys shout, "Keep going after him, keep going after him. You really got a leg up, Jack." You knew it was the debate. . . .

T.W.: That was the quantum jump?

P.S.: That was it. The ball game was over. Of course, there was the second debate, when the Nixon people tried to freeze the studio. They had them turn the temperature down to forty degrees or something. When you walked in there, you needed a parka, a fur coat, in the goddamn joint.

T.W.: I think Nancy [Mrs. White] has got one thing that perhaps you should put in the record. We spoke to Rose Kennedy sometime after that. She said, "I felt so sorry after that first debate. I felt I should say something to Mrs—"

NANCY W.: "No, no. [She said] "I felt so sorry for Nixon's mother."

T.W.: Yes, She felt sorry for Nixon's mother because Nixon had lost the debate.

NANCY W.: The most motherly comment I ever heard.

I ended the first of my several tapes with Theodore White with this account, then only five years old, of my recollection of the last few days and nights of the 1960 presidential campaign.

P.S.: [Two nights before the election] we ended up in Waterbury, Connecticut, at 4:00 A.M., and found forty thousand people who had been waiting for five hours, standing in front of this hotel. Kennedy was late.

T.W.: One of the great nights in the campaign.

P.S.: Absolutely the greatest night in the campaign.

T.W.: With every fire engine out alongside the road.

P.S.: So he got up on the balcony of this hotel and gave this fantastic speech. He went to bed at 4:30 or 5:00 A.M., feeling great, and had to get up at 6:00 A.M. to start campaigning again. So we rolled into Boston election eve. There was a great rally at the Boston Gardens. . . . I was so tired that night, I didn't even go to the goddamn rally in Boston Gardens. I watched it on television. After, about a half dozen reporters were clubbed by the Boston police. I was insulted by the press again for not being there to defend their lives. The next morning, he voted and went up to the Cape.

T.W.: Tell it slowly and with joy. Go ahead.

P.S.: I had set up this deal for the press at the Armory. I had run about three direct lines from the Armory into the Kennedy house, the ambassador's house. I guess I stationed Don Wilson and Andy Hatcher at the Armory, and I went over to spend the night at the Kennedys'. It started out like gangbusters; it started out like we were going to win by a landslide. In fact, the computer said we were. Then everything started to go bad all over the place. By midnight, it was a real dog race.

   JFK would come over for a while, and then he would go back to his house. He would come over to watch for a while and then he would go back. Finally, about 2:00 A.M., he came over and stayed until about 4:00 A.M. Nixon came on the screen and said that he wouldn't concede. Kennedy said, "If I were he, I wouldn't concede, either." Then he started to walk off, and I said, "What am I going to tell the press?" I hadn't even been down to see them yet. He said, "Tell them I went to bed. Wake me up if anything happens."

   So I went down to the Armory and held a press conference that lasted a half hour to forty-five minutes. Finally, I got to bed about 6:00 A.M.

T.W.: I have a complete videotape of that press conference of yours. If you ever want it for your private collection, I can give it to you.

P.S.: I'd love to have it sometime.

T.W.: I've got it.

P.S.: I looked so tired that night.

T.W.: You looked beautiful; you looked so young. You were cupping your hand over your ear like this to listen to questions. I suppose you were tired. But you were beautiful that night. Go ahead.

P.S.: Six A.M. I went to bed, and 6:45 or 7:00 A.M., a guy called me and said, "Kennedy just carried Minnesota. He's the President of the United States." Incidentally, we had gone to bed thinking he had carried California. So I said, "Well, God, I had better get over there and tell him that he's President."

I got in my car and left the Yachtsman. I started to drive. I had gotten about a block and a half from Kennedy's house when I was stopped by a man whom I'd never seen before in my life. He was wearing a suit; he was very well-dressed. He said, "Oh, Mr. Salinger, go ahead." This was my first encounter with the Secret Service. The fascinating thing about it was that they had studied the Kennedy staff completely. They knew all of our names; they knew what we looked like; they knew who should have access to the President.

When I got there, I found that Sorensen had beaten me there by about two minutes and had told Kennedy that he was President.

CHAPTER SEVEN

"PIERRE, I WANT you to stay on as my press secretary, all right?" It was Wednesday, the day after the election, and JFK and I were walking across the lawn toward his father's house. The President-elect had called a morning meeting to begin the work of setting up his presidency.

"*All right?*" If I hadn't been so thrilled at his words, I would have laughed out loud. It was a dream come true.

My response was honest, if unoriginal: "I would like that very much."

"It's yours, then," said Kennedy. "I'll let you pick your second in command."

I told him I would like to name Andy Hatcher, who'd been my backup man all through the campaign. "He's very able, and very loyal," I said.

"You've got him, then," said Kennedy, and, having just transacted the most important business of my entire life without so much as breaking stride, we continued to walk across the lawn. The process was characteristic of John Kennedy, characteristic of his basic decency. There were people who'd said—even to me—that while it was good of JFK to let me handle press relations during the campaign, if he won he would surely pick someone with more experience, or someone with a "name." (NBC correspondent Sander Vanocur was the person most often mentioned.)

Now, I will confess that there were times when this reasoning struck me as plausible. While I knew that JFK valued loyalty almost as much as any other attribute, I wasn't entirely sure that he would reward the loyalty of one who so clearly was an outsider. By doing so, he gave me the chance, and the job, of a lifetime. (In allowing me to choose Andy Hatcher as my top assistant, JFK made history, for Andy thereby became not just the first African-American ever to serve as an Assistant White House Press Secretary, but the *only* one.)

JOHN F. KENNEDY, PRESIDENT OF THE UNITED STATES OF AMERICA, to PIERRE E.G. SALINGER, of California, Greeting: REPOSING special trust and confidence in your Integrity, Prudence, and Ability I do appoint you Press Secretary to the President of the United States of America, authorizing you, hereby, to do and perform all such matters and things as to the said place or office do appertain, or as may be duly given you in charge hereafter, and the said office to hold and exercise during the pleasure of the President of the United States for the time being. IN TESTIMONY WHEREOF, I have caused the seal of the United States to be hereunto affixed. DONE at the city of Washington this twenty-first day of January, in the year of our Lord One Thousand Nine Hundred and Sixty-One, and of the Independence of the United States of America the one hundred and eighty-fifth.

It will surprise no one to learn that all of us, the entire White House staff having been sworn in in a single ceremony, had our commissions framed— and carried them with us to all the offices we ever occupied.

In addition to Nancy and the three Salinger kids, I'd invited a small crew of people to the inaugural events—Mother and Jerry, my brothers and their wives, and my half sister, Anne, and her husband, Nate, who, had he been a Catholic, I would have described as a man of the cloth.

Today, Anne lives in the beautiful leisure-world community of Laguna Hills, south of Los Angeles. She has been widowed three times. In 1960, she was married to her first husband, Saul Appelbaum. Anne was kind enough to share her memories for this book. Many of them remain quite vivid, despite the passage of more than three decades.

She remembers that she met John Kennedy for the first time early in the campaign. "He came to Rockford, Illinois, where I lived before moving back to California, to barnstorm the state, to decide if he should get into the primaries. I met the *Caroline*, his private plane, out at the airport, and then we all went down to the Shrine Auditorium. I remember JFK coming through the room, yelling, 'Hey, Pierre, your brother-in-law the rabbi is looking for you!'

"The night of the election," Anne recalls, "you [Pierre] called me at four o'clock in the morning. You probably don't remember, but I remember, because I had friends over, and we were cooking eggs and watching television. And at four in the morning, you called to say, 'Kennedy won— but *I* can't make any announcement until the morning!' You had to tell somebody. So we stayed up all night!"

All my inaugural guests who made it to the balls had a great time mixing with the odd and wonderful conglomeration of politicians and celebrities, and statesmen and artists that made up that oh-so-special celebration.

The inaugural balls were simply wonderful. I've never cared for the name Camelot as an accurate description of the Kennedy years, but the festivities on the night before the inauguration were, in fact, the stuff of which myths, and also dreams, are made. For one thing, it all began with a huge snowstorm that after threatening to cancel everything, instead merely postponed the galas into the wee small hours, where they took place in a fairyland setting.

Leonard Bernstein, the great musician, who was to conduct Washington's National Symphony Orchestra at the D.C. Armory that night, described (in 1965, in his interview for the Oral History Program of the JFK Library) the events as being, initially, "a fearful evening . . .":

> It was a madhouse because we had been rehearsing there all day—Bette Davis, Laurence Olivier, etc., millions of people—and this blizzard began to fall in the afternoon and nobody could get back to his hotel, to say nothing of getting back to the Armory. But we tried and were stuck in the middle, as were all the cars in Washington. I was stuck in Bette Davis's car. There were about six of us all being asphyxiated in this limousine, which couldn't move. Cars had run out of gas and were blocking the streets, and this blizzard kept falling. We never got to the hotel, but stopped off near where we were stalled, in somebody's apartment. Somebody in our car knew somebody who lived nearby, and we went up there to use the phone. We called the White House to come rescue us and get us back to the Armory so we could perform, but all their cars were out picking up people who had been stranded.
>
> Finally, we got the police cars to come and they drove us there on the sidewalks because you couldn't go through the streets, as the streets were all blocked with cars. Oh, it was

ghastly! We drove between the trees on the sidewalk in this insane police car back to the Armory, unwashed, unchanged, un-black-tied. And everybody was in kind of a special blizzard festival mood. It made the occasion more exciting actually than it might have been. It was gay, the way a city becomes festive when a blizzard falls on it and everybody feels helpless anyway and perfect strangers embrace and everybody becomes friends and sings and jumps in the snow. It was also rather nerve-racking, in addition to being festive, because of the tension and not knowing whether we could get back to the Armory or whether we were going to be stranded forever in the middle of Washington.

But get back they did, and were greatly surprised at the huge number of people awaiting their scheduled performance of Bernstein's own "Fanfare," which he'd written for the occasion, and the Hallelujah Chorus from Handel's *Messiah.*

It all began two or three hours later than it was supposed to. But it went off beautifully and I saw the President afterward at a party that was given at some hotel. In fact, I made the inexcusable blunder of cutting in as he was dancing with a friend of mine with whom I wished to dance, and since people were cutting in all over the floor, I thought nothing of doing likewise, except that I was cutting in on the *President.* He did look pale for a moment, but he got over it, and it didn't injure our relationship. He was very sweet about it.

Q.: He didn't make any quips?

BERNSTEIN: No, but the girl was furious. She made lots of quips. That was fun, that evening, I must say.

On Inauguration Day, having listened with rapt attention to the new President's stirring address (and watching with increasing sympathy as Robert Frost tried gamely to read the poem he'd written for the occasion, despite an electrical fire in his lectern), I slipped away from family and friends for a moment in the early afternoon, when we got back to the White House.

I wanted to find my new office and try it on for size. Jim Hagerty, that wonderful man who had served President Eisenhower so well for eight long years, had emptied the office down to the bare bones. (He had, however, left me his trusty wooden cudgel, with a note that instructed me to use it as a last resort in dealing with the press.) There were no files in the file cabinets and no books in the bookshelves, and the bank of buttons on the phone were all unlit and quiet. Behind a massive glass-topped oak desk, two long windows gave a view out over the gardens and toward Pennsylvania Avenue and Lafayette Park.

I leaned back in the swivel desk chair, put my feet up on the empty desk, and, taking out a fresh cigar, prepared to pollute the office of the press secretary to the President of the United States for the very first time. It was a glorious feeling.

Later, I snubbed out the cigar, left it in the huge ashtray that had providentially appeared on the desk since the last time I'd been there (visiting Jim Hagerty), and went out to join Nancy and our various relatives. Soon the revelry was in full swing.

The weather, however, continued to assert its dominance. My sister, Anne, remembers that I got them seats "right across from the reviewing stand. It was *so freezing* that when the band from Lompos, which is right above Santa Barbara, passed by, my husband said, 'We've seen it all, and we've been loyal to California. Now we can leave.' "

Then, all of a sudden, the festivities were over and it was time to go to work.

Much has been written in recent years about the "revolution" that Ronald Reagan brought to government. Well, the Kennedy administration also had its share of revolutionary changes, not the least of which took place in the office of the press secretary. Before getting into specifics, however, I need to stress the obvious yet crucially important point that the day I became the press secretary to the President of the United States, I was in an entirely different world from the one I'd been in the day before. Even though I was dealing with the same people, *I* was no longer the same person— because I was suddenly in the position where I was no longer speaking for a man who aspired to be President, but for a man who *was* President.

And that, as the poet wrote, makes all the difference. Overnight, the things the press secretary says weigh heavily, not only in the United States but also all around the world. Getting used to that took some doing, more so for me than for the press corps.

One of the greatest differences between my operation and that of all the presidential press secretaries who have held that position since the end of the 1960s is that I had more power because I had more access to my boss, the President. In fact, I had *total* access to the President. I didn't have to ask anyone if I could see him. I simply walked into the office of Evelyn Lincoln, his personal secretary, and if Kennedy wasn't busy, I could just go right in and start talking to him.

When I was press secretary, there was no communications director— that post was created under Richard Nixon in 1969—which meant that I was fully in charge of *all* communications. What's more, I was also in charge of all the departmental press secretaries, such as those of State, Defense, and Health, Education and Welfare (which is known today as Health and Human Services). Whatever news they wished to release to the press and the public had to be cleared through my office.

An indication of the problems caused by the limiting of the press secretary's power can be seen in this brief excerpt from *Speaking Out,* the 1988 book by Larry Speakes, who became President Reagan's de facto press secretary after the shooting of Jim Brady (and who also served in the press offices of Presidents Nixon and Ford). Describing a tiff between himself and David Gergen, he wrote, "I felt from the minute Brady was shot, Gergen had his eye on [the press secretary's job]. . . . Gergen was named director of White House communications, with control over the speechwriting unit and the out-of-town press corps, while I was appointed deputy assistant to the President and principal deputy press secretary. This was a bizarre arrangement that had me dealing with the Washington reporters for out-of-town newspapers, while Gergen dealt with reporters from the same newspaper who called from their home offices. Under Gergen's plan, he and I also shared briefing room duties, with me briefing the press three days a week and him two."

From what I've been told, Mr. Speakes, who held the job longer than anyone since Jim Hagerty, was a pretty good press secretary. Unfortunately, his place in history will be marked by his too-candid admission, in his book, that at times he made up presidential quotes. He told the media that Ronald Reagan had said things Ronald Reagan had not said.

Obviously, that was no way to run a railroad, or a White House press operation.

The first impression I formed of the White House press corps was that I was definitely dealing with an establishment, and an establishment that preferred its own routine. Over the years, the members of the White House press corps had figured out how they liked to cover Presidents, which was, essentially, to try to mold the press secretary so that he would see things *their* way. I quickly learned that a presidential press secretary who attempts to make changes that favor the President, and not the press, runs a very definite risk.

In 1960, the White House press corps consisted of approximately twelve hundred members, but the real inner circle was made up of no more than fifty members, at most. As far as the Establishment was concerned, there were layers within layers, but the inner, inner circle in those distant days was composed of the wire-service reporters, the folks who covered the White House for the Associated Press (AP) and United Press International (UPI.) In 1960, those posts were held, respectively, by Marvin Arrowsmith and Douglas Cornell, and, later, by Al Spivak and Merriman Smith. They felt, and were not at all shy about arguing the point, that because they reached so many more readers than did a sole correspondent for a single paper, for *any* single paper, that they had a special relationship with whoever happened to be occupying the White House.

No matter how competent or how great the reporter from, say, the *New York Times* or the *Philadelphia Bulletin* happened to be, they argued, he could write for but a fraction of the readers reached by any wire-service reporter. What made it so hard to dispute this line of reasoning was that essentially it happened to be correct.

That is not to say there was no opposite point of view. In fact, the first real problem I faced on starting my job was the competing claim voiced by reporters for the *New York Times,* the *Washington Post,* and the *New York Herald Tribune* that because they had fifty or sixty papers tied to their news services, they were, in effect, also reaching vast numbers and thereby entitled to the same consideration as AP and UPI.

What did this consideration mean? In practical terms, it meant that AP and UPI were included in every single pool—a small group of reporters who would observe events and later share their coverage with the rest of their brethren—we had, whether it was riding in the President's plane, or in the car behind his, or being one of three or four people at a foreign meeting. (For example, when JFK met Khrushchev in Vienna, there wasn't enough room on the steps of the American embassy for all the press who wanted to be there, but I made sure we accommodated AP and UPI.)

Bit by bit, however, I began to expand that pool, with the eventual goal of having the two wire services, all four networks (Mutual Broadcasting System considered itself the fourth network, so I did, too), as well as the international news services.

I also tried, whenever possible, to fit in reporters from the major foreign papers and news organizations, such as Reuters, Agence France Presse, or Tass. (I think I was the first press secretary in history to include a Tass correspondent in a White House pool, which I did when Gromyko visited JFK.) It may seem hard to imagine, given all the changes in the media in the last several decades, but all of these initiatives were opposed by the Establishment. I went ahead with them, anyway. It was a time for change.

A huge cry of protest went up when I announced that I was moving the presidential press conferences from the Indian Treaty Room in the Executive Office Building (where they'd been held since the Truman administration) to the State Department Auditorium, in order to make room for all the media people who wanted to attend. You'd have thought I was committing a treasonous act!

"You're ruining the *atmosphere* of the presidential press conference," one correspondent shouted at me angrily. Apparently, by moving to a big room, I would also be destroying the *intimacy* of the event. These arguments fell on deaf ears (mine)—as much as I appreciated atmosphere and intimacy, I wanted to serve as much of the press as possible, and not just the Establishment.

That protest was minor compared with the one that arose when I told the media that President Kennedy's press conferences would be carried *on live television*. That was, of course, an invasion of the rights of what was then called the pen-and-pencil press. I was told that this move, too, would "ruin" the press conference because it would turn everyone into actors and actresses. I do not exaggerate when I say that the entire pen-and-pencil press was after my scalp. One of the most vociferously angry was Bill Lawrence of the *New York Times*. I remember him literally screaming at me, "You're *killing* the writing press!"

It has always amused me that Lawrence, one of the ringleaders of the "scalp Salinger" set, did a 180-degree flip on this issue four months later when he left the *Times* to become chief White House correspondent for the American Broadcasting Company.

Actually, I had more than a little to do with Bill Lawrence's career move. When Jim Hagerty left the White House and went over to ABC, it was clearly in third place among the television networks, and Hagerty asked me to keep an eye out for any good print correspondents who might be interested in the newer medium. In 1961, when President Kennedy was getting set to leave on his first big trip to France, Austria, and England— to see De Gaulle, Khrushchev, and Macmillan—Lawrence walked into my office in a real snit. It was two days before we were set to leave, and he'd just been informed by the *Times* that he wasn't going; the paper would use its reporters who were based in Europe. Realizing that Bill's outrage was genuine, I said, "Relax. I have an idea. Come back and see me at four o'clock." As soon as he'd left, I picked up the phone and called Hagerty, who was delighted to hear that a real pro like Bill Lawrence might be interested. Promptly at four that afternoon, a radiant Lawrence strode into my office and said, "You'll never guess! I'm going on the trip—as a correspondent for ABC!"

Aligned with Lawrence, at least originally, were people like Eddie (Edward T.) Folliard, of the *Washington Post*. He had covered Presidents since the days of Woodrow Wilson, and I always had the greatest admiration for him (but he accused me of bringing the institution of the presidential press conference "to perdition"). Pete Lisagor, of the *Chicago Daily News*, also attacked me for having a televised press conference, and then, four short years later, he attacked President Lyndon Johnson for *not* having one. Obviously, time marches on.

Initially, I came up with the idea for televising the press conferences, then passed it on to JFK. The President, who had been a journalist himself briefly and who counted a number of journalists among his close friends, was immediately receptive to the idea. The inner circle, however, was not of one mind on this issue. Ted Sorensen, McGeorge Bundy, and Dean Rusk were dead set against it, and Ken O'Donnell was not noticeably enthusiastic. They all worried that if the President made a "live" error, the global results could be cataclysmic. Fortunately, this argument did not sway President Kennedy, who felt strongly that we should go ahead with this plan.

His reasoning, like mine, was that the TV debates had been such a big plus for him that he would be missing a golden opportunity if he didn't utilize his easy mastery of the medium. He also felt, as did I, that television would be the ideal vehicle for going directly to the American people—and over the heads of the nation's editorial writers, who were universally opposed to a Democratic administration. It's important to remember that in those days only three or four newspapers carried the full transcript of a presidential press conference, so the American people got to see and read only what the newspaper determined was the crucial distillation, a decision with which the administration often disagreed. We believed the people should have the opportunity to *see* the press conference in its entirety.

In those days, the President could reach, via television, an average viewing audience of 6 million families, or roughly 18 million people. Compared with the *Ed Sullivan Show,* to cite the leading example, which drew 50 million viewers each Sunday night, that did not exactly make for a great rating, but it was an enormous number of people nonetheless, people who would be able to see and hear an entire presidential news conference. Today, thanks to us, that ability to reach large numbers of the populace is standard.

The final important change we made in the way the White House press operation was run, and the one that most infuriated the Establishment, was our turning the White House into an open beat. Basically, what we did was to say that any reporter could go directly to any member of the White House staff and interview him or her on any subject without having to clear it with the White House press secretary.

This represented a radical change in policy. Under the old rules, a reporter needed an explicit okay from the press secretary before he could interview any staff member, which meant that the reporter would often have to sit around outside Jim Hagerty's office waiting to be anointed. Instead of this archaic arrangement, I had turned the White House into an open beat, wherein a good reporter—one who was willing to do a little work—could beat his colleagues to a good story.

The better reporters, like Tom Wicker and Sandy Vanocur, welcomed the change, but there were others who had gotten used to being recipients of handouts, and had forgotten how to be reporters. They reacted to this change as if the White House had just been taken over by some nut. I can't say that we ever did win them over to our way of thinking.

These are but three examples of how the old order resisted the new.

A final, and almost frivolous, example has to do with the large room across the hall from my office where the regular White House press worked. The room hadn't changed in the better part of a century. It was, in a word, a disgrace. There were spitoons *on top of tables*, and disarray everywhere. We shoveled out the mess, cleaned up the room, and put in cubicles, whereupon the working press—ever annoyed at change—dubbed the place "Salinger's Loan Company," claiming that's what the cubicles made it resemble. Five years later, when President Johnson's people did an even more thorough modernization, the White House press corps didn't like that, either. They called it the "LBJ Hilton." Obviously, there's no pleasing some people, especially if they are media people.

The bottom line, however, remained: A new day had dawned, and it would be seen and felt throughout the White House and official Washington.

President Kennedy had been in office just over a year when he was asked at a press conference how he viewed his treatment by the press. The first line of his answer got a big laugh: "Well, I am reading more and enjoying it less . . . but I have not complained, nor do I plan to make any general statement to the press. I think that they are doing their task, as a critical branch, the fourth estate. And I am attempting to do mine." His last line also brought forth laughter: "And we are going to live together for a period, and then go our separate ways."

The President wasn't the only one who had to learn how to deal with an inquisitive press. His press secretary was a student in the same class. A few excerpts from a couple of my early press conferences indicate that I was also learning the ropes, but for me the problem was compounded by the fact that I had switched sides. Instead of asking the questions, I was required to answer them, *but only to the extent the President wanted them answered.* Trying to determine that extent was probably the toughest part of my job.

At ten minutes after noon on Saturday, April 29, 1961, I met with the press for a news conference.

MR. SALINGER: I have the release on the appointment of Robinson McIlvane as United States Ambassador to Dahoney.

Letter to the President from Julius Raab.

Text of the Message from the President on the occasion of the dedication of Kings Point Inter-faith Chapel at Kings Point, New York.

And we have the text of the speech in Chicago last night, as actually delivered. [Laughter]

Q.: Were there some changes?

MR. SALINGER: There were some minor changes....

I went on to tell them about the President's appointment schedule for the following Monday, but I was soon interrupted with questions about a meeting of the National Security Council that happened to be taking place on a Saturday, an unusual occurrence. I'd said nothing about the meeting, but a number of the reporters had already learned of it.

Q.: Have you got any news?

MR. SALINGER: No.

Q.: [Will you] Have anything later on what's going on?

MR. SALINGER: I may have in general, be able to say in a general way the subjects discussed, but I don't think I will have any specifics.

Q.: Do you have an exact and definitive list of who is involved this morning?

MR. SALINGER: Yes, I have the list of those. We have the statutory members, the President, the Vice President, the Secretary of State, the Secretary of Defense, and the Director of OCDM, Mr. Ellis.

Others present are Mr. Douglas Dillon, Secretary of the Treasury; Mr. David Bell, Director of the Budget; Admiral Arleigh Burke, Acting Chairman of the Joint Chiefs of Staff; Allen Dulles, Director of CIA; Edward R. Murrow, Director of USIA; Chester Bowles, Undersecretary of State; Roswell Gilpatric, Deputy Secretary of Defense; U. Alexis Johnson, Deputy Undersecretary of State ...

Q.: For what? Does he have a portfolio?

Q.: Political. [At times, to speed things up, reporters answer one another's questions.]

MR. SALINGER: ... McGeorge Bundy, Special Assistant to the President; Jerome B. Weisner, Special Assistant to the President; Walt W. Rostow, Deputy Special Assistant to the President; George McGhee, Counselor of the Department of State; Paul Nitze, Assistant Secretary of Defense; Lieut. Gen. Lionel C. McGarr, Chief of the Military Assistance Group in Vietnam; Frederick E. Nolting, Jr., US Ambassador to Vietnam ...

Q.: Pierre, is the Attorney General there?

MR. SALINGER: He was here earlier this morning. I don't know if he has been in or—

Q.: His car is still outside.

MR. SALINGER: The meeting is still going on.

Q.: Could you add him?

MR. SALINGER: I saw him earlier. I do not know if he is in the meeting.

Q.: Sorensen?

MR. SALINGER: I don't believe so.

Q.: Could we find for sure about the Attorney General?

MR. SALINGER: I will find out, when the meeting breaks up.

> Mrs. Kennedy and Caroline will leave for Glen Ora at 1:00 p.m. They will be accompanied by Lem Billings.

Q.: Doesn't he have a more formal name than that?

MR. SALINGER: K. Lemoyne Billings. (laughter)

Q.: Oh.

Q.: Of New York?

MR. SALINGER: Yes.

Q.: Friend of the President?

MR. SALINGER: Friend of the President. It is possible the President may go with them at that time. If not, he will go later.

Q.: Drive?

MR. SALINGER: He will go down in the helicopter himself.

That kind of simple exchange went on all the time in press conferences. Soon we were back on more substantial grounds, despite my wish not to be. The reporters wanted to know more (than I wanted to tell them) about what was going on in the meeting of the NSC. Fortunately, this time they were satisfied by my promise to tell them more as soon as I could. Several days before that, they hadn't been.

I had been asked a question about a *Herald Tribune* story that had said—inaccurately—that close advisers of the President had urged him to use American troops in Cuba.

MR. SALINGER: I would like to go off the record—

Q.: On the record, you have no comment?

MR. SALINGER: On the record, I won't have comment—

Q.: On the record, you won't comment?

MR. SALINGER: I will say, off the record—and it is understood that this is off the record now?—just for your guidance—the story is completely inaccurate. The problem is, if I am talking on the record, it produces a new story. So I tell you off the record it is inaccurate . . .

I'd had much the same problem several days earlier.

Q.: There was a specific report this morning by Marquis Childs that the President has offered American NATO forces to General De Gaulle should he feel it necessary, and also that these paratrooper planes are on their way to Paris—

MR. SALINGER: I would like to go into background on this, if everybody will agree to that?

Q.: This is for use—by background you mean—

MR. SALINGER: Why don't we go off the record for a minute and then come back on the record? Everybody agree to that?

The problem I have [is that] I might deny Childs' story, and everybody will write a story saying—in other words, it builds an inaccurate story on top of an inaccurate story, which is what I am trying to prevent.

The suggestion that we offered them any NATO troops is off the record, but for me to say that on the record immediately makes my denials a major story, so what I am trying to do is starting you off running the story without making an official story of it.

Q.: That is off the record or on the record?

MR. SALINGER: What I just said?

Q.: I am confused . . .

Minor quibbles aside, working for John F. Kennedy in the White House was every bit as wonderful as I had hoped—and expected—it would be. One of the reasons why is that for the first time in decades, it was inhabited by a real family. The White House is an odd place to live, but the Kennedys managed it with characteristic aplomb. Nonetheless, I always got a kick out of the fact that the Kennedy children, little Caroline and her toddler brother, John, would frequently walk their father to work.

Fortunately, some of the other problems we had to deal with in the White House were on the humorous side. For example, in early 1962 we engineered the Great Starling Caper. When it comes to disrespect for historical edifices, be they statues or buildings, the starling is right up there, so to speak, with its larger cousins, the pigeon and the seagull. Thus when we encountered a mass migration of starlings to the White House and its grounds, we soon found evidence of the seriousness of the problem. I bought a hat, but that proved to be merely a protective, and not a preventive, measure.

To our immense relief, some genius in the National Park Service came to our rescue with a recording of a starling in distress, which we played, night and day, over loudspeakers hung from trees on the grounds. The birds bought our act, and left for quieter, less distressing haunts.

The episode was memorialized at one of my press conferences.

Q.: Is it true that the White House has been playing a recording of a distressed starling on the lawn, and has it been successful in its purpose?

MR. SALINGER: The White House has had a problem for some time with starlings who have created nuisances in front of the White House. For the last two days we have been playing a record of a distressed starling to discourage other starlings from appearing on the premises.

Q.: Has it worked?

MR. SALINGER: It has so far.

Q.: What does a starling in distress sound like, Pierre?

MR. SALINGER: I have the record here and I am going to play it for you. But first I have to tell you that they had to get the call of a distressed Washington, D.C., starling, because any other starling would be ineffective in this plan.

Q.: How do you tell a D.C. starling from an out-of-town starling? Are they square? Do they hang out in the wrong places?

MR. SALINGER: You can always tell people from out-of-town. I will play for you now the call of a distressed starling.

I did, and the piercing wail of a *very* distressed bird soon filled the room—whereupon I made the wonderful discovery that the recording had the same effect on the press as it did on the birds.

Another problem with a humorous ending cropped up in the second year of JFK's administration. We had been giving a series of lunches for small groups of journalists on a state-by-state basis, and they were going well—except for a small problem. One day the President said, "Pierre, I've just been told that each time we have one of those lunches we lose an alarming amount of silverware. The journalists are taking pieces home as souvenirs. See if there's anything you can do about it, short of frisking people."

I did, and there was, and the problem disappeared. If I do say so myself, it was an ingenious solution. The Secret Service found me a "retired" pickpocket, who mingled with the guests as they were about to leave, and deftly retrieved our silver. People must have been very surprised when they got home, but no one ever called to complain.

JFK's day began between 7:30 and 8:00 A.M., with a breakfast tray and a big pile of newspapers. As he ate two soft-boiled eggs, bacon, toast, and freshly squeezed orange juice, followed by a cup of coffee that he would overload with sugar and cream, he'd scan the papers, often making notes or picking up the phone to call one of us and inquire as to how something he wanted held for a while had gotten into print. He also read while taking his morning bath, and it was not at all unusual to get a sheet of paper from him that was wet because it had fallen in the tub. Then, just about nine o'clock, the children would accompany him, hand in hand, on his stroll from the West Wing living quarters to the Oval Office in the East Wing.

There have not been children of comparable youth in the White House since the Kennedy era, so it is hard to make comparisons, but I doubt if any First Lady could have been more protective of her children and their privacy than was Jackie Kennedy.

Much has been written about Jackie Kennedy's voice, which *was* unusual—somewhat high-pitched, breathy, and at times almost little-girlish. I've always thought it rather interesting that her handwriting had similar characteristics, almost as if it were the physical manifestation of her voice. Among my treasures are a number of the notes she wrote me on her pale blue White House stationery.

One shows her frustration with attempts to use her daughter for commercial gain. In her characteristically elliptical phrasing, it reads:

Pierre,

They are now selling Caroline *dolls—with wardrobe &* Jacqueline *dolls with* STATE *wardrobe at F.A.O. Schwartz [sic]—which is the first time it has gotten into the really available—rather proper domain—They are in window displays or were—Can you do something about this—John McInerney did some law work on this problem for me once—If a call such as you made to the sunglass people doesn't work will you try Clark Clifford—McInerney or Better Business Bureau—*

A company called Ideal Toy Co. is trying to pressure me (through Tom Walsh) into endorsing a Caroline doll that would have our backing & all royalties would go to charity & there would be no other dolls—I would rather have a doll a month than endorse one—

But this is irritating—so please do see what you can do— Call FAO Schwartz—N.Y.C. I guess— JFK said to write you this.

Jackie

When an unauthorized picture of Caroline playing on the White House lawn appeared in papers across the country, Jackie was not pleased. This time, however, her mood was a little more positive, for she'd written across the top, "Don't worry—a nice calm memo!"

> *Pierre—*
>   *Your policy of no peep shows has worked marvelously all Fall—now if they get away with this I am afraid they will start up in full force again—so could you berate the fotog—or the AP for buying it—if it was taken by a tourist.*
>   *Guards should be told to watch for people photographing through grilles—The guards at the gate could have stopped this—If necessary one can patrol up & down outside by S.W. gate—I don't think we need one at end of s. lawn yet as its so conspicuous—but the minute any fotos get taken from there lets put a guard out there too—*
>   *Do speak to present guards—This must have been taken on that blocked off street by JFK's office—or out of Old State Dept window—They should watch for people there—climbing on cars to take pictures etc.*

As I was putting away the file in which I'd kept these memos for three decades, a small card tumbled out onto my desk. It was a note Jackie had written me in November of 1961 after the immensely successful Pablo Casals cello concert at the White House. She wrote:

> *Dear Pierre,*
>   *Last night was an incredible dream—and all because of you—the only thing that broke my heart is that you weren't there after with Casals—Jack had said you & Abe Fortas were coming—when I sent someone scurrying for you—you had disappeared—Please know how much we missed you & thank you for what was really an historic evening.*
>
>   *Love, Jackie.*

I've read many descriptions of that fabulous evening, but never one to compare with that of Leonard Bernstein.

BERNSTEIN: Being at the Casals dinner in November, 1961, when there were many artists about, I couldn't help comparing it with the last time I had been in the White House, which was during the reign of Eisenhower when I had played, with about thirty members of my orchestra, parts of a Mozart piano concerto and an abbreviated version of the "Rhapsody in Blue." . . . It was a State Dinner and I was the entertainment. To compare that dinner with the Casals dinner is to compare night and day.

Eisenhower's was definitely not Lenny's kind of dinner:

. . . For one thing, you couldn't smoke, that was number one on my mind. You couldn't smoke at the dinner table, you couldn't smoke before dinner and you couldn't smoke after dinner. I am an inveterate smoker, and I had to perform afterwards, and I got more and more nervous. There were no drinks served before dinner, either. The guest line formed by protocol, not by alphabet. Everything was very different then; it was very stiff and not even very pleasant. Dinner was at a huge horseshoe-shaped table at which seventy-five or so people were seated so that nobody could ever really talk to anybody.

Q.: Again, the table was arranged by protocol?

BERNSTEIN: Yes, and the food was ordinary, and the wines were inferior, and you couldn't smoke. By the time I got to play, I was a wreck, and by the time I finished playing, I was more of a wreck . . .

The contrast is just extraordinary. Compare that to the Casals dinner at the White House in November, 1961 at which you were served very good drinks first; where there were ashtrays everywhere just inviting you to poison yourself with cigarettes; where the line is formed alphabetically; and where, when you do line up, you are in a less querulous mood because you have a drink and a cigarette; where, when the moment comes for you to greet the President and the First Lady, two ravishing people appear in the doorway who couldn't be more charming if they tried, who make you feel utterly welcome, even with a huge gathering—there were at least as many people at this as there had been at the Eisenhowers'. You are then brought in to dinner. Dinner turns out to be not at a horseshoe table but many little tables, seating about ten people apiece, fires roaring in all the fireplaces, and these tables are laid in three adjacent rooms so that it's all like having dinner with friends. The food is marvelous, the wines are delicious, there are cigarettes on the table, people are laughing, laughing out loud, telling stories, jokes, enjoying themselves, glad to be there.

I'll never forget the end of that evening, when there was dancing. The Marine Band was playing waltzes or something, and Roy Harris and Walter Piston and people like that were kicking up their heels in the White House, a little high, just so delighted to be there, so glad that they had been asked, feeling that they had finally been recognized as honored artists of the Republic. You know, I've never seen so many happy artists in my life. It was a joy to watch it. And the feeling of hospitality, or warmth, of welcome, the taste with which everything was done, the goodness of everything—it was just *good*. The guests were so interesting, and most of all the president and Mrs. Kennedy. It was like a different world, utterly like a different planet. I couldn't believe that this was the same White House that I had attended a year ago and performed in.

The Casals concert was indeed a most successful event. One of the byproducts for the President was that it gave him an instant, if undeserved, reputation as a lover of classical music. A few weeks later, having had just about enough of this, Jackie, who truly did love good music, was heard to remark, about her husband, "The only music he really appreciates is 'Hail to the Chief.' "

I believe my help in arranging the concert by Pablo Casals—the first time he'd played in the White House since 1904!—cemented the bond that had been growing between Jackie and me. I believe she now realized that I had always had her interests, as well as the President's, at heart.

Slowly but surely, as the first year of the Kennedy administration forged ahead, my relationship with the press improved. Although in May, *Newsweek* reported that the consensus of the Establishment was that I had "not yet acquired the sure touch of [my] predecessor, James C. Hagerty," some of the gurus were more positive. UPI's Merriman Smith gave me a left-handed compliment: "He seldom commits the same error twice." Bill Lawrence, who was at that point still with the *New York Times*, told *Newsweek*, "He's off to a good start. There's been no attempt to fence the President off."

I appreciated that comment, for it went to the essence of what I considered to be my role. And the *Washington Star's* Mary McGrory, in a widely disseminated article, was more than kind (if not uncritical) in her comparison and contrast of myself and Mr. Hagerty. She wrote:

> Pierre Emil George Salinger is a roly-poly, cigar-smoking piano player with dark blue eyes, pointed ears, and a sense of proportion unusual in one of his calling. Some people think he resembles Napoleon without the imperial dyspepsia; others think he looks like Grover Cleveland without the moustache.
>
> What interests the Washington press corps much more, however, is his professional resemblance.
>
> It is generally agreed he bears practically none to his immediate predecessor, James C. Hagerty, who not only enunci-

ated Eisenhower policy, but, by President Eisenhower's own admission, helped to make it. Salinger does not help make White House policy; occasionally he doesn't even know what it is, and what's more he admits it.

The truth of McGrory's last comment—in particular the part about my sometimes not even knowing what White House policy was—would soon become obvious. But this time, there would be nothing funny about it.

CHAPTER EIGHT

AT THE TIME I became White House press secretary, my budget was $125,000 a year, and I had a staff of twelve. By contrast, that of the public information office of the Department of Defense (read Pentagon) was about $25 million, and they employed about one hundred people. Perhaps that's one of the reasons why our first military crisis became, also, a public-relations nightmare.

The first news of a military action in the Caribbean burst upon the national consciousness on April 17, 1961, with the information that a small number of B-26's flown by defecting Cuban airmen had conducted a series of almost totally ineffectual bombing raids on several Cuban beaches. That was followed by an exercise whose goal was nothing less than the overthrow of Fidel Castro. This operation failed miserably.

The plan of attack, which had been drawn up in the waning months of the Eisenhower administration, then shined up—no, *burnished*—for President Kennedy by the Central Intelligence Agency called for U.S. planes to drop fifteen hundred Cuban exiles on supposedly strategic spots along the Bahia de Cochinos, the Bay of Pigs.

Supported by American aerial might, the men were to take the beaches and then begin their march on the capital and on Cuba's Red-loving premier. The invasion was the culmination of a long period of planning and intrigue that had become an open secret in Cuba itself, and widely, if speculatively, reported in numerous newspapers both at home and abroad. Despite that openness, however, all questions were met with firm and immediate denials. For example, on April 12, five days before the invasion, during a presidential press conference called in response to the news that the Russians had put a man (Yuri Gargarin) in space, JFK was asked about the rumored invasion of Cuba by the United States. "There will not be," said President Kennedy, "under any conditions, an intervention in Cuba by the United States *armed forces* [my italics]."

So secretive and evasive was the President's conduct, and so trusting his reliance on the CIA and its information, that as the agreed-upon date of the invasion drew near, among those who *should have been* in the know but were not were Kennedy's secretary of state, Dean Rusk, his UN ambassador, Adlai Stevenson—and his press secretary.

On Sunday afternoon, April 16, the phone rang at my house in Georgetown. It was the President.

"Pierre," he said, in a serious tone, "I want you to stick close to home tonight. You may have some inquiries from the press about a military affair in the Caribbean. If you do, just say you know only what you read in the newspapers."

When I heard the words "military affair in the Caribbean," a chill went through me. You didn't have to be the President's press secretary to have heard rumors of an American invasion of Cuba—but if you were the President's press secretary, you sure as hell ought to know whether they were true or false!

Be that as it may, when I got to the White House on Monday morning, the first thing the President did was to tell me sternly, "We'll have no comment on what's happening down there. We're watching developments down there—that's *all*!"

John Kennedy had decided that the less I (and Dean Rusk and Adlai Stevenson) knew, the better. That way, I could not later be accused of lying to the press. Nonetheless, some of the fat that was soon in the fire of national scrutiny was most definitely mine.

Three days after the rebels landed, their mission was over, a dismal failure. During that time, on instructions from the President, I revealed nothing of what we knew was going on (and going south.)

With his own jets and Khruschev's tanks, Castro was having no trouble in crushing the rebels.

As JFK had pledged that we would not intervene militarily, all we could do was to stand idly by and watch the news get worse and worse. Each morning, the President would grab the first page of the copy as it came off the ticker from one of the four wire-service machines we had set up in my office, scan the first paragraph, and then, disappointed and dis-

gusted, hand it to me. That seventy-two-hour period from landing to sur-
render was the grimmest time in all my months in the White House.

Today, reading back over the transcripts of my mid-April 1961 press
conferences, I find it nothing short of amazing that I was able to keep as
much from the press as I did. (I suppose that continues to reflect how little
I knew.)

The first brief exchange was on Monday, April 17.

Q.: Any comment on the Cuban situation?
MR. SALINGER: No, I wouldn't have any comment on it.
Q.: Can you tell us, Pierre, what disposition is being made of the fliers
    [Cuban airmen who'd sought political asylum in the U.S.], where are
    they, and who has control over them?
MR. SALINGER: I have no idea.
Q.: Didn't you say it would be through Immigration Service?
MR. SALINGER: It would be handled by Immigration Service.
Q.: Pierre, any chance they will produce them at the UN?
MR. SALINGER: I have no idea.

And that was it for the first day. After that, though the queries got tougher,
they never really got *too* tough, probably because the press was being kept
in the dark so effectively. (It is not my fondest memory today, but at the
time I was actually almost proud of my ability to keep the press hounds
at bay.)

The next three days brought only a couple of easy questions on Cuba,
having to do with White House statements that we were monitoring the
situation by way of the wire services. Obviously, no one had much to go
on, other than the increasingly bad news that the attack had failed and that
Castro was in the process of mopping up the floor with the rebels.

I opened my afternoon briefing on Wednesday, April 19, with a short
statement on the issue, and I got only two softball questions. The next day,
Thursday, there was no question on the Bay of Pigs, and only one lengthy
exchange on Friday. But that Q and A session had to do with the hurried
visit to Washington of José Miró Cardona, the head of the Cuban Revolutionary Council; if the press had known the details of the (CIA-
controlled) role played over the last few days by Cardona and his fellow
council members, they could have uncovered the whole sordid mess.

We put out the news that Señor Cardona was in Washington to brief
the President on the status of the obviously failing, if not already failed,
mission. In fact, however, his visit involved damage control of the highest
order.

On Friday morning, the end of what had been his toughest week in office, the young President went before live television cameras to begin a press conference for which Arthur Schlesinger, Dick Goodwin, and I had briefed him *hard.* "I know many of you have further questions about Cuba," he said, then masterfully deflected all but one of them by declaring, "but I do not think that any useful national purpose would be served by my going further into the Cuba question this morning." (Imagine a President, *any* President, trying that today!)

The single question he took had to do with whether or not it was true that both Dean Rusk and Chester Bowles were against the invasion. JFK's answer would become one of his most-quoted lines: "There's an old saying that victory has a hundred fathers and defeat is an orphan."

Then he did one of the smartest things he would do in his entire presidency: He took the full blame for the fiasco in the Caribbean by saying, "I am the responsible officer of this government."

Later, in the relative privacy of the Oval Office, he expanded on this, saying, "I'm the President of the United States. I made this mistake, and I take full responsibility for it."

As he spoke, I kept another of his statements firmly in my mind, and I underlined it with hope. At the conclusion of our briefing session that morning, John Kennedy had said, "Memory is short. If we just sit tight for about three weeks, things will cool off and we can proceed from there."

He was right, at least in general, but several years later, in *With Kennedy,* I would assess the matter this way: "The Bay of Pigs was JFK's first major defeat as President and the greatest disaster of his entire administration. He was to suffer the scorn not only of the Communist world but of the [Cuban] exiles themselves. Our own allies began to question the wisdom of his leadership. Neutral nations were now more receptive to overtures from the Kremlin. Castro was stronger than ever and would find Khruschev more willing to listen to his plans for nuclear missiles 'to defend' Cuba. But the crisis that would provide was still eighteen months away . . ."

One of the real problems of the modern presidency is that the President must make decisions based on the information and advice of men he does not really know. So it was in the tragedy that came to be known in history as the Bay of Pigs.

I will never forget the night that the Bay of Pigs came to its dismal conclusion on the beach in Cuba. At two o'clock in the morning, four of us—Arthur Schlesinger, McGeorge Bundy, Dick Goodwin, and I—gathered in the Oval Office. After we'd talked to the President for about a half an hour, he left us and walked out the French doors and onto the south lawn of the White House. There he walked, completely alone, for an hour.

From time to time, we could see him through the windows as he walked by. I doubt if any of us had ever seen, or would ever see, a more dramatic example of the loneliness of the presidency, and the lonesome burden of ultimate responsibility, than the sight of President Kennedy walking, alone and resolute, around the south lawn of the White House on the night the Bay of Pigs failed.

A lesser man who had this experience in his first three months in office might well have seen his presidency begin to slide straight downhill. But John F. Kennedy somehow found some resource of strength that enabled him to pull himself back to his normal level of control and confidence.

The first evidence I saw that he had grasped the lesson of the Bay of Pigs with great clarity occurred in June of that same year, 1961, when he went to Vienna to meet with Chairman Khrushchev. It was supposed to be just a get-acquainted meeting, but I believe that Khrushchev thought he saw a chance to take advantage of the young President, who had just suffered an international humiliation. I think he figured that Kennedy would be so down after the Bay of Pigs that he, Khrushchev, could strike a blow or two in his relentless war against the free world.

The first day's meeting was in the American embassy, and on the second they switched to the Soviet embassy. In the last hour of the second day, it became very apparent from his comments that Mr. Khrushchev was going to make a drive in the latter part of that same year to sign a separate peace treaty with East Germany and to close off access to West Berlin.

The meeting ended with Khrushchev on his feet, telling a seated Kennedy that he was going to accomplish this by the winter. To this pronouncement, the President replied, "Well, then it's going to be a very cold winter."

Upon his return to the United States, Kennedy swiftly mobilized public opinion and sent two U.S. Army divisions to Europe. Out of that show of strength, the winter passed without Mr. Khrushchev carrying out his threat to recognize East Germany.

In July 1964, while on a fact-finding trip to the Far East as part of my campaign for the United States Senate, I gave a speech in Tokyo to the Foreign Correspondents Club of Japan. This is what I had to say, in part, about the Cuban missile crisis, which at that time was not even two full years old.

"The real test [of whether or not JFK had learned anything of value from the Bay of Pigs fiasco] came in October of 1962, and it turned out to be a test not just for the free world but for *all* mankind."

I continued, "It was the day on which we discovered, by our military overflights, that missile sites were in the process of construction. I believe that historians will look back and say that the ten days that followed were crucial for the history of the world."

Over those ten days, as the President met in the Cabinet Room of the White House with the executive committee of the National Security Council, the secretary of state, the secretary of defense, Ambassador Stevenson, and all the others, one could see firsthand that the lessons of the Bay of Pigs had been learned.

Every single course of action was tested and cross-tested, and every single assumption that was made was sent back to be retested. Every single scenario was taken to its logical extreme in an effort to see what might happen, and in our effort to avoid the nuclear confrontation which at that point seemed almost certain to occur. And in the end, Mr. Khrushchev decided to withdraw his missiles from Cuba, and the free world was able to breathe more easily.

As a result of those ten days, I believe we came to a point where we realized that we must find some way, while maintaining the strength and resolve of the United States, to sit down around the world and discuss these great issues that divide us. Because, certainly, in those ten days we were as close to nuclear war as anybody would ever like to imagine.

It all began on Tuesday, October 16, 1962, the minute I walked into the President's office to brief him on the day's schedule of appointments that I would be reading to the press at my regular 11:30 press conference. In place of the jaunty, debonair, and cheerful chief executive I saw on most mornings, I was met by a grim-visaged JFK, who was clearly *not* in a good mood.

"I haven't time to hear the rest of it," he said, cutting me off in midmessage. "But I have one you can put on top of this list. I'm going to see Gromyko here Thursday."

"What does he want?" I asked, knowing the reporters would be asking me the same question.

"I don't know what he wants," said the President. "He's coming on his initiative, not mine."

Clearly preoccupied with something, Kennedy stood up behind his desk. "There's another thing. I expect a lot of traffic here this week—Rusk, McNamara, Stevenson, the Chiefs of Staff. If the press tries to read something significant into it, you're to deny that anything special is going on."

Uh-oh. I hadn't heard that for a while, not since the Bay of Pigs. And back then, as a result, we'd had one of our few direct confrontations. Several days after things had calmed down, I'd gone in to the Oval Office and told the President that I simply would not be able to do my job if he was going to keep me out of the loop in regard to important events and developments.

"Mr. President," I said, trying to keep my voice steady, "if you can't promise me that in the future I will be kept informed of such important matters, then I'm afraid I will have to resign."

"Pierre," he said in a voice much steadier than mine, "the Bay of Pigs was a disaster from start to finish. I listened to the wrong people and took the wrong course of action. You have my word that in the future you will always be fully informed."

I was greatly relieved by the President's words. Our relationship remained on a high plateau, both professionally and personally.

Shortly after the Bay of Pigs, JFK got off a good line in response to my telling him that as a result of the swift and decisive manner in which he'd taken responsibility for the failure of the Bay of Pigs, his standing in the Gallup poll had improved dramatically, to 83 percent.

"Let's hope," he said, "that in order to remain popular I don't have to keep doing stupid things."

(It was also at about this time that President Kennedy said to me privately, in reference to the Bay of Pigs, "Winning isn't everything, but losing is *shit!*")

This time, by telling me to fend off the press, he was indirectly saying that something important was afoot. I knew that he would tell me what it was, but not immediately. However, I sensed it was something big.

On Wednesday, the seventeenth, the President flew to Connecticut for a couple of political events, but we returned to Washington late that same evening. Over the next two days, as a parade of high-ranking aides and officers filed in and out of the Oval Office, I managed to keep the increasingly obvious from the forefront of media attention. Fortunately, JFK's travel on behalf of Democratic candidates running in the off-year elections provided the press with a lot to do.

On Friday, we flew to Chicago, but we had not been there for long when he learned that the Cuban missile situation was heating up. The President still hadn't taken me into his confidence—despite a week of meetings with his highest-level brass—but I was not ready to push him on it. The calls from journalists were pouring in (an apt verb considering how much leaking was going on) and I kept holding them off. However, when I got back-to-back calls from two very different sources (one a government spokesman and the other a newspaperman), each one asking if it was true we were about to invade Cuba, I figured it was time someone let me inside the tent.

I went up to the President's suite and found him, in his boxer shorts, on the phone to Washington. Ken O'Donnell was with him. I told the

President of the two calls, and he instructed me to return one of them and Ken the other. We were both to deny the invasion rumor.

My call brought a skeptical response: "Maybe we're not going to invade, but something big is up."

I went back upstairs and asked Ken O'Donnell, who'd been present at all the high-level meetings over the past week, if he could tell me what was happening. "I'm flying blind with the press," I explained.

He said, "All I can tell you is this: The President may have to develop a cold somewhere along the line tomorrow. If he does, we'll have to cancel out the rest of the trip and head back to Washington.

"If I were you," he said gravely, "I'd stay away from the reporters tonight—"

"I can't," I interrupted.

"—even if you have to hide out somewhere."

"I can't do that," I repeated. Perhaps if we were back in Washington, I might have been able to get away with it, but not in Chicago, with a long-planned dinner with four heavy hitters from the press, one of whom was the columnist Irv Kupcinet.

Over brandy, Kup looked at me and said, "How's your supply of Cuban cigars holding out, Pierre?"

When I responded that I hadn't been able to find any in months, he leveled his gaze and said, "Better get used to the domestic variety."

The next morning, Saturday, I was interrupted halfway through a routine press briefing (in which I was outlining the President's western itinerary) by an aide who whispered I was to go to the President's suite immediately.

"I have a terrible cold," said an unshaven, pajama-clad JFK. "You'd better go downstairs and tell the press I'm returning to Washington on the advice of Dr. Burkley," and he nodded toward Rear Adm. George G. Burkley, the White House physician.

I must have shown some surprise before turning to do as bidden, because suddenly the President said, "Wait a minute. Let's be sure we're all saying the same thing."

With that, he whipped around, grabbed a piece of Sheraton-Blackstone stationery, and quickly wrote, "99.2 temperature. Upper-respiratory infection. Doctor says he should return to Washington."

"There," he said, handing me the sheet. "Go back to your press conference and tell them that."

Immediately after that, President Kennedy canceled the West Coast leg of our trip and, pleading a bad cold, flew back to Washington.

At one point, finding him alone in his private compartment in the plane, I asked, "Mr. President, you don't have that bad a cold, do you?"

"I've had worse," said JFK.

Going right for it, I said, "Then there's something else?"

John F. Kennedy was as eloquent a man as I've ever met, but in making his point he could also be downright earthy.

"Something *is* going on," he said. "You'll be briefed when you get back to Washington, and when you find out—grab your balls."

Later, a U.S. Marine Corps helicopter deposited us on the White House lawn. As we were walking away from it, the President took my arm and asked if I would "be around."

"Of course," I assured him.

I went to my office and held a brief press conference on the President's cold, after which I sent the staff home, mainly to give the impression that there was nothing unusual in the offing on this lovely fall weekend afternoon.

The rest of the day and evening raced by as we tried to fend off reporters who were discovering sievelike leaks all over Washington.

At 2:30 P.M., the secretary of defense, the attorney general, the new chairman of the Joint Chiefs of Staff, and the director of the Office of Emergency Planning slipped through a side door of the White House and went in to meet with the President.

At three, one of my assistant press secretaries, who'd been standing by in the White House Situation Room, called to tell me that U.S. intelligence had reported a massive buildup of Soviet warplanes in Cuba. A number of them were capable of delivering a nuclear strike.

Ten minutes later, Ed Folliard of the *Washington Post* called to ask if there was any connection between JFK's coming back early from his trip because of a cold and LBJ's cutting short his junket to Hawaii, also because of a cold.

"Coincidence," I told him.

At 5:30, the session with EXCOM, the executive committee of the National Security Council, ended. Ken O'Donnell called to say the President wanted me to go home (again, mainly for the sake of appearance) but also to stay close to the phone.

"Not to worry," I told him.

I went home and tried to be nice to Nancy and the children, but my mind was ninety miles off the coast of Florida.

The President called me at 9:38 to see if I'd had any more calls from the press. I told him I hadn't, and then said, "Mr. President, I'm still in the dark."

There was a pause, and then Kennedy said, "I know. Consider yourself lucky."

Half an hour later, I got a call from Folliard telling me that an hour ago at a Georgetown dinner party, Walter Lippmann, the famous and influential columnist, had told a *Washington Post* editor that the United States was "on the brink of war."

I immediately called the President, whose angry response was, "This town is a sieve!"

Moments later, a somewhat calmer Kennedy said, "Pierre, how much longer do you think this thing can hold?"

I told him that there were too many good reporters chasing it for it to hold much longer.

"I would say through tonight, and maybe tomorrow."

"All right, Pierre," said the President, "I'll have Bundy fill you in on the whole thing in the morning."

At nine o'clock the next morning, presidential assistant McGeorge Bundy gave it to me straight.

We were on the verge of nuclear war. Soviet missiles located in Cuba were capable of destroying Washington, New York, and all the other major cities on the Eastern Seaboard, from Florida to Maine.

Our intelligence indicated that while they were not yet fully operational, they would be within just a few days. We had—somehow—to force their removal before that point.

"The President," said Bundy, "should reach his final decision today and announce it on national television tomorrow. The next move is Khrushchev's, but, frankly, we don't know what he's likely to do."

While President Kennedy, with the help of EXCOM, was deciding on which course of action to take, I had several very important tasks. They involved the general areas of maintaining the President's communications with the American people and making certain that no information was released (or got out) that might be of use to the enemy.

My first task was to ready the implementation of our national emergency information procedures, which we had been updating ever since the election with the expert help of Col. Justice Chambers, the deputy director of the Office of Emergency Planning (and a Congressional Medal of Honor winner in World War II). Our task that morning was simply to jump-start the plan and get it going.

Next, I had to help summon to Washington the horrible-sounding entity known as the Censorship Advisory Board. A bit of an anachronism in a nuclear age, the fifteen-member panel was composed of well-known news executives who would have the necessary but unenviable job of implementing national news censorship during wartime, were we to reach that horrific stage. Even if things did not go that far, the board might still have to be activated, and official censorship needed, in case the President had to declare a state of national emergency. As a measure of my respect for him, I brought in Jim Hagerty, Ike's press secretary, to chair that board.

The President himself had a direct role to play in this effort to maintain secrecy. On Sunday night, he called the editors of both the *New York Times* and the *Washington Post* and basically told them not to publish any information until after he had given his speech on Monday night. He convinced them of the vital importance of not letting the Russians know what we were doing.

I also had to help in arranging the logistics whereby a number of radio stations in South Florida would be able to receive the President's speech and rebroadcast it to Cuba in Spanish.

Finally, and obviously I'm only mentioning the major tasks, I had to make the arrangements for the President's speech to the nation the next night.

At noon on Monday, I called in Bob Fleming, ABC's White House bureau manager (and chairman of the special network advisory committee that handles sudden requests from the White House for television and radio airtime).

"The President would like to go on the air tonight to discuss a matter of the highest national urgency," I said.

"Do you have a time preference?" asked Fleming, cutting right to the heart of the matter and not bothering with any superfluous questions.

"Seven o'clock, across the board," I said, meaning a simultaneous broadcast across all the time zones so that all Americans could hear the President at the same time.

"I'll get back to you," said Fleming.

Next, I called the press into my office for the regular morning briefing. My initial announcement was the first official word I'd given them that we had a major crisis on our hands.

I said, "We have just submitted to the networks a request for a half hour of time at seven tonight for the President to make an address to the nation on a subject of the highest national urgency. We expect to hear from the networks in the next fifteen or twenty minutes."

"Do you think they'll give it to you?" asked a reporter with a sense of humor.

"I have a feeling they will," I replied.

With that, the phone rang. It was Fleming, saying yes.

President Kennedy had the amazing ability not simply to appear, but actually to become, calm once he had made a difficult decision. This night was no exception. He began speaking to the nation from the Oval Office at exactly 7:00 P.M. In the back of the room, I stood to one side, mesmerized. (An historical footnote: Standing not far from me, and present because of my personal invitation, was the Washington correspondent for Tass. I figured this was the ideal time, with President Kennedy speaking not just about but really *to* Premier Khrushchev, to break the ban on Soviet journalists inside the Oval Office.)

> Good evening, my fellow citizens: This government, as promised, has maintained the closest surveillance of the Soviet military buildup on the island of Cuba. Within the past week, unmistakable evidence has established the fact that a series of offensive missile sites is now in preparation on that imprisoned island. The purpose of these bases can be none other than to provide a nuclear strike capability against the Western Hemisphere. . . .

After announcing "a strict quarantine on all offensive military equipment under shipment to Cuba," he went on to say something that caused the hair on the back of my neck to stand up: "It shall be the policy of this nation to regard any nuclear missile launched from Cuba against any nation in the Western Hemisphere as an attack by the Soviet Union on the United States, requiring a full retaliatory response upon the Soviet Union." He continued: "Each of these missiles, in short, is capable of striking Washington, D.C., the Panama Canal, Cape Canaveral, Mexico City, or any other city in the southeastern part of the United States, in Central America, or in the Caribbean area. . . ."

After calling on Khrushchev to abandon "this course of world domination, and to join in an historic effort to end the perilous arms race and to transform the history of man," the President closed with two short paragraphs that were quintessential JFK.

> The path we have chosen for the present is full of hazards, as all paths are, but it is the one most consistent with our character and courage as a nation and our commitments around the world. The cost of freedom is always high, but Americans have always paid it. And one path we shall never choose, and that is the path of surrender or submission.
>
> Our goal is not the victory of might, but the vindication of right; not peace at the expense of freedom, but both peace

and freedom, here in this hemisphere, and, we hope, around the world. God willing, that goal will be achieved.

Never in my life was I more anxious or more active than I was over the course of the next six days, which were certainly the grimmest of the thousand days of John Kennedy's presidency. Yet I never knew him to be more in command of himself or of events. And I will never forget his courage, his smile, and his optimism that this crisis, too, would pass.

At one point, on Friday, October 26, I went for a walk with JFK in the Rose Garden. He was silent for quite a while, and then he suddenly said, "You know, if we don't succeed in bringing this crisis to an end, hundreds of millions of people are going to get killed."

Saturday evening, President Kennedy said to me, as he did to all the other scared and weary aides, "Pierre, go home and see your wife and kids. Tonight we decide whether to make war or not." (By that point, I'd been at the White House, and sleeping on my office cot, for seven straight days.)

Later that same day, acting on the instructions of my government, I handed my wife an envelope that had been given to me by the Secret Service. I told her that while she was not to open it unless and until she received explicit instructions from Washington, I could tell her what was in it. When I did so, Nancy's face blanched.

What she was holding in her hands was the evacuation plan for families of high-level government officials in case of a nuclear attack. Under the plan, the President and certain other top government officials, myself included, were to be taken to a remote spot in the mountains of a nearby state, from which safe haven they would run the government. Nancy's instructions under the plan were to take the children and drive to a designated spot "outside the nuclear impact area of Washington."

"Oh my God, Pierre," she said, "this means war, doesn't it?"

"No," I said quickly, and then added, "but it could."

Even in the best of family times, this would not have been an easy message to receive. Unfortunately, these were no longer the best of times for us. Nancy, an artistic person—she was a very talented potter—did not take to life in the fast lane in Washington. I happened to love it. When we'd met, I was a journalist turned congressional investigator, and now I was the press secretary to one of the two most powerful men in the world. It was heady stuff, and I reveled in it. Ironically, Nancy would probably have been happier if we had been ordered to go to the countryside outside of Washington and *stay* there.

* * *

John F. Kennedy's native optimism prevailed. Six days after his speech, Soviet Premier Khrushchev ordered the withdrawal of the missiles from Cuba. The collective sigh of relief that followed could be heard around the entire world because it *came from* the entire world.

My first call was to my wife. "Nancy," I said, "you can smile—the war's over."

Next, I called Art Buchwald. On the previous Monday, October 22, the last entry in my day book had read: "8:00 P.M. 'Fat Fingers' Buchwald's. Poker. 3102 Cleveland Ave., N.W."

Not long after my press conference announcing that the President would be going on television to discuss a matter of national security I'd had a call from Art. A good friend, Art had not pushed me. He'd simply asked, "Should I go out and get the food and drink for tonight?" I had replied, "No, Art. There won't be a poker game this week."

So, right after speaking to Nancy, I called "Fat Fingers" Buchwald and told him he could go out and buy food and drink for next Tuesday's poker game. For the remainder of its existence, our gathering was known as the Cuban Missile Crisis Poker Club.

In 1989, twenty-seven years later, in Moscow, Premier Mikhail Gorbachev convened a unique gathering of thirty. There were ten Soviets, ten Americans, and ten *Cubans* at the meeting. All of us were veterans, in one sense or another, of the crisis. Among the Americans were Ted Sorensen, Robert McNamara, McGeorge Bundy, and I. I thought I knew pretty much all there was to know about the Cuban missile crisis. I was amazed to learn how mistaken I had been to believe that.

What so amazed me was to hear what we had *not* known at the time of the crisis.

For example, while I had heard of the existence of Operation Mongoose (the JFK-approved, CIA-run plan for the overthrow of Fidel Castro), I had not known until I learned it in Moscow in 1989 that Cuban intelligence had been able to penetrate the CIA and get some documents on Operation Mongoose.

One of the documents they obtained said, in effect, "If Castro is not out of power by October 1962, then the United States will have to do something tougher." Cuban intelligence passed that information to the KGB, which handed it over to Khrushchev. That information was the basis for Khrushchev's belief—no, his *conviction*—that the United States was going to invade Cuba in October 1962.

The second fascinating discovery was learning the true account of Soviet troop strength in Cuba in the fall of 1962. The CIA had reported there were ten thousand. We learned in Moscow in 1989 that there had been *fifty thousand.* Not only were there five times as many as we'd been led to believe; these troops were equipped with nuclear weapons. This meant that if we had invaded Cuba—as so many high-level people in both the legislative and the executive branches were urging—we would have lost a tremendous number of our own soldiers, sailors, and airmen.

The third absolutely fascinating revelation was that early in the affair, Castro had tried to convince Khrushchev to start the attack, launch the missiles of October. Had that happened, it is entirely possible that the world as we knew it then would no longer exist.

Finally, we learned that Castro was enraged when he learned that a deal—to remove the missiles—was done between Kennedy and Khrushchev as a result of negotiations *that did not involve Cuba.* What so angered Castro was his firm belief that if he and his people had been part of the negotiations, they could have wrested some concessions, such as a U.S. agreement to pull out of its naval base at Guantánamo Bay. To this day, the fact that the Cubans were not even consulted rankles Castro. With the collapse of the Soviet Union, it must aggravate him even more.

CHAPTER NINE

MY PRESS CONFERENCE, which immediately followed JFK's speech on the Cuban missile crisis, was a tumultuous and at times acrimonious affair. For well over half of it, I escaped the question I'd been dreading, but suddenly there it was.

The reader should not miss the sarcasm embodied in the initial wording.

Q.: Is it still true that he came back, that the President came back, because of a cold?
MR. SALINGER: I will let you answer that.

If I do say so myself, that was a nice try. But it didn't work.

Q.: Wait a minute. I think that is important. I would like to know. Did the President come back because of this crisis?
MR. SALINGER: The President had a cold.
Q.: Did he come back because of this crisis?
MR. SALINGER: The President had a cold. I am not going to go beyond that.

A bit later in that same (October 22) press conference, I got a chance to clarify my answer somewhat, for the record.

Q.: When you stated to UP and AP and me that there was no other reason for his return, were you aware of this crisis?

MR. SALINGER: I was stating my knowledge at the time.

My original answer about the President's cold as the reason for his hasty return from the Midwest on October 20 would come back to haunt me. Just weeks later, using that statement as the basis of its accusation, the subcommittee on Freedom of Information of the U.S. House of Representatives, chaired by Congressman John Moss (D-CA), charged me with "deliberately" lying to the press, and, therefore, to the American people.

My response was the simple truth: On the morning of October 20, I had no knowledge of the Cuban missile crisis—and even if I had, it would not have been in the national interest of the United States for me to reveal that information. I say that because the President had yet to make his decision as to how we should respond to our discovery of the missiles— and neither the Russians nor the Cubans knew we had made that discovery. While it is true that no declaration of war had been made (and, thank God, one never had to be), it is also true that the guidelines, such as they were, for the official censorship of news had come about during conventional wars, and that is hardly what we were facing during the Cuban missile crisis. The U.S. Supreme Court once said, in a case involving capital punishment, "Death is different." So is nuclear war.

One of the main reasons why President Kennedy was successful in dealing with the missile crisis is that, by design, the announcement, and the simultaneous implementation of, the blockade of Cuba caught both the Russians and the Cubans by surprise. I very much doubt we would have had that same success had we not kept a lid on certain information.

Compounding our problem at the time of these charges of lying to the press was the wide dissemination of a story that I believed to be false. It involved a statement allegedly made by Assistant Secretary for Defense of Public Affairs Arthur Sylvester. The story, which ran in a number of papers, and which Sylvester totally denied, stated that he'd said the government had a basic right "to lie to save itself when it is [involved] in nuclear war."

I was not called before Congressman Moss's committee, but Arthur Sylvester was. The statement he gave before that committee struck me as exactly right. He said, "The government does not have a right to lie to the people, but it does have a right in facing an enemy [to put out] information [that] is not accurate and is intended to mislead the enemy. I think that any people will support their government in not putting out information that is going to help the enemy, and, if necessary, misleading them."

There is no point in my trying to deny that once the President had made his announcement of the blockade we controlled the extent of the news that got out. Our intention was to give the press as much information as we could in a crisis situation, while still protecting information that the enemy would view as being of a vital nature to them. Clearly, this was a tightrope situation, where we were trying to achieve a delicate balance. I decided that I had better go directly to the leaders of the press and explain what we were about.

If my press conference immediately following the President's speech was tough, this meeting, held at six o'clock the next day, was as close to brutal as I ever want to experience. Back in 1962, we didn't use the term *media* to the extent it is used today, but that meeting was definitely a media event. In addition to the pen-and-pencil press, there were top representatives of the nation's radio, television, and wire-service organizations.

Among the assembled honchos were Ben McKelway, who was the editor of the *Washington Star* and the president of the Associated Press; Wes Gallagher, the AP's editor and head of its Washington bureau; several top people from UPI, including Merriman Smith; and at least two people from each of the three television networks (including my predecessor, Jim Hagerty, who was with ABC). In addition to myself and Andy Hatcher from the White House press office, I'd invited Pentagon spokesman Arthur Sylvester and Bob Manning, the top information officer at the State Department.

"Obviously," I said, "we are not at war. However, we are by no means overstating the case to say that this crisis could lead to nuclear war. Because of that, while we *do not* want to impede the orderly flow of news, we do not, at the same time, want to give the enemy—and there's no point in using any other word—any information that would be helpful to them. Knowing that all of you and the organizations you represent are as patriotic as the government, and knowing that in the past you have cooperated with the government to avoid helping the enemy, I'm going to assume that you will cooperate now."

That said, I informed the group that we were instituting a general policy based on a list of twelve points that the government considered information that would be helpful to the enemy (such as discussions of plans for employment of U.S. strategic or tactical forces; estimates of the destructive power of our weapons; intelligence estimates of targets; our intelligence of enemy plans or capabilities; and details of movements of any and all U.S. forces).

Then I told them that the next day we'd be issuing that twelve-point list to their organizations. At the same time, I told them, the Department of Defense would be putting out a similar list to all of its commands, informing them this was the type of information they should *not* give out.

This information did not exactly thrill the assembled throng. Nor did my statement that the guidelines were only advisory in nature mollify them to any noticeable degree. There were some complaints, thinly disguised as questions, as to why the navy had refused to allow reporters on the ships that sailed from Norfolk, Virginia, to form the blockade. I replied that unlike such approved coverage during the wars they claimed as precedents, the information they would have reported back clearly fell within the twelve-point guidelines. They also wanted to know why reporters were not allowed to go to the naval base at Guantánamo Bay. I replied that they would be able to go there "at the proper time."

In the end, the organizations did promise to send our guidelines around to all their affiliates and bureaus—not exactly an ironclad guaranty of cooperation, however. I came away from the meeting with something less than general satisfaction. There had been, on the part of a few of the more senior participants, a definite hostility. I'm afraid they considered limited censorship akin to limited pregnancy. I disagreed, but before dropping off to sleep that same night, I did reflect on how much my views had changed since I had become someone in charge of putting out the news, rather than someone responsible for gathering it—or ferreting it out.

The word *coexistence* has often been used to describe relations between the United States and the Soviet Union, but it is also an apt word for the kind of strained relations between the American government and the American press that prevailed in the latter part of 1962. Frankly, I think the whole situation would have been a lot better had not Arthur Sylvester made another comment, this time on October 29, that riled the press lords and may well have bothered a lot of American citizens (I know it bothered *this one*).

Sylvester's line that caused the most consternation was: "generation of news . . . becomes one weapon in a strained situation." It took but a few weeks for that phrase to be transliterated into the more easily understood—and more sinister-sounding—"management" of news, and we were beaten over the head with it for the rest of the Kennedy presidency.

I can't say I blame the press entirely, nor can I say I believe we did everything just right. But I think the ongoing bad rap we received was just that, a bad rap.

As usual, it was the President himself who put the matter in its proper perspective—at his November 20 press conference, his first since the crisis—and he did so with characteristic directness and verbal ease.

"We did not want to indicate to the Soviet Union or to Cuba, or anyone else who might be our adversaries," he said, in explaining why the U.S. government had not announced the discovery of the missiles to its citizens as soon as it had verified the information, "the extent of our information until we had determined what our policy would be and until we consulted with our allies and members of OAS and NATO. So, for these very good reasons, I believe this matter was kept by the government until Monday night."

JFK continued: "I have no apologies for that. I don't think that there's any doubt it would have been a great mistake and possibly a disaster if this news had dribbled out when we were unsure of our response and when we had not consulted with our allies, who might be involved in great difficulties as a result of our action."

Later, after having said that once the United States had Premier Khrushchev's initial message regarding the withdrawal, our government had endeavored to "speak with one voice," he made his main point: "I can assure you that our only interest has been, first, during this period of crisis and over a longer period, to try—not to have coming out of the Pentagon information which is highly sensitive, particularly in the intelligence areas, which I can assure you in my own not too distant experience has been extremely inimical to the interests of the United States."

More than thirty years have passed, and I have covered and written about a number of other military crises, but I can still say with pride that during the Cuban missile crisis we acted in the very best interests of the American people.

I doubt that I would get much, if any, disagreement with the statement that the Cuban missile crisis was the scariest time in recent history. Even the tragic war in Vietnam, with its huge loss of life (some 58,000 Americans alone), did not create the same kind of fear in the general world populace as did the very real threat of nuclear warfare. So I think it only fitting that after recounting that terrifying event I turn to a light topic. Indeed, the tale I'm about to retell involves one of the funniest things that happened in the JFK White House. I am speaking of my near humiliation at (almost) being forced to participate in the by-now-infamous event known as the fifty-mile hike.

In February of 1963, President Kennedy somehow got it into his head that his administration had to make a very public showing of the importance of being physically fit. Personally, I'd kept in shape by indulging in the occasional run to the corner for cigars. Unfortunately, for me, JFK did not consider that sufficient exercise for an American male in his midthirties. So he made an example of me, and it took most of my guile and cunning to escape his well-intentioned clutches.

It all began innocently enough. President Kennedy was a voracious reader and was forever coming up with fascinating bits of information, especially from American history. One day, he ran across a letter written by President Theodore Roosevelt in which the old Rough Rider suggested to the commandant of the Marine Corps that it would be a good idea if his men would occasionally take a long hike to prove they were in good physical condition. TR's idea of a good long hike? Would you believe *fifty* miles?

Kennedy was so taken with this idea that, in a nimble example of (harmless) news management, he sent the Teddy Roosevelt letter and the following memo to *his* Marine Corps commandant. "Why don't you send this back to me as your own discovery? You might want to add a comment that today's Marine Corps officers are just as fit as those of 1908, and are willing to prove it. I, in turn, will ask Mr. Salinger for a report on the fitness of the White House staff."

The commandant wrote back to say that a detachment of U.S. Marines would set off on a fifty-mile hike the next week.

"You realize, of course," the President said when he gave me the commandant's letter to release to the press, "that someone from the White House will have to go down there and march with the marines." I became immediately disconcerted when I realized that as he said this, JFK was staring at my waistline.

I immediately volunteered . . . Presidential Assistant Ken O'Donnell, who was always in top shape.

"No," said the President. "It should be somebody who *needs* the exercise, somebody who would be an inspiration to millions of other out-of-shape Americans."

It was begining to dawn on me that Kennedy was dead serious about this, and I was struck by the realization that if I tried to hike fifty miles, I would be dead—serious! In a burst of inspiration, I reminded the President that when Teddy Roosevelt had charged up San Juan hill, he had been astride a horse, not on foot.

"Perhaps," I said, "that's the way we should all remember him."

JFK, his eyes still on my corpulent midriff, said no, then added ominously, "There's no escape, Pierre."

Back in my office, I did a quick reality check of my physical-fitness history, such as it was. Back in college, I had been, believe it or not, a cross-country runner, and I had even won two tenth-place ribbons. (However, in both races, the eleventh man in a field of eleven had been unable to finish because of blisters.) After the war, I tried out for the boxing team at the University of San Francisco. One of my first opponents was a foreign exchange student from Austria. I was plump, but he was fat. In the first round, I threw an uppercut that ricocheted off his paunch and hit me squarely on the chin. I was out cold for much longer than the count of ten. When the coach finally brought me around, he made the tactful suggestion that a self-inflicted one-punch knockout was the proper note of glory on which to end my pugilistic career. I quickly agreed.

My only physical exertions since then had included an infrequent round of golf (riding in an electric cart whenever possible); an even more infrequent tennis match (conceding to my opponent the entire forecourt and both sidelines); contests of strength with stubborn wine corks; an exhausting Bach arpeggio on the piano; and weekly weight-lifting exercises with the ponderous Sunday edition of the *New York Times*.

I was thirty-seven years old, five foot nine, and twenty pounds overweight at 185. I was never without a cigar, a thirst, or an appetite. Clearly, I was not a fit representative of the New Frontier.

Yet I had no choice but to start training immediately in the event the President did send me to Camp Lejeune. I had a date for lunch that day at the Hay Adams Hotel, a full block and a half away from the White House, and decided to walk both ways. I was footsore on my return and immediately informed the President of that fact.

"Try it again tomorrow," he said, "and report back."

"If I may, sir," I replied, "I should like to remove myself as a volunteer."

"You are the only man on the staff," he said, "who has shown sufficient interest in the hike to open training. You are still very much in the running."

This was beginning to get serious. I decided my best bet was to find an able substitute, and I got the President to agree to sending his air force aide, Brig. Gen. Godfrey T. McHugh, into the game for Salinger. A handsome, older bachelor (with a *very* active social life), McHugh was in such good shape that the previous spring he had, at the age of fifty-one, graduated from the parachute school at Fort Benning along with a class of teenage recruits.

I came up with McHugh's name because that morning's *Washington Post* had carried a story in which he was quoted as having said, at a cocktail party, that it would be "loads of fun to go on a fifty-mile hike every day." The minute I read the story, I literally ran into the President's office, waving it.

"All right," said Kennedy, "you're off the hook. You can tell the press McHugh is our man." And then he added, "But let him know first."

I dialed McHugh's extension with some reluctance and was overjoyed to find him out of his office. I tried, though not very hard, to find him, and when I couldn't, I happily announced his name to the press as my substitute.

McHugh, on learning from the press that he was to be the sacrificial hiker, counterattacked, and within minutes he was off the spot and I was back on it. (I was shocked to hear that he had accused me of having "self-serving motives.") McHugh told the press not only that he would lead the way but that he was challenging me to match his pace—"if he can."

The reality of what I was about to undergo was beginning to sink in as I announced, a week ahead of time, that the actual hike would begin on Friday morning, February 15, at seven o'clock in the morning.

Gloating over my discomfort, the White House reporters had a field day. They kept dropping by my office with "fun" gifts—a pair of crutches, a compass, rubbing alcohol, and other aids for the footsore and bedraggled. Unfortunately for them, they went too far. At my afternoon press briefing, I announced that I expected any reporter covering the hike to do so fully, from beginning to end. "When I walk," I said grandly, "everybody walks."

Their response was another barrage of jokes, but I could tell I had scored a direct hit. Their questions began to reflect an increasing nervousness. Many of the reporters were much older than I, and most were in not much better shape. (It should be remembered that this was 1963, well before the so-called fitness craze.)

When one of them asked how long the hike would last, I replied, "Up to three days." There were groans around the room, but more than fifty reporters signed up to go along (most at the urging of their editors, who of course would remain safely desk-bound). I knew I would have big trouble trying to keep up with McHugh, but I figured I could more than hold my own with most of the reporters.

The Sunday before the hike, I did a practice run with my family around Lake Barcroft, the northern Virginia suburb where we had bought a house on the lake in 1962. I felt quite good reporting that I had traversed the five-and-one-half-mile course in just under two hours. Then I got the news that Bobby Kennedy, the attorney general, and a true sports and fitness nut if there ever was one, had on that same day begun a fifty-mile hike from Washington to the presidential retreat at Camp David, along with Justice Department spokesman Ed Guthman (a sturdy type) and former Olympic hockey player David Hackett, the executive director of the President's Committee on Juvenile Delinquency.

The next evening, as I sat watching the news, a glass of red wine in hand and cigars at my side, I was startled to hear that Bobby had made it—alone. Guthman and Hackett, clearly my physical superiors, had dropped out at the seventeen-mile mark!

If that wasn't bad enough, Art Buchwald predicted in his column the next morning that the hike would literally be the death of me and that I would go down in history as a martyr to fat men everywhere. Seeing as Buchwald's waistline was clearly in excess of mine, I was surprised when he offered to go the full fifty miles with me. But then he added that he would be riding in a horse-drawn surrey, eating cold chicken and sipping champagne.

At my first press briefing of the day, UPI's Merriman Smith asked me, "With Bob Kennedy and all the other volunteers getting into the fifty-mile-hike act, do you think your own participation is still necessary?"

MR. SALINGER: Are you asking that question from the standpoint of self-interest?
Q.: I am.
MR. SALINGER: Have you been assigned to cover this?
Q.: Not yet. But if it becomes necessary, shouldn't you consider an age limit, saying nobody over fifty could go?
MR. SALINGER: How about nobody over thirty-five?
Q.: We're all for that.

I then revealed to the assembled group of reporters that I had taken a practice spin around Lake Barcroft.

Q.: How far did you go?
MR. SALINGER: Five and a half miles.
Q.: Did you have a support unit?
MR. SALINGER: No.
Q.: Did you actually hike around the lake or just among the homes of friends?
MR. SALINGER: I resent that implication.

What I truly resented more than anything else was the fact that the hike was to take place the very next morning. Whether I could make it was not the right question; I knew I could not. The right question was how could I get out of it. The comedian Lenny Bruce had a line that perfectly described the approach I suddenly decided to employ. Lenny's line was: "Be a man—sell out."

I went in to the President and blurted out, "I can't walk fifty miles. If you bet on me against McHugh, you will be backing a loser."

"You're sure?" asked President Kennedy, a grin starting to come across his face.

"Yes, sir."

"Well, all right. If you can't, you can't. But, Pierre, you're going to have to come up with a good reason for calling it off."

I went back to my office, my entire being flooded with relief, and tried to do just that. It wasn't easy. After a couple of very weak attempts, I hit upon an idea that had the twin benefits of being logical and (almost) honest. I grabbed the phone and called Dick Snider, the director of the President's Council on Physical Fitness. (The fact that today it is known as the President's Council on Physical Fitness and Sports has had absolutely nothing to do with me.)

I told him the White House felt that the whole fifty-mile-hike business was getting out of hand, then asked, "Isn't there a danger that people with bad hearts or other infirmities might do permanent harm to themselves by attempting hikes that are clearly beyond their capacity?"

When he said something that sounded like agreement, I raced on. "In that case, wouldn't it be in the national interest for the President's Council on Physical Fitness to advise unfit people against such hikes?"

"Pierre," said Dick Snider after a long silence, "are you speaking for yourself or for the President?"

"I am speaking for myself," I said, and then hurriedly added, "but I can assure you that the President is aware of my interest in this matter."

Snider said he would think about issuing such a statement "at the appropriate time."

"The appropriate time is right now!" I told him, and to his everlasting credit, he not only agreed to put out a statement within the hour but he actually did so.

The council gave its advice at eleven, and I took it at twelve. I gave the press the statement from the President's Council on Physical Fitness, and they immediately grasped its significance, both for me and for them, too. There was general merriment and laughter.

MR. SALINGER: May I make my statement, please? The President's Council on Physical Fitness this morning issued a statement commending those in the nation who are successfully attempting the fifty-mile hikes, but warning that those who are not in good shape should not attempt such a feat. My shape is not good. ("Q. Are you referring to your condition or your proportions?") May I finish my statement? While facts laid out by the President's Council have been apparent to others for some time, their full significance was pressed upon me as a result of a six-mile hike last Sunday ("Q. You have gone up half a mile.") I have done little walking since, except to go from my office to the White House dispensary. Even that trip required the use of an elevator. I believe the fitness of this administration has already been amply demonstrated by the Attorney General. ("Q. When he walks, he walks for others.")

MR. SALINGER: A further demonstration on my part would be superfluous and possibly dangerous. I am therefore rescinding the hike previously announced. I may be plucky, but I am not stupid.

Q.: Hear! Hear!

UPI's Merriman Smith, who traditionally closed each of my press conferences, did so again, but this time with a most heartfelt "Thank you, Mr. Secretary, in more ways than one."

One of the best things about writing a memoir as opposed to a more formal book that covers both history and politics is that the rules aren't as rigid. For example, one doesn't feel compelled to stick to a strict chronology, and in that spirit I am going to slip backward in time in order to tell the story of how I eventually came to spend fourteen hours with Nikita Khrushchev.

In January 1961, to the surprise of many (including President Kennedy), the astonishment of several, and the anger of a few of my fellow members of the Kennedy administration, I was invited to go to the Soviet Union.

Without getting into *too* much detail, I should at least set the stage. Shortly after I became the presidential press secretary, I was approached by an NBC producer named Lucy Jarvis with the idea of a televised debate between me and my Soviet counterpart, a man by the name of Alexei Adzhubei, who happened to be married to Khrushchev's daughter. Although I thought the chances of this ever coming about were slim to none, I agreed.

To my surprise, when I stepped off the plane in Vienna in June 1961 (where I was accompanying President Kennedy for his first and only summit meeting with the Soviet premier), there was Lucy Jarvis at the airport. Seeing her was the first surprise; the second was her news that the Soviets had agreed to the idea of a debate between the two press secretaries.

That was the beginning of a whirlwind of activity. Here's how Patrick Anderson encapsulated the swift sequence of events in his book *The Presidents' Men*:

> Salinger's most surprising role . . . was as an impresario of Russian-American relations. He fell into this role more or less by accident during the Kennedy-Khrushchev meeting in Vienna in June 1961, and in rapid succession he debated two leading Russians on American television, became a drinking companion of Khrushchev's son-in-law and his press spokesman, served as a courier of secret messages between Kennedy and Khrushchev, arranged the first interview of an American President by a Rus-

sian journalist, and climaxed his adventures by spending four-teen hours with Khrushchev himself.

No previous Press Secretary, and no White House aide since Harry Hopkins, had been as directly involved in inter-national diplomacy. The fact that Salinger was the emissary rather than some more solemn figure such as Bundy, tended to detract from the fact that his exchanges with the Russians, and particularly with Khrushchev, were an invaluable source of in-formation to Kennedy. Salinger was not the man Kennedy would have picked for the job . . . but the Russians liked Sal-inger and Kennedy would have been foolish not to make the most of this informal link with the Kremlin.

When I spoke with Lucy Jarvis at the airport, she told me that Khrush-chev's spokesman, Mikhail Kharlamov, was waiting for me at his hotel. We met, exchanged greetings, and he told me that the Soviets had accepted NBC's offer and that he and Alexei Adzhubei would go to Washington in July to debate me and an American journalist (to be chosen by me and the network).

I told him how pleased I was and extended an invitation to him and to Adzhubei to visit me in Washington after the debate. I said that while we would thereby be able to continue our discussions of the problems of press relations betwen the two superpowers, I also intended for it to be a social visit. I could tell that this met with his approval, as he accepted immediately.

The debate took place on July 24, and it went very well. My partner was Harrison Salisbury, the *New York Times'* Russian expert. For over an hour, we debated our relative positions on freedom of the press. The Rus-sians were hard and dogmatic opponents, and it was soon quite evident that our positions were light-years apart. As the debate had been prere-corded for broadcast the next night, once it was over I put on my social hat and went around to make sure everyone knew when and how to get to my house in Washington the next evening.

The party at my house on Lake Barcroft was a great, and boisterous, success, and one my neighbors talked about for weeks, if not months, afterward. I'd invited a number of people, including Ed Murrow and Mer-riman Smith, as well as Georgi Bolshakov (officially the editor of a leading Russian magazine but in fact a KGB agent who would later prove a quite effective back-channel operative for communications between Kennedy and Khrushchev), who had translated for Adzhubei and Kharlamov, and a fourth Russian, Mikhail Sagatelyn, Tass's Washington correspondent.

Spotting the lake a short distance behind my house, the Russians immediately expressed a desire to immerse themselves and escape the oppressive heat and humidity of Washington in July. I lent them bathing trunks, and soon they were splashing merrily, shouting Russian imprecations into the fetid air.

I made a slight miscalculation as to how long it would take to cook chicken on the grill, and as a result I served up a platter of semidone chicken, parts of which were noticeably red and probably raw. But by this time, there had been *many* vodka toasts, and the Russians were so hungry that they demolished the birds with gusto.

Then we all crowded around a portable television set on my patio to watch the broadcast of the debate, immediately after which I got a call from the President. "You and Salisbury were great," he said. "I thought you won hands down. Tell him that for me." By evening's end, there had been many *more* vodka toasts, much laughter, but also much good, serious talk, and the Russians had experienced their first (and probably their only) suburban American cookout.

From the time the limousine I'd arranged for had picked them up at National Airport until the time it dropped them off there, the Russians had spent three days as my guests. I didn't make any converts to our system of government, of course, but these individual Russians did get to know individual Americans as people and did get to see how they lived. It was good for all of us.

Over the next year, I continued my contacts with Adzhubei, Kharlamov, and Bolshakov. In September of 1961, Kharlamov accompanied Foreign Minister Andrey Gromyko to the United States, and while in New York he gave me a message from Khrushchev that I was to give to President Kennedy.

Just weeks later, I met Bolshakov in the Carlyle Hotel in New York, where he handed me a twenty-six-page letter from the Soviet premier to the American President. Two weeks later, I had one for him to take back to the Soviet Union. That was the start of an historically amazing interchange of private communications—forty-four in all—that went back and forth between the two world leaders until JFK's assassination.

Dated September 29, 1961, and addressed to "His Excellency Mr. John F. Kennedy, President of the United States of America," Khrushchev's first letter began:

Dear Mr. President,

At present I am on the shore of the Black Sea. When they write in the press that Khrushchov [sic] is resting on the Black Sea it may be said that this is correct and at the same time incorrect. This is indeed a wonderful place. As a former Naval officer you would surely appreciate the merits of these surroundings, the beauty of the sea and the grandeur of the Caucasian mountains. Under this bright southern sun it is even somehow hard to believe that there still exist problems in the world which, due to lack of solutions, cast a sinister shadow on peaceful life, on the future of millions of people.

But as you fully understand, I cannot at this time permit myself any relaxation. I am working, and here I work more fruitfully because my attention is not diverted to routine matters of which I have plenty, probably like you yourself do. Here I can concentrate on the main things.

I have given much thought of late to the development of international events since our meeting in Vienna, and I have decided to approach you with this letter. The whole world hopefully expected that our meeting and a frank exchange of views would have a soothing effect, would turn relations between our countries into the correct channel and promote the adoption of decisions which would give the peoples confidence that at last peace on earth will be secured. To my regret—and, I believe, to yours—this did not happen.

I listened with great interest to the account which our journalists Adjubei [sic] and Kharlamov gave of the meeting they had with you in Washington. They gave me many interesting details and I questioned them most thoroughly. You prepossessed them by your informality, modesty and frankness which are not to be found very often in men who occupy such a high position.

My thoughts have more than once returned to our meetings in Vienna. I remember you emphasized that you did not want to proceed towards war and favored living in peace with our country while competing in the peaceful domain. And though subsequent events did not proceed in the way that could be desired, I thought it might be useful in a purely informal and personal way to approach you and share some of my ideas. If you do not agree with me you can consider that this letter did not exist while naturally I, for my part, will not use this correspondence in my public statements. After all only in confidential correspondence can you say what you think without a backward glance at the press, at the journalists.

As you see, I started out by describing the delights of the Black Sea coast, but then I nevertheless turned to politics. They say that you sometimes cast politics out through the door but it climbs back through the window, particularly when the windows are open. . . .

Khrushchev's letter, which continued on for another twenty-two pages, was warm in tone but tough in content, and it was clear the two had the possibility of a long correspondence ahead of them, which is just what happened. President Kennedy's letter struck much the same tone.

Dear Mr. Chairman:
I regret that the press of events has made it impossible for me to reply earlier to your letter of last month. I have brought your letter here with me to Cape Cod for a weekend in which I can devote all the time necessary to give it the answer it deserves. My family has had a home here overlooking the Atlantic for many years. My father and brothers own homes near my own, and my children always have a large group of cousins for company. So this is an ideal place for me to spend my weekends during the summer and fall, to relax, to think, to devote my time to major tasks instead of constant appointments, telephone calls and details. Thus, I know how you must feel about the spot on the Black Sea from which your letter was written, for I value my own opportunity to get a clearer perspective away from the din of Washington.
I am gratified by your letter and your decision to seek this additional means of communication. Certainly you are correct in emphasizing that this correspondence must be kept wholly private, not to be hinted at in public statements, much less disclosed to the press. For my part the contents and even the existence of our letters will be known only to the Secretary of State and a few others of my closest associates in government. I think it is very important that these letters provide us with an opportunity for a personal, informal but meaningful exchange of views. There are sufficient channels now existing between our two governments for its more formal and official communications and public statements of position. These letters should supplement those channels, and give us each a chance to address the other in frank, realistic and fundamental terms. Neither of us is going to convert the other to a new social, economic or political point of view. Neither of us will be induced by a letter to desert or subvert his own cause. So these letters can be free from the polemics of the "cold war" debate. . . .

The importance of this additional attempt to explore each other's view is well-stated in your letter, and I believe it is identical to the motivation for our meeting in Vienna. Whether we wish it or not, and for better or worse, we are the leaders of the world's two greatest rival powers, each with the ability to inflict great damage on the other and to do great damage to the rest of the world in the process. We therefore have a special responsibility—greater than that held by any of our predecessors in the pre-nuclear age—to exercise our power with the fullest possible understanding of the other's vital interests and commitments. As you say in your letter, the solutions to the world's most dangerous problems are not easily found—but you and I are unable to shift to anyone else the burden of finding them. You and I are not personally responsible for the events at the conclusion of World War II which led to the present situation in Berlin. But we will be held responsible if we cannot deal peacefully with problems related to this situation.

The basic conflict in our interests and approach will probably never disappear entirely, certainly not in our lifetime. But, as your letter so wisely points out, if you and I cannot restrain that conflict from leading to a vicious circle of bitter measures and countermeasures, then the war which neither of us or our citizens want—and I believe you when you say you are against war—will become a grim reality.

I like very much your analogy of Noah's Ark, with both the "clean" and the "unclean" determined that it stay afloat. Whatever our differences, our collaboration to keep the peace is as urgent—if not more urgent—than our collaboration to win the last world war. The possibilities of another war destroying everything your system and our system have built up over the years—if not the very systems themselves—are too great to permit our ideological differences to blind us to the deepening dangers of such a struggle. . . .

President Kennedy closed his first letter, dated October 16, 1961, and running about one-third as long as Khrushchev's, by saying it was his "deepest hope that, through this exchange of letters . . . we may improve relations between our nations and make concrete progress in deeds as well as words toward the resolution of a just and enduring peace. That is our greatest joint responsibility—and our greatest opportunity."

* * *

The invitation for me to visit the Soviet Union was an outgrowth of all these official and unofficial contacts by which certain people on *both* sides—from the very top down—were trying to do whatever they could to improve U.S.-Soviet relations during the first time in world history when mutual annihilation was no longer something out of science fiction but a horrendous possibility.

Whenever he visited my home in Falls Church, which he did on three different occasions, Alexei Adzhubei was quite taken with my children. I remember in particular his playing an impromptu game of hide-and-seek with ten-year-old Suzanne and his praise for fourteen-year-old Marc's talent as a violinist. We had discussed plans to exchange sons—for a month. Marc would spend part of his summer vacation in Moscow with the Adzhubeis and their oldest son, Nikita, would spend part of his with us.

Just before he left, Alexei invited me and my entire family to come to Moscow for a visit. Frankly, I'd thought he was simply being polite, but as I would soon find out, the offer was indeed genuine.

In January, when I learned that Alexei Adzhubei and his wife, Rada, Khrushchev's daughter, were in Havana on the last stop of a South American tour, I immediately suggested to the President that he invite them to the White House for lunch.

He did, and the event was a great success. President and Mrs. Kennedy were even more charming than usual, and it was easy to see that Rada Adzhubei was enjoying herself thoroughly, as was her husband. As a result of their earlier interview for *Izvestia*, JFK already knew that a meeting with Alexei Adzhubei was an indirect meeting with Nikita Khrushchev, and he made the most of the pleasant opportunity.

The luncheon with the Adzhubeis came at a propitious time. The United States and the Russians were in the middle of very serious negotiations over an equally serious proposal: that Kennedy and Khrushchev take part in a series of "television exchanges." The planning, which had to be done in secret, had already necessitated a fast trip to Paris for myself and Ed Murrow.

In addition to setting up the debate, I discussed an idea that seemed to me to make eminent good sense—a "hot line" between Washington and Moscow. One of my Russian friends liked the idea immediately, but his government decided it was too novel, too different. Later, after the Cuban missile crisis had almost blown the world apart, the Russians called and said, "How soon can we install it?"

During the luncheon, which I attended, I was thrilled to hear the President say to Mr. Adzhubei that Mr. Salinger would be happy to accept his kind invitation to visit the Soviet Union in May.

The President also said I would be going alone. As he had already nixed the plan for my son and Adzhubei's to trade vacation visits (on the grounds that it would be a security nightmare in both countries but especially in the United States because Nikita was the grandson of the Soviet premier), I wasn't surprised when he also decided against my family's going with me to Moscow.

While my happiness at learning I was to go prevailed, I did have a fleeting thought that Nancy would probably be relieved rather than disappointed. Unfortunately, our differences were becoming greater. Her main passion was for pottery, an art that demands solitary effort, whereas mine was for politics and for people, and the grander the scale, the better. I guess if I had been a better husband, I would probably not have looked forward to the trip as eagerly as I did. But there it was.

When I made the announcement of my own upcoming trip to the Soviet Union, for the purpose of trying "to achieve a freer exchange of information between Moscow and Washington," the news was met with some interesting reactions. The idea of a presidential press secretary acting as a foreign emissary was almost without precedent, as I well knew, so I could understand their surprise. At the press briefing where I made the announcement, there were all sorts of questions about protocol and procedure, plus one that had never entered my mind: Would I be meeting with Premier Khrushchev?

Hardly, I replied.

So much for prognostication.

THE MOMENT I entered the bar in the basement of the Hay-Adams Hotel, I could see Georgi Bolshakov waving to me nervously. In fact, I'd never seen him so nervous.

I had called him earlier in the day because I wanted to discuss the possibility of Mrs. Kennedy and Mrs. Khrushchev taking part, briefly, in their husbands' upcoming television exchange. As it happened, he was at home, fighting off a cold, but he insisted on meeting me, suggesting 6:30 P.M. at the Hay-Adams. I was not prepared for a scene out of James Bond, but that's what was in store for me.

Bolshakov held a large glass of clear liquid, which I did not think was water, and I noticed that his hand shook as he raised it to his lips.

Georgi had said he had bad news for me, bad news he felt he had to give me in person.

"What is it, Georgi?" I asked. "Won't your party officials allow Mrs. Khrushchev to take part in the show?"

"It's worse than that," he said, shaking his head. "There isn't going to be any show."

"What? What are you talking about? Everything's set."

"My government wants to call off the whole Kennedy-Khrushchev exchange," he said.

"Why?"

"The fault is your own President's," he said, "for deciding to resume the nuclear tests. [Following Russia's lead, several weeks earlier we had announced our intention to resume atmospheric testing.] The Soviet people would not understand it if their premier would consent to a joint appearance with him at a time like this."

Noticing that there were a number of newsmen in the bar, I kept my voice low, but it wasn't easy, for I was upset. The Russians had broken the moratorium first, so how could the collapse of the program be *our* fault?

"Relax, my friend," said Bolshakov. "None of this affects your visit to the Soviet Union. We still want you to come."

"It sure as hell *does* affect my visit," I said, banging my fist on the table, for the moment forgetting all about the reporters in the room. "What's the use of trying to open up lines of communication if your people are going to behave this stupidly?"

I got up and left without even saying good-bye. I hurried across Lafayette Park and walked right into JFK's office. When he heard the news, he got even madder than I had.

At first, he wanted me to refuse to go to Russia, but, after he'd talked with Chip Bohlen, the State Department's expert on Soviet affairs, he changed his mind. He instructed me to tell Georgi Bolshakov that the cancellation of the television exchange would be announced by both governments, with no explanation of what had caused it. In fact, he said, "*insist*" on it.

To my surprise, Bolshakov agreed immediately, then reminded me once again that my trip was still on.

"I don't think so," I said angrily.

"I know there are always some people who feel that Americans are always young and inexperienced, and foreigners are always able and tough and great negotiators," said JFK. It was his next nationally televised press conference, and he was reacting to the barrage of Republican criticism following the news that he was sending me to the Soviet Union. One of the most vocal critics was an archconservative congressman from Texas, Bruce Alger. As usual, President Kennedy was defusing a tense situation with deft humor.

"But I don't think the United States would have acquired its present position of leadership in the free world," he continued, "if that view were correct. Now [Congressman Alger] also said that Mr. Salinger's main job is to increase my standing in the Gallup poll. Having done that, he is now moving up to improve our communications."

The need for the President's special way with humor had arisen because there was criticism over the fact that a "mere press secretary" was going to be a special envoy for the United States. Yes, the Russians had renewed their invitation to me, and JFK, knowing that any legitimate (even if unusual) channel of communication with the Soviet Union was worth trying, told me to go.

There was a lot of lighthearted bantering, especially from the press, about my trip, which of course didn't bother me. I have to admit, though, that I didn't particularly like what my White House colleague Kenny O'Donnell said to me: "It isn't important whether you can carry the mission off successfully or not, although I think you'll do all right. Just the announcement that you're going has already been a political minus for the President." (Well, Ken's job *was* to worry about just that, and not my feelings.)

Opposition also came from certain vested interests outside the White House but within the administration. For example, the opposition from the middle echelons of the State Department was much more subtle—and always anonymous. There were the inevitable leaks to the press that high-ranking diplomats were "viewing [the trip] with alarm" and that the President was "privately regretting his decision."

This came as no surprise. Old hands at State were still shaking their heads over my television debate with Alexei Adzhubei and Mikhail Kharlamov. Nor did they approve of my role in arranging Adzhubei's *Izvestia* interviews with President Kennedy. It was clear to me they felt that White House personnel—and frequently the President himself—had no right to meddle in international affairs. I still have a vivid recollection of a conversation I had with a very senior State Department official about a month after JFK took office. The President had told me to relay a rather pedestrian message to him.

"I don't know if I should follow through on this or not," the official said.

"But it's the President's policy," I replied.

"It may be the President's policy," he bristled, "but is it the State Department's?"

In fact, JFK finally did begin to have some doubts of his own about my impending trip, but he felt my plans were too far along to call things off without offending the Russians. He did tell me, however, to leave my family behind.

"That way, at least, they won't be able to call it a social jaunt at government expense."

To be perfectly candid, I had a few misgivings myself, but I felt considerably better after a lunch I had, just before I left, with the new Soviet ambassador to the United States, Mr. Dobrynin. His first words to me were, "Please call me Anatoly, and I shall call you Pierre." He went on to say, in reference to some of the negative things that had been written about my trip, "We diplomats have been talking to each other for years, and not very much happens. The only way Americans can understand Russia is to go there and talk to the people and find out what they are thinking."

Misgivings aside, on May 5, 1962, I took off for the Soviet Union, by way of Bonn and Amsterdam. The last leg of the trip was on a Russian airliner, an Aeroflot TU-104, which took but 150 minutes to fly more than sixteen hundred miles.

"Adzhubei insists on taking you from here to the government dacha outside the city," said U.S. Ambassador Llewellyn Thompson as he pulled me aside from the welcoming crowd at Sheremetyevo airport, a group led by my friends Adzhubei and Kharlamov.

"You will spend," Tommy Thompson almost whispered, "most of tomorrow there with Khrushchev." Now *that* truly surprised me. Apparently, the Soviet premier had suddenly decided that I was to be shown some Russian-style hospitality—with him as the host.

I gulped. Not only was this not going to sit well with the Republicans but JFK would have a *fit*. He'd sent me to the Soviet Union to do media work, not to talk to Khrushchev!

We had already assured our Republican critics that I would be meeting only with my counterparts in communications. Well, criticism or no criticism, I could hardly refuse.

The two-story dacha on the Moscow River was an impressive, if somewhat incongruous, building; it had six dining rooms but only two bedrooms. My Russian hosts led me to the largest of the dining rooms, where we proceeded to put away an astonishing amount of food—and drink (vodka, of course)—over the next three hours. Still full the next morning, I asked for a light breakfast, and I was served twelve pancakes, with sausage on the side! (All the others ate heartily.)

After the meal, we took a walk in the cold air, and even stopped for a small contest in marksmanship at an amusement park–style shooting gallery on the grounds of the dacha. Then, shortly before noon, we all gathered in front of the main building as the official limousine rolled up, bearing the Soviet premier.

If I hadn't been warned about his mercurial temper, I'd have thought I was meeting the jolliest of men. Khrushchev bounded out of the limo, a smile stretching from ear to ear, and his first words to me were, "I thank your President for having my daughter to lunch at the White House. No other American President has had the courage to do that."

The first order of nonbusiness was a cruise up the Moscow River. Khrushchev waved to Russians on the shore with all the political familiarity of Tip O'Neill on the streets of Boston. As soon as we were back on land, he began trudging through the woods, with me and our pair of translators semitrotting to keep up with this sixty-eight-year-old former miner. (The thought crossed my mind that if the Russians had come up with the idea of a fifty-mile hike, Khrushchev would have done it himself!)

Once again, we made a marksmanship stop, but this time the rifle play was skeet-shooting. Khrushchev hit a very impressive eight out of ten, but I could smash only one clay bird in six attempts. My host consoled me by saying, "Don't feel bad. I've got generals who can't hit anything, either."

Next, the Soviet leader led us back to the wooded paths for an even longer hike. We must have walked at least five miles. All along the way, he talked. His discourse, which was almost completely *non*political, centered on two subjects, Berlin and Soviet agriculture. At one point, seeing the blank look on my face after his words on the latter topic had been translated into English, he said, "I don't know why I waste my time explaining all this to you. You don't know anything about agriculture."

No, I admitted, I didn't.

I was rewarded with a big smile. "That's all right," he said. "Stalin didn't, either."

We got back to the dacha about 3:00 P.M., to find an enormous tableful of food and drink awaiting us.

A happy Khrushchev slapped me on the back. Instead of using the Russian word *Tovarich,* which is reserved for addressing members of the Communist party, he said, "Sit down, Gospodin [Mr.] Salinger. You have worked for your lunch and now you shall have it." Reaching for the vodka bottle, he said, "I have escaped my doctors today, and I'm going to have a good time."

And that is exactly what we did. From three until six, we sat and ate, along with Kharlamov, Adzhubei, and a number of other Russians, in addition to the two translators, and of course we had vodka toasts, one after another. There were also many jokes told, and not only did Khrushchev tell most of them but he told the best ones. He was a born storyteller, and I could tell, despite the language barrier, that the laughter of the others was genuine and not brought on simply because the joke teller was their leader.

Just when I thought all the food had been served, and certain I could eat no more, a huge platter of a succulent lamb and rice dish arrived from the kitchen.

"Gospodin Salinger and I will eat this together," said the premier, and though convinced that I could not, I did. However, I managed to skip the rich dessert, but Khrushchev demolished his—along with *five* cognacs.

Suddenly, there appeared one of the famous Khrushchevian mood shifts I'd been warned to look out for.

"Your President has made a very bad mistake, for which he will have to pay!" His voice had dropped several notches, the Russian words sounding almost guttural as he spat them out, and his eyes locked onto mine. "He has said that you will be the first to use the bomb."

It turned out that the premier was referring to an article in *The Saturday Evening Post* in which the writer (Joseph Alsop) had quoted the President as to the conditions under which he would feel he'd be forced to use nuclear weapons in Europe.

I hastily explained—or as hastily as one can when speaking through an interpreter—that JFK had quickly clarified his quoted remarks. I assured him that American policy remained unchanged, that we would use such weapons of destruction only if we or our allies were "the target of mass Communist aggression."

A still-angry Khrushchev replied that he had seen and dismissed that statement. He said that he believed President Kennedy had announced a new policy. He then warned me sternly, and despite the fact he called me *mou dpyg* ("my friend"), that he would employ the same policy if his people or their allies were attacked by us.

I glanced at my translator, but he was so mesmerized by what Khrushchev was saying that he missed my look. I had a sudden flash of what it must have been like to have been a young Richard Nixon in the famous Kitchen Debate during the Soviet leader's visit to the United States in 1956.

"We Russians have suffered three wars over the last half century— World War One, our civil war, and World War Two—but you Americans have never had to fight a war on your own soil, at least not in the past fifty years. You've sent troops overseas to fight in two world wars, and you've made a fortune as a result. America has shed few drops of her own blood while making billions by bleeding the rest of the world dry."

Once I realized he had finished, I tried to formulate a response, but suddenly, Khrushchev broke into his famous gap-toothed grin. As quickly as his anger had flared up, it went away, and a big smile creased his face.

He clapped his beefy hands together. "I am going to tell you an official state secret." He brought up the 1961 incident at the Brandenburg Gate of the Berlin Wall, where American and Soviet tanks had faced off against one another at point-blank range. Khrushchev put the entire blame for the incident on Gen. Lucius B. Clay, U.S. Army, stating loudly, "Clay is as much a general as I am a shoemaker."

He went on to explain that he'd held an emergency consultation with his minister of defense, telling him, "Even a schoolboy knows that tanks can either go forward or backward. They do not like to stay in one place.

A couple of good Scouts—my brother Herbert and I, circa 1938.

The four Salinger boys at about the time of our father's death in an auto accident in 1940.

June 6, 1945. Twenty-year-old Lieutenant Junior Grade Pierre Salinger receiving the Navy and Marine Corps Medal. Years later, in the White House, JFK (who'd won the same medal) and I would joke about which one of us was the bigger hero.

1957. I testify as a staff investigator on the Senate Rackets Committee, where I worked for Robert Kennedy and met his brother John.
COURTESY UNITED PRESS TELEPHOTO.

Advice from my predecessor, James C. Hagerty, Ike's press secretary, was always welcome and always excellent. Here he briefs me immediately after the election.

Post-election, pre-inauguration press conference in Florida. Note my concept of casual beachwear. The picture was taken by the famous Palm Beach photographer Mort Kaye.
COURTESY MORT KAYE STUDIO, PALM BEACH, FLORIDA.

Fore! Golfing with JFK. My son Marc, who loved to caddy for the President, is immediately to the left of Kennedy. Because of my many errant shots, the Secret Service eventually banned me from the presidential foresome. COURTESY WHITE HOUSE PHOTOGRAPHER CECIL W. STOUGHTON.

In the Oval Office with Kennedy, whose bad back would not allow him to sit up straight for very long.

Press secretary to the President of the United States. Photo by the famous Karsh.
COURTESY KARSH.

The press secretary's crowded office. Note the *Life* cover story on the July 2, 1961, suicide of Ernest Hemingway.

Jackie's note to me reads, "To Pierre, from the biggest cross he has to bear, Jackie 9-21-60."
COURTESY LIFE PHOTO BY
ED CLARK.

A White House party for the President's birthday.

Helping Agriculture Secretary Orville Freeman (second from right behind me) celebrate a fishing festival in his home state of Minnesota. COURTESY HUGH SKRASTINS FILM, MINNEAPOLIS, MINNESOTA.

General Douglas MacArthur, shown here leaving the White House, had just met with the President. He told him the Bay of Pigs was Ike's fault, not JFK's—and warned him not to get involved in a land war in Southeast Asia.

July 24, 1961. Harrison Salisbury of *The New York Times* and I debate Alexei Adzhubei, the editor of *Izvestia*, and Mikhail Kharlamov, Khruschev's press secretary.

May 1962. At a Moscow airport, following my visit to the Soviet Union, I compare notes with Alexei Adzhubei and the U.S. Ambassador to Moscow, Llewellyn Thompson. The man on the far right is my interpreter.

When I did poorly at skeet-shooting, Khruschev said, "Don't feel bad. I've got generals who can't hit anything either."

Watching the 1963 America's Cup races with the President aboard the USS *Joseph P. Kennedy, Jr.* COURTESY R. L. KNUDSEN, PHC, USN, OFFICE OF THE NAVAL AIDE TO THE PRESIDENT.

The press secretary, far left bottom, says good-bye to his Chief.

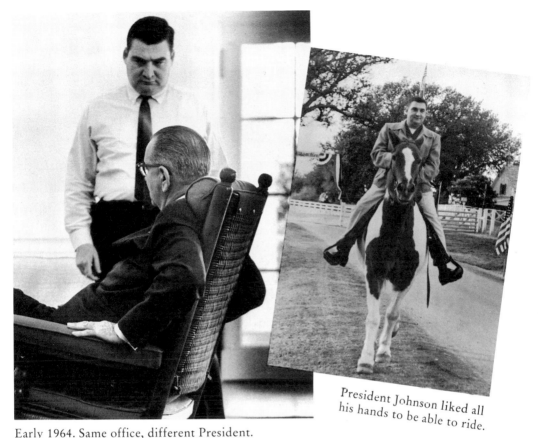

President Johnson liked all his hands to be able to ride.

Early 1964. Same office, different President.

With LBJ aboard Air Force One.

Dr. Martin Luther King, Jr., kindly came to a fund-raiser for me in L.A. in 1965 to help reduce my senatorial campaign debts.

P.S. and *L'Express* editor Philippe Grumbach, with "The Greatest."

Partners in The Factory, L.A.'s first, and hottest, discotheque, sometime in the late 1960s. From left, Jerry Orbach, P.S., Paul Newman, Peter Lawford, Peter Bren, and Ronald Buck, with Sammy Davis, Jr., seated (and Tommy Smothers, missing). COURTESY LANE KASTENDICK, LOS ANGELES, CALIFORNIA.

Under sail off the island of Skorpios—P.S., John Kennedy, Jr., Jackie, and Caroline.

Aboard the *Christina*, on the cruise Jackie hastily arranged after the accidental death of Ari's son, Alexander, in a helicopter crash in 1973. My wife, Nicole Gillman Salinger, is at the far right. The woman next to her is an American; she and her husband also made the trip, but I've forgotten their names. My apologies.

One of my favorite pictures of Jackie and Ari. We're in a limo in Paris, on our way to Maxim's. Two years later he was gone, a terribly swift victim of myasthenia gravis. COURTESY RUPER.

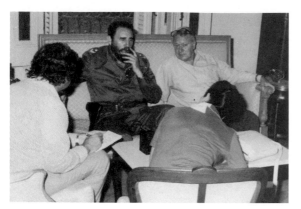

Interviewing Fidel Castro, 1975.

Also in 1975, I interviewed former President Gerald Ford for *L'Express.*

1988. My French Legion of Honor *Chevalier* is "upgraded" to *Officier.*

Back in the White House (after a fourteen-year lapse) to interview President Jimmy Carter. COURTESY KARL SCHUMAKER, THE WHITE HOUSE.

Greeting Egyptian President Anwar Sadat, whom I also interviewed for ABC-TV.

Nineteen seventy-nine book jacket photo taken by the famous French photographer Bernard Charlon.

Paris, 1979. I check the news of the release of the first group of American hostages.

February 15, 1988. Ted Koppel and I interview Austrian President Kurt Waldheim. We both won Emmies for this show.

My interview with press magnate Robert Maxwell took place in 1990, the year before he died at sea mysteriously.
COURTESY MIKE MALONEY, *DAILY MIRROR*.

November 26, 1991. Interviewing Libya's Col. Gadhafi in a tent in the countryside somewhere beyond Tripoli.

Early September 1982. Ten days after my interview with Princess Grace (at the Royal Palace in Monaco) she was killed when her brakes failed on a mountain road.

The couple who lied about their ages—my mother and her second husband, Jerry Carlson.

Covering the one-hundredth
anniversary of the Statue of
Liberty for ABC, in 1986.
COURTESY STEVE FENN/A.B.C.

Poppy, my fourth and final
wife, in a nice hat.

If the tanks went forward, it was war. If they went backward, it was peace. West Berlin means nothing to us. So I told Malinovsky [his defense minister] to back up our tanks a little bit and hide them in buildings where the Americans couldn't see them. If we do this, I said to Malinovsky, the American tanks will also move back within twenty minutes and we will have no more crisis."

Then, with a look of something like satisfaction on his face, he added, "I personally ordered the construction of the wall. A state is a state and must control its own borders."

There was a moment's lull after his last statement had been translated, and I stole a glimpse out the window. It was now just past six o'clock, and as dark out as the bottom of the river just yards away. I wondered what would come next.

At that, Khrushchev stood, and again clapping me a good one on the shoulder—but this time without smiling—said, "Come, Gospodin Salinger, it is time that we speak to each other privately."

Outside the dacha, seated in a small arbor and alone except for a small contigent of security agents and one translator, Nikita S. Khrushchev and I talked for the next hour and a half. It was a wide-ranging discussion that covered a number of topics (including his preference for John F. Kennedy over Richard M. Nixon, both politically and personally) but often came back to two topics. One was the situation in West Berlin, and the other was Khrushchev's unwavering belief that President Kennedy had actually meant what Joe Alsop had reported (in *The Saturday Evening Post*) regarding an American nuclear first strike.

During those ninety minutes, there were, again, the mercurial mood shifts, but for the most part he was serious, almost grave.

As Khrushchev began to talk about American Presidents and politicians, I became transfixed. The chilly air could have dropped another twenty degrees and I'm sure I wouldn't have noticed it. Talk about a history lesson!

"If I had to compare the two American Presidents with whom I dealt, Eisenhower and Kennedy, the comparison would not be in favor of Eisenhower. Our people whose job it was to study Eisenhower closely told me they considered him a mediocre military leader and a weak President. He was a good man, but he wasn't very tough. There was something soft about his character.

"As I discovered in Geneva—when he would have to read a note from John Foster Dulles before making a single decision; it was hard for me to believe that a head of state could allow himself to lose face like that in front of delegations from other countries—he was much too dependent on his advisers. It was always obvious to me that being President of the United States was for him a great burden."

He then proceeded to take credit for JFK's victory over Richard Nixon.

"When I met Kennedy in Vienna, he impressed me as a better statesman than Eisenhower. Unlike Eisenhower, he had a precisely formulated opinion on every subject. I joked with him that we had cast the deciding ballot in his election to the presidency over that son of a bitch Richard Nixon. When he asked me what I meant, I explained that by waiting to release the U-2 pilot Gary Powers until after the American election, we kept Nixon from being able to claim that he could deal with the Russians. Our ploy made the difference of at least a half a million votes, which gave Kennedy the edge he needed."

Khrushchev paused just long enough to look at me and grin hugely.

"You know I had met Kennedy during my visit to America. The Senate Foreign Relations Committee gave a reception for me, and Lyndon Johnson introduced us. I was impressed with Kennedy. I remember liking his face, which was sometimes stern but often broke into a good-natured smile."

"What about Richard Nixon?" I ventured while he paused for breath.

"Nixon? I had been all too familiar with him in the past. He was a puppet of Joseph McCarthy's, but when McCarthy's star started to fade, Nixon turned his back on him. So he was an *unprincipled* puppet—the most dangerous kind. I was very glad Kennedy won the election, and I was generally pleased with our meeting in Vienna. Even though we came to no concrete agreement, I could tell he was interested in finding a peaceful solution to world problems and in avoiding conflict with us. He was a reasonable man, and I think he knew he wouldn't be justified in starting a war over Berlin."

Then his mood darkened again momentarily.

"It is unwise to threaten us with war, unwise to attempt to keep us from signing a peace treaty [with West Germany] with threats of war. I repeat, we do not recognize and cannot recognize the right of the Western powers to keep their troops in West Berlin, with its two and a half million people. Adenauer himself [the West Berlin chancellor] says that not a single fool wants to fight over West Berlin. But if the Germans themselves say this, certainly the United States even more so will not fight over West Berlin, which it needs like a dog needs five legs.

"We cannot foresee what steps will be undertaken by the American government, but we are prepared for anything. We wish to be correctly understood in the United States. It would be silly on our part to attempt to frighten you, exactly as it would be foolish on your part to frighten us.

We have already fought more than once and well know what war is, and therefore do not want it.

"Although both the Soviet Union and the United States possess completely adequate means of destruction, at present it is indispensable to measure our forces not by the quantity of weapons but by the quantity and quality of reason on both sides. That is the main thing."

We also talked about the possibility of reviving the idea of the Kennedy-Khrushchev exchange on worldwide televison, and the Soviet premier surprised me by not opposing it out of hand. Interestingly, he thought that a visit to the Soviet Union by JFK ought to be a precondition.. "We want to invite Kennedy to the Soviet Union not to insult him," he said, "but so that his trip would contribute to improving relations between our countries."

Of course no such trip ever took place, but from time to time I am reminded of it, and am always intrigued anew by the idea of what might have happened if it had.

The significance of what I had experienced was just beginning to dawn on me as the visit ended and Khrushchev and I were walking back to the dacha. He approached the waiting limousine, then suddenly turned to his son-in-law, Alexei Adzhubei, and said, "What is Gospodin Salinger doing for lunch tomorrow?"

Alexei replied that he was taking me to a famous Georgian restaurant in Moscow.

"No," said Khrushchev. "I have had such a good time today, I think I will do it again tomorrow. You will bring Gospodin Salinger here for lunch."

And so Adzhubei did, and once again we walked and talked and ate and ate and drank and drank. It was marvelous.

This time, as we started our trek into the forest, Khrushchev said, again clapping me on the shoulder, "We walk twice as far as yesterday, yes?"

The premier's first topic of conversation was government control over newspapers, especially their editorial content. He found it very hard to believe that I, as the press secretary to the President of the United States, did not have veto power over what the American papers printed. "Adzhubei does," he assured me, in reference to his son-in-law's position as editor of *Izvestia*.

After a long hike, in which the conversation never slowed, we came to the edge of a collective farm. Khrushchev stopped and stared out at the fields for a few moments before speaking. Then he said, "When I first came here fifteen years ago, this farm was in terrible condition. I went to Stalin and I said I wanted to do something to help that farm, and Stalin wouldn't let me. Wasn't that awful? But now," he said, winking, "*I* give the orders, and I have done many things to help this farm. I have even planted trees— myself!"

Instinctively, I replied, "A moment ago you were discussing death-dealing bombs and now you speak with much greater interest of planting trees."

"Of course. Trees are life, but weapons are death."

Years later, when the Communist party leaders deposed Khrushchev, it did not exactly surprise me. I remembered his fondness for that collective farm. He had been the first Communist dictator to try to create reform in his country, and he had worked to cut back the power of the Party in certain economic facets of the Soviet Union. Clearly, he had pushed too hard.

It had been drizzling during our walk, a fine Russian mist, but now it changed to rain, and the premier, with some reluctance, announced that we would return to the dacha. There, we discovered Llewellyn Thompson, the American ambassador to Russia, and his wife, as well as the Russian foreign minister and his wife, Mr. and Mrs. Gromyko.

I didn't know if what we were being served was a late lunch or an early dinner, but there was more than enough food for both meals. Without exaggeration, there were almost ten courses, and each one was accompanied by a glass of vodka and a toast.

As usual, there was a round of jokes, and, also as usual, Khrushchev's were the funniest. One was about an American and a Russian arguing over which country was the more democratic. The American said that his country was so open and free that he could walk into the office of the President of the United States and "criticize everything he's doing, and the President will still receive me well and shake my hand when I leave." The Russian replied, "It's the same in the Soviet Union. I can walk into Stalin's office, criticize everything the American President is doing, and Stalin will still receive me well and shake my hand when I leave."

When the meal was over and it was apparent that my visit was about to end, I was surprised to realize I was feeling more regret than relief. I had come to like Khrushchev very much. Later, after he'd left amid warm and friendly farewells, it struck me that in the almost *fourteen* hours I'd spent with Nikita Khrushchev, he had never left his guests to confer with a staff person or a security guard or anybody, nor had he taken a single telephone call.

"You will come back," Khrushchev had said to me, "and we will have more fun." But I did not, at least not while he was still the most important and powerful man in the Soviet Union. Two years later, he was deposed (which meant my friends Adzhubei and Kharlamov were also gone). By early 1965, he had become what the Russians refer to as a "non-person."

When the former Soviet leader's memoirs (*Khrushchev Remembers*) were published in 1970, I rushed to get a copy. One of the book's many fascinations for me was its author's remembrance of the late President Kennedy. Khrushchev wrote, ". . . his death was a great loss. He was gifted with the ability to resolve international conflicts by negotiation, as the whole world learned during the so-called Cuban crisis. Regardless of his youth, he was a real statesman. I believe that if Kennedy had lived, relations between the Soviet Union and the United States would be much better than they are. . . ."

In that same volume, Khrushchev discussed something that he had also mentioned to me, the fact that he was trying, toward the end of his chairmanship, to reform the Communist party and to reduce its power over the country's internal economic matters. He said he was hoping to see such decision-making become much more public. He wasn't talking about anything as radical as privatization, but clearly he saw a need to cut back the power of the Party. Unfortunately, in 1964 the Communist party bosses learned he was serious and that they were about to lose a significant amount of their power, so they got Nikita Khrushchev before he could get them.

A final footnote to my Russian trip. "Gospodin Salinger," said the Soviet premier shortly before I was to leave, "I hear you are a great lover of cigars. I do not smoke cigars myself, but I just received a wonderful present, which I have decided to give to you. It's from my friend Fidel."

With that, he handed me a huge box containing 150 Cuban cigars! I was stunned. My first thought was, My God, these are illegal—because of our embargo against Cuban goods. I can't take these into the United States. But my next thought was, Hey, wait a minute. I've got this incredible presidential passport—I'm on a foreign mission for the President of the United States. I'm not going to get stopped at customs. *And,* the President loves cigars, too, so he's going to be very happy.

I packed the cigars, beautiful box and all, in my luggage, and, sure enough, I had no problem. I sailed through customs and went straight to the White House. The minute President Kennedy heard I'd arrived, he sent for me so I could give him an immediate briefing on my trip and my discussions with Khrushchev. I gave him a very detailed report, at the end of which I told him I had a special surprise.

"What is it?" he asked.

"I've got one hundred and fifty Cuban cigars!" I said, hardly able to contain myself.

Instead of smiling, as I'd anticipated he would, JFK frowned and said, "You didn't smuggle those into the country, did you?"

"No," I said, somewhat aggrieved, "I brought them right through customs."

"Pierre," the President said in a lecturing tone, "do you realize what a scandal it would be if the media found out about those cigars?"

"How are they going to find out, Mr. President? There are only three people in the world who know about it, you, me, and Khrushchev."

"No, no, no," he said, shaking his head. "And because I don't trust you on cigars, I want you to go to the head of U.S. Customs and turn those cigars over to him personally. And because I think you might take some of those cigars out of the box, I want him to count them and then sign a paper saying all one hundred and fifty survived the trip."

So, sadly, I went to the head of customs, turned over the cigars, which he counted, and signed a paper certifying that, yes, all 150 were there. As I walked out, I said to the man, "What are you going to do with those cigars.' "

"Why, destroy them," he said in an official tone.

"I know," I said, "one by one."

Relenting, but only a bit, this hard-hearted civil servant said, "Here, take the box." My hopes leapt, but he took the box, turned it over, and dumped out all 150 cigars. It was, however, a lovely box, and I have it to this day.

By the spring of 1963, I had become something of a non-person myself. Professionally, I was a great success, in the sense that I had one of the most fascinating jobs in the world, certainly one of the most fascinating in the United States. Personally, although I lived but a short ride from my work, I was in effect an absentee husband and father. Thanks mainly to Nancy, the kids were fine, but I saw little of them, and when I was home, I almost always got phone calls from the office. It was becoming increasingly clear that my wife was uncomfortable with our life and with my work.

I also had family problems of a different sort. After years of fighting the bottle, my brother George, then in his early thirties, took a turn for the worse. He began to experience longer and longer periods of blackout, times in which he didn't know where he was and what he was doing—or with whom. Rock bottom arrived when, during a particularly long and drunken spree, he woke up one morning beside a woman he'd married the night before in front of a justice of the peace. George had neglected to mention—or perhaps could not remember—that he was already married. My mother, who refused to believe that one of her children could truly be an alcoholic, as opposed to having "a problem with alcohol," was pleading with me, as the oldest son, to see if I could do something to help George. For my part, I had about written him off.

One day, during this same period, I waited for just the right moment and went in to the President's office. I wanted to talk to him about my future. The previous year, we'd had a somewhat related conversation. I'd asked him what he thought he would do after his presidency was over (by then, everyone in the White House assumed he'd be reelected in 1964).

"I've actually given that some thought," he said, "and what I'd like to do is to buy a newspaper in New England—and make you its editor." That was an intriguing idea, but we'd never talked about it again, and I was never really sure he had been serious when he said it. Also, I doubted if the world would allow such a capable and charismatic figure as JFK to assume the relatively obscure role of newspaper publisher.

This time, I had a statement instead of a question. "Mr. President," I said, "I will work as hard as I possibly can to get you reelected, but after that, I would like to move on. I think it would be better for you, as well as for me, if you had a brand-new press secretary for your second term in office." Kennedy looked at me, the slightest of smiles on his face.

"I think that's a good idea. Because I have a new job in mind for you."

Oh? This was the first I'd heard of it. "What is that?" I asked. I had absolutely no idea what he was going to say. His smile growing broader, he said, "I'm going to name you ambassador to France."

For more years than I care to remember, I received the excellent Executive Desk Diary that was put out by *The Saturday Review.* Always bound in leather, the handsome eight-by-ten-inch volumes bear my name embossed in gold leaf. On a shelf in my library, four books await their eventual transfer to their final home in the John F. Kennedy Library. These are the volumes for 1960, 1961, 1962, and 1963.

When the book is opened flat, it provides space to list an entire week's appointments. In the volume for the year 1963, the one which I return to far more than I do the others, there are the usual assortment of entries, both for myself and for the President.

For example, on Monday, April 8, I noted in red pencil: "1–5—JFK—Baseball opener"; and on Wednesday, August 7, it indicates that all of my scheduled appointments were canceled because I went with the President to "Hyannis/Boston."

The entry I least like to read, but the one I find myself returning to again and again over the years, is the entry, in plain pencil for Friday, November 22, 1963, which reads, simply, "JFK—Texas."

Two days earlier, there's a similar single note that reads, "PS / Japan." That was my destination, along with most of the cabinet of the United States, when we got word that President Kennedy had been shot in Dallas.

The last time I'd seen him had been at 7:30 on the night of the nineteenth, when I'd stopped in his office to remind him that I was to leave for Japan, by way of Hawaii, later that night.

My first impression was that JFK looked very tired. He'd been reading from a pile of papers on his desk, and his glasses, which he never wore in public, rode low on the bridge of his nose.

"I just stopped in to say good-bye," I said. "I'm off later tonight. The Texas trip is all set, as far as my office is concerned. Mac Kildruff is going with you, and Andy Hatcher will stay here in Washington. I'll be back in ten days, in time to go to the army-navy game with you."

Looking up, he asked who was going to take care of the press for the visit of the West German chancellor, Ludwig Erhard.

"Andy will handle it."

"Okay, fine," said JFK.

He continued to look at me. It was again apparent that his recent and unusually heavy travel schedule had fatigued him. I was certain that was why he said what he did, which was: "I wish I weren't going to Texas."

"Don't worry about it," I said reflexively. "It's going to be a great trip and you're going to draw the biggest crowds ever. Going with Mrs. Kennedy will be terrific."

He looked up, smiled that wonderful smile, and said, "Well, hurry back."

As I left the Oval Office, I wondered if I should have told him about the letter I'd received the day before. It was from a woman in Dallas, and she'd written, "Don't let the President come down here. I'm worried about him. I think something terrible will happen to him."

I hadn't told him about the letter because I didn't think it was warranted. True, there had been trouble in Dallas—both Chief Justice Earl Warren and United Nations Ambassador Adlai Stevenson had run into right-wing hecklers there. But I had had no hard reports of any impending trouble.

I'd answered the woman's letter the same day: "I appreciate your concern, but it would be a sad day for this country if there were any city in the United States he could not visit without fear of violence. I am confident the people of Dallas will greet him warmly."

Another reason I hadn't shown the letter to President Kennedy is that he would have dismissed the warning out of hand. He'd often said to me, or to anyone who'd tried to get him to be more careful in public, "If anyone is crazy enough to want to kill a President of the United States, he can do it. All he must be prepared to do is give his life for the President's."

Two days later, the Hawaian portion of our trip concluded (we'd gone there for another in a series of important meetings over the situation in Vietnam), I was at 35,000 feet above the Pacific on the way to Japan. In addition to the crew, there were twenty-eight people on board, about half of whom, my wife, Nancy, among them, were spouses of White House personnel or cabinet officers.

On the trip were Secretary of State Dean Rusk, Secretary of Defense Robert S. McNamara, Secretary of the Treasury C. Douglas Dillon, Secretary of the Interior Stewart Udall, Secretary of Commerce Luther Hodges, Secretary of Agriculture Orville Freeman, and Secretary of Labor Willard Wirtz.

I was trying to decipher the ponderous prose of a briefing book on U.S.-Japanese economic relations when Assistant Secretary of State for Public Affairs Bob Manning tapped me on the shoulder.

"The secretary wants to see you up forward," he said.

As the senior cabinet officer aboard the flight, Secretary of State Dean Rusk was in the up-front section normally used by the President. This large and luxurious private cabin was, in effect, a flying conference room. It also had a small anteroom fitted out with an array of telecommunications equipment, including a wire-service Teletype machine.

Rusk was seated, and looking for all the world as if someone had clubbed him into his chair. He held a yellow sheet of Teletype paper in his hand. He was waiting for two other men to arrive, and he said nothing, but, sensing this was a grave matter, I looked over his shoulder.

Whoever had sent the message had done so hurriedly, as there were misspellings—and one did not send misspelled messages to *this* aircraft.

I read, . . . LASTTHREE SHOTS WERE FIRED AT PRESIXENT KENNEDY'S MOTORCADE TODAY IN DOWNTOWN DALLAS. . . . KENNEDY SERIOSTY WOUNDED. MAKE THAT PERHAPS PERHAPS SERIOUSLY WOUNDED. . . . KENNEDY WOUNDED PERHAPS FATALLY BY VASSASSINS BULLET.

"Situation Room, this is Wayside [my code name]. Can you give me latest situation on Lancer [President Kennedy's code name]?" I was in the communications section, which was just through the forward cabin, and the communications sergeants had within seconds put me in touch with the White House Situation Room, at that very moment the operating nerve center of the United States—and, along with a certain hospital room in Dallas, Texas, the most tension-filled space in the world.

The answer was immediate. "He and Governor Connally have been hit in the car in which they were riding."

"Please keep us advised," was my instant response. "Secretary Rusk is on this plane headed for Japan. We are returning to Honolulu. Will be there in about two hours. We will need to be advised to determine whether some members [of the cabinet] should go direct to Dallas."

As I left the tiny room, I told the communications sergeant to keep the line open and to call me instantly when there was more information.

I relayed the news to the secretary of state. Rusk was doing an excellent job of figuring out our options—and an even better job of taking control. He said that he and Bob Manning and I should go to Dallas, but that after our plane had refueled in Hawaii, still some eight hundred miles away, all the others should head back to Washington.

Within minutes, there was more information, as relayed by the Situation Room back in Washington. Explaining that he was about to read from the Associated Press bulletin, the sender forged right ahead: " 'Kennedy apparently shot in the head, Mrs. Kennedy cried out ... Connally half-seated slumped to the left, blood on face and forehead.' Nothing further."

Then, after only a brief pause, the voice came through again: "President and Governor Connally were rushed to Parkland Hospital near Dallas Trademart. ... Will contact you if we get more."

The "more" everyone was dreading began to come in a few minutes later when the radio crackled, just as I was about to go back into Secretary Rusk's cabin. It was the Situation Room.

"Stand by for a moment, Wayside. Waiting for confirmation of something. ... Hear you loud and clear. ... Nothing further for you."

I could not make myself leave. Ten seconds passed. Fifteen. Thirty.

Then a voice said, "Wayside, this is Situation Room. We have conflicting reports now; getting no confirmation. Will call you again when we get confirmation."

Oh God! What is going on? How is he? Could we be at war? My thoughts rushed on, incoherent. I'd never been so frightened in my life.

The next message came very quickly. It was instructions for Rusk, from Acting Secretary of State George Ball, to tell the plane to return to Washington with everyone aboard. We were not to go to Dallas.

That frightened me even more.

Crackle, crackle. Almost immediately after the last message, the bottom dropped out.

"Situation Room relays following to Wayside. Have report quoting

Kildruff in Dallas that Lancer is dead. That he died about thirty-five minutes ago . . ."

The tears were streaming down my face as I left the communications center and walked into Rusk's cabin, where all the cabinet members had gathered.

"The President is dead," I told them.

Dean Rusk got up and walked to the front of the plane. He picked up the microphone, fiddled with it for a moment to see how it worked, and then said to the twenty-eight passengers in the main cabin, "Ladies and gentlemen, this is the secretary of state speaking. We have received official confirmation that President Kennedy is dead. I am saddened to have to tell you this grievous news. We have a new President. May God bless our new President and our nation."

A horrible sound went up in the small cabin, a strangulated sob. Spouses rushed to hold one another. Nancy came up to me. She, too, had tears running down her cheeks. We hugged briefly, and then I turned and went back to work. It was all I could think of to do.

But there was a long flight ahead of us, and little, if anything, that any of us *could* do. Finally, out of desperation, I suggested we play poker. Suddenly, there were half a dozen of us or more, all sitting down and pulling bills out of our pockets. It swiftly became a poker game out of Kafka or Ionesco—bizarre. We played for table stakes, and money flew back and forth across the table. But there was no bantering, no conversation, just low-voiced, dead-serious betting. From time to time, one or another of us would turn from the table, put his head in his hands, and sob. Time passed incredibly slowly.

Then, all of a sudden, the game was over, and all the money was sitting in a pile in front of me. I counted it, and there was more than eight hundred dollars. I had won everyone's money. This was terrible. I shouldn't have won: I should have *lost*. I was appalled.

Eight hours and thirty-one minutes after refueling in Honolulu, our plane touched down at Andrews Air Force Base in Washington. It was 12:31 A.M. The field was ablaze with the lights of the television cameras. I have no idea how I got through that gauntlet. I know I heard Rusk make a brief statement on behalf of the cabinet, and then, to my immense relief, I heard the voice of my driver, calling, "Mr. Salinger, Mr. Salinger." I fell into the car for the short ride to the White House.

At 4:25 A.M., a black hearse arrived at the White House. It rolled through the northwest gate, where a military guard was hastily forming.

Still another honor guard, ramrod-straight, was inside the north portico and all along the corridors leading to the East Room, to which four men, representing each branch of the military service, carried the casket containing the body of John F. Kennedy, my President, my boss, my friend. One thought kept pushing forward: I had been in *so* many towns and cities of America with John Kennedy, *but I was not with him in Dallas, Texas, on November 22, 1963.*

I went to the East Room, where a Mass was said for the slain President. After it was over, Jackie came up to me. She still wore the pink suit that bore her husband's blood, a gory emblem of everyone's loss. She put an arm around my shoulder, and said, "Pierre, I can *see* this has been a terrible day for you. You look exhausted. I want you to spend the night here in the White House."

She said much the same thing to Ken O'Donnell and Larry O'Brien, and the three of us were led to the bedrooms on the third floor, above the presidential living quarters.

The day before, as the President stood in the tail section of *Air Force One* and looked out at Dallas, he'd kidded with George Thomas, his butler and valet for more than twenty years. Thomas was from the tiny crossroads town of Berryville, Virginia, and the President had said, "You know, George, I think this is a bigger town than you come from."

Now, George Thomas was trying to work through his grief. He helped us out by mixing drinks, turning down our beds, and laying out our clothes for the next day, the same tasks he'd performed countless times for the man whose body now lay in a casket two floors below.

None of us could sleep, so we sat on the edges of our beds, talking and talking and talking about the past twenty-four hours, the worst day any of us had ever experienced.

Of course sleep took forever to come. Finally, at about 7:00 A.M., I drifted off.

I could not have been asleep for more than an hour when the phone beside my bed began to ring. It was a White House operator.

"Mr. Salinger, the President is calling."

I picked up the phone, to hear a familiar voice with an unmistakable regional accent.

"Pierre, this is Lyndon Johnson."

CHAPTER ELEVEN

As THE WORLD knows, Jackie Kennedy was magnificent in the days and weeks immediately following her husband's assassination. She was especially wonderful to me. A couple of days after the funeral, having sorted out her husband's possessions, Jackie personally chose something that had belonged to John Kennedy and gave it to each person on his staff as a memento. To me, she gave a small leather case for a pair of cigars, with the initials JFK, and a touching note, which read, "For dear Pierre, I know you carry more cigars than this but I thought you might like to have this cigar case that belonged to Jack—it comes with all my love and appreciation for all you did to make his days here so unforgettable. Jackie." Wherever I have worked since, that cigar case has been in the top drawer of my desk.

Another person who was wonderful to me was Lyndon Baines Johnson. While it is well known among people who follow politics that there was no love lost between LBJ and a number of the Kennedy lieutenants— his feud with Bobby Kennedy is common knowledge—it is less well known that to some of us he was just great. I came away from my short experience of working for him with renewed respect and admiration.

"Pierre," he'd said on November 23, in his very first phone call to me as President, "I know how much President Kennedy meant to you, and I know how you must feel now. But I want you to stay on the job."

Then he said something I found to be very interesting. He said, "I need you more than he ever did."

My response was to say I would stay on, and he replied, "Come over and see me as soon as you can." Thus began an intense and intriguing four months that would end with my realization that I had to leave the White House because I could not overcome the memory of JFK.

On my way to see President Johnson—God, that sounded strange—that first morning, I noticed that the door to JFK's office was slightly ajar, so I looked in, and I was immediately sorry I had. All of President Kennedy's possessions had been removed during the night—the ship models, the sea pictures, framed photographs of his children, and the famous rocking chair. The barrenness of the office underlined the fact that it was waiting for its new tenant. The transition had begun.

I became the first press secretary in history to serve two Presidents—and I soon realized it was not a particularly good idea.

I told LBJ he should think about replacing me with someone with whom he'd had a longer and deeper relationship. I suggested two candidates, George Reedy, a longtime Johnson aide who had the respect of the working press, and Carl Rowan, under Kennedy the head of the United States Information Agency and also a former ambassador (to Finland). LBJ said he'd think about it, but he urged me to stay with him for as long as I could.

One of the things I liked best about Johnson was that he made it so easy for me to do my job. I was the only staff member who had open access to his office. He was also very good about taking advice, often saying simply, after hearing me out, "If you think it's the right thing to do, go ahead and do it."

He was gracious to me in other ways. He had Nancy and me to dinner at the White House, and, almost on a whim, we decided to reciprocate, at least by making an offer. We hardly expected a positive response, seeing as we'd never had President and Mrs. Kennedy to our house for dinner. One Saturday morning, I asked LBJ if he and Lady Bird would like to come over sometime for dinner, and he called back minutes later to ask if that same evening would be convenient.

We had a great time. We ate off dishes that Nancy, a skilled potter, had made, and when LBJ made a big fuss over the fact that he could drink coffee from one of her ceramic cups without burning his lips, she promptly gave him the cup. For weeks after that, he would tell me he used it every morning, and the next time he saw Nancy, which was months later, after I'd left the White House, he immediately told her, "I still have that cup, and I'm still using it."

When Chancellor Ludwig Erhard made a state visit to America, LBJ took him to Texas and entertained him royally. One event turned out to be special for me. After Van Cliburn, the pianistic whiz kid who was a longtime Texan, had just concluded a concert of highly difficult Chopin pieces before an audience of some six hundred people, the President picked up the microphone and boomed out an order: "Now, would Mr. Salinger please go to the piano?"

After I'd finished (I played one of my own compositions so no one could make comparisons with any other pianist's performance of the same work), Chancellor Erhard was generous in his praise, which proved to me that he had absolutely no future as a music critic.

As I returned to my seat, I noticed that LBJ was at the mike again. In a somewhat incongruous comment, given the occasion, he suddenly said, "I don't have to tell you that Mr. Salinger was John F. Kennedy's press secretary . . . and I don't know what I would have done without him, night and day, over this past month."

If President Johnson was kind to me, he was simply wonderful to Jacqueline Kennedy. It is apparently not very well known that Jackie, who gave long interviews about her husband and their years together to the JFK Library's Oral History Program but banned their release until fifty years after her death, *did* grant an interview for the LBJ Library. It was a clear mark of how much she thought of both LBJ and Mrs. Johnson.

Referring to the Johnsons in the days immediately following the assassination, Jackie (who by then was Mrs. Onassis) said:

> I tell you, they were wonderful to me. Lyndon Johnson was extraordinary. He did everything he could to be magnanimous, to be kind. It must have been very difficult for him. I don't know exactly how long [it was] before I could move. I moved out of the White House as quickly as I could, but it was a period of about ten days. That's a rather long time, isn't it? Now that I look back on it, I think I should have gotten out the next—I didn't have anyplace to go.

The interviewer, Joseph P. Frantz, interrupted kindly, saying, "You were in an extraordinary position. Most widows don't immediately have to vacate." Jackie then repeated her last sentence:

> And I didn't have anyplace to go. It was Ambassador Galbraith who asked the Harrimans [if Mrs. Kennedy and the children could stay in their Georgetown house for a while]. I suppose one was in a state of shock, packing up. But President Johnson made you feel that you and the children [could stay],

a great courtesy to a woman in distress. It's funny what you do in a state of shock. I remember going over to the Oval Office for two things. They were two things I thought that I would ask him as a favor. One was to name the space center in Florida Cape Kennedy. Now that I think back on it, that was so wrong, and if I'd known it [Canaveral] was the name from the time of Columbus, it would be the last thing that Jack would have wanted. The reason I asked was, I can remember this first speech Jack made in Texas was that there would be a rocket one day that would go to the moon. I kept thinking, That's going to be forgotten, and his dreams are going to be forgotten. I had this terrible fear that he'd be forgotten, and I thought, Well, maybe they'll remember someday that this man did dream that. I think that was a wish that [President Johnson] could have easily said, "Look, my dear, that's impossible—" But he didn't. He called Governor Collins on the phone right away. . . . When I was back in the house within an hour or so, he called me and said it was fine.

The other two instances mentioned by Jackie were LBJ's immediate action to extend the life of one of her pet projects, a commission that was involved in renovation efforts in the nation's capital, and his personal intervention that resulted in an historic chandelier being returned to the White House from the vice president's office in the U.S. Capitol.

Later, she described how taken she was with Lady Bird Johnson from the beginning of their friendship.

Right after the nomination, the Johnsons came up to Hyannis to stay with us. It's a rather small house we have there, and we wanted them to be comfortable so we gave them our bedroom. But we didn't want them to know it was our bedroom, because we thought they might feel they were putting us to trouble. There was a lot of moving things out of closets so there'd be no trace of anybody's toothbrush anywhere. I remember that evening how impressed I was with Mrs. Johnson. She and my sister and I were sitting in one part of the room, and Jack and Vice President-elect Johnson and some men were in the other part of the room. Mrs. Johnson had a little spiral pad, and when she'd hear a name mentioned she'd jot it down.

J.F.: Actually, she was in the conversation with you but kind of listening to them?

J.O.: Yes. They were sort of at the other side of the room. Or sometimes if Mr. Johnson wanted her, he'd say, "Bird, do you know so-and-so's number," and she'd always have it down. Yet she would sit talking with us, looking so calm.

J.F.: After you moved out of the White House, did you have much contact with the Johnsons?

J.O.: President Johnson used to call up. He used to really call up quite a lot in the beginning. He was so nice. They'd always ask me back to the White House, but they understood that I really didn't want to go back. I don't think I ever would have gone back if I could have helped it, but when our portraits were presented, I sort of had to.... But anyway, they would call up. Luci came when we were still in the Harrimans' house, bringing Christmas presents. The Cabinet gave me this beautiful gold coffee set inscribed with the names of the President and the Cabinet members and close aides, at sort of a surprise party when I moved to my new house in Georgetown. I think Bobby and Ethel organized that. The President came to that, completely by surprise. He just went out of his way to do everything like that....

The man had incredible warmth, didn't he? I really felt they were warm. I almost felt sorry for him because I knew he felt sorry for me. There wasn't anything anyone could do about it, but I think the situation gave him pain and he tried to do the best he could. And he did, and I was really touched by that generosity of spirit, or whatever you would call it. I always felt that way about him.

Asked about the frequent press reports that there was friction between the old Kennedy staff and the new, incoming Johnson staff, Jackie said that she was aware of that type of story, but said:

I never felt that while Jack was alive. Afterwards I was really in my own shell of grief, and when all those things are written, do they come through to your consciousness or not? I mean, nobody from the Kennedy staff was saying that to me. But I suppose it's natural in one sense. It was such an awkward way to come to the presidency, wasn't it? There should be a dividing line; this was an unnatural division.

And then President Johnson asked the staff to stay on. Well, that was generous of him. I suppose he had to have the people there in the beginning, but—I'm just thinking this now as you ask me—it was just difficult, humanly difficult.

J.F.: Well, he wasn't their president.

J.O.: Yes, and they were all lost. I suppose it was mostly with the Irish ones, wasn't it, that they'd say it. You know the closeness of the Irish in everything, and then their man they loved gone in the most tragic way. It's just human. . . .

I talked with Jackie many times in the years between 1963 and her death in 1994, and she was always candid with me. But there are some things in this interview that I'd never heard her say before. For example, this is what she had to say about her feelings for the White House after she had moved out. It came in answer to a question as to whether the Johnsons had invited her to come back to 1600 Pennsylvania Avenue after they'd become the First Family.

> They'd ask me to every state dinner automatically. Then Mrs. Johnson kept the restoration committee going, and I'd always be asked to that, but I explained to her in writing and on the telephone that it was really difficult for me and I didn't really ever want to go back. I think she understood, but out of courtesy they just kept sending me the invitations. . . . It was just too painful for me to go back to that place.
>
> I suppose again that's where the press makes things very difficult. That was so generous of Mrs. Johnson to name the garden after me. I almost don't approve of a garden being named. I don't think it is anymore now. That was so nice of her, but she didn't have to do that. So I suppose if [the press] were all saying how awful of me not to come, I can see that was an uncomfortable position for her. I just couldn't go back to that place. Even driving around Washington I'd try to drive a way where I wouldn't see the White House.

Lyndon Johnson was a fascinatingly complex man. One of the many things that intrigued me about him was that he was as grateful to Jackie Kennedy and her late husband as she was to him. Often, and in very emotional terms, he'd tell me how much he appreciated how kind they had always been to him. In early 1964, he told me he wanted to "do something nice for Jackie—I'll name her ambassador to France." I carried the message to Jackie, who appreciated the gesture but declined. LBJ was fond of telling people, "She always made me feel at home."

It seems odd, but I spent a lot more time with LBJ on a day-to-day basis than I had with JFK. Often, he'd ask me to swim with him in the White House pool, and sometimes we'd do that twice in one day. These swims would always be accompanied by long and frequently heartfelt conversations. His admiration for President and Mrs. Kennedy was a frequent topic. Unfortunately, so was his dislike for Bobby Kennedy. I tried to explain that Bobby did not bear him any ill will, but there'd been too much water flowing over that dam for too long, and LBJ simply remained convinced that Bobby had always had it in for him. As far as I know, he carried that belief to his grave.

I believe I served President Johnson well in the few months I was his press secretary. He'd come into office with his own distinct way of dealing with the press, and while it was not what you might call high-handed, it was perhaps a bit imperious, given all the years he'd spent in the Senate. I got him to broaden the formats he chose and to make better use of television, as well as to have a select group of reporters into the Oval Office from time to time.

Eventually, however, when the post-assassination honeymoon was over and the inevitable problem of White House leaks arose anew, LBJ became more and more secretive with the media. It was not a good development, and it would only get worse in later years as he sunk further into the quagmire of Vietnam. On the day I started to walk into his office only to be told by his secretary that in the future I was to call for an appointment, I knew I would not be around the White House much longer.

One of the reasons that I spent more personal time with LBJ than JFK, mealtimes and swims and things of that sort, was that Johnson was the type of President who expected his press secretary to be at the White House when he woke up and still there when he went to bed. I found that gruelling. What I finally found *grating* was the way he treated so many of his top people. I know it sounds crude, but LBJ thought nothing of summoning a cabinet member into the bathroom for a talk while he was defecating. And, despite his good start, he soon began treating the press badly, which was such a contrast to Kennedy's methods. The final straw was when I discovered the reason why it took one of the female staff members two hours each afternoon to deliver papers from my office to the President—they were having an affair.

On top of everything else, and for reasons that included assassination and assignation, I was drinking a bottle of scotch a day. On balance, LBJ had been very kind to me, but it was time to stop the drinking, and time to get out of the White House, where the memories of JFK were simply too overpowering.

Most of the people I meet who recognize my name say they remember me because I was JFK's press secretary, and a few recall that I was also press secretary to Lyndon Johnson, but *very* few people remember that I was a United States senator. The reason for that, in addition to the passage of time, is that I held that exalted office by appointment, and for only five months. Nonetheless, it remains one of my fondest memories, and an accomplishment of which I am very proud. It also gave me, when the voters failed to elect me to a full six-year term, the opportunity to borrow that marvelous crack made by Dick Tuck when he, too, lost an election: "The people have spoken—the bastards!"

Given my long involvement in politics, and especially after I went to work in the White House, I would occasionally be asked if I had any interest in holding office myself. My standard answer was a fast no. I'd thought about running for Congress from San Francisco in the mid-fifties (against another political tyro by the name of Caspar Weinberger) but decided investigative reporting was more exciting. In 1962, while working for JFK and living in Falls Church, Virginia, I'd been approached about running for Congress against Joel Broyhill, a particularly nettlesome conservative Republican incumbent. My widely reported answer would later cause me some embarrassment: "You're looking at a fellow who will never run for public office."

In the summer of 1963, I was handed an opportunity that would eventually become very hard to resist. Sadly, my longtime friend Clair Engle, Democratic senator from California, was operated on for a brain tumor, and the prognosis was not good. He had been considered a shoo-in for reelection, but this bad news changed the picture. Quite possibly, there was going to be an opening in the United States Senate from my home state of California.

Three candidates expressed interest. One was the attorney general, Stanley Mosk, another was Congressman James Roosevelt, FDR's oldest son, and the third was Alan Cranston, the state's controller. In September 1963, two months before he was killed, I had accompanied President Kennedy on a flight to California to dedicate a dam, and Pat Brown, the governor, was along for the ride on *Air Force One*.

JFK told Governor Brown he was concerned that a three-way fight among Democratic hopefuls might send the seat across the aisle to the Republicans.

Jokingly, Pat Brown said, "What do you think, Pierre?"

My response also brought laughter: "I think that if you guys don't stop fooling around, I might come out and run myself."

At that time I was just kidding, but half a year later, wanting to get out of the White House, and seeing the same possibility of us Democrats losing the seat, I began to take a serious look at the situation. Engle was even sicker than he had been, but he had not officially dropped out. By February, of the three most talked-about contenders, only Alan Cranston, the controller, had announced; Mosk and Roosevelt were undecided.

Early that same month, on an official trip to Los Angeles to advance a joint visit there by President Johnson and President López Mateos of

Mexico scheduled for the twenty-first, I attended a dinner honoring Stanley Mosk. The attorney general and I were both seated at the head table, and at one point he turned to me and said, "You know, Pierre, you're wrong about being ineligible to run."

Earlier that year, when a U.S. House seat from San Francisco opened up, I'd put out a statement that I was ineligible to run because I voted in Virginia.

"You're wrong," said Mosk. "I checked it out, and you're eligible to run for federal office from California."

I thanked Stanley for the information, and then said, only this time I was no longer entirely kidding, "I promise never to use it to run against you."

As winter ended and spring began its normally glorious arrival in Washington, I sent out a few feelers on the question of my eligibility. I noted, as I waited for the answers, which involved legal research, that I was becoming increasingly anxious to leave the White House. I saw the ghost of John F. Kennedy wherever I turned.

Then something most unusual occurred. In Los Angeles on the night of the Johnson–López Mateos visit, I attended the joint address given by the two men to the student convocation at UCLA. Johnson and Mateos then went into the Student Union to meet the university chancellor, so I left to join the huge traveling press corps. As I walked out of the building, there was a large group of students waiting to catch a glimpse of the two leaders, and when they saw me, they broke into applause, and some of them started chanting, *"Salinger, Salinger."*

I was stunned, but I kept my composure long enough to wave in reply. Later, I got to thinking: If *students,* always a hard sell in California, as in most places, thought enough of me to, one, recognize me, and, two, applaud me, then maybe this White House tour of duty had given me what the pols call "voter appeal." Hmmm.

At that point, things began to escalate. The day after I got the word that Mosk had decided not to run, James Roosevelt lost the endorsement—to Cranston—of the California Democratic Council (CDC), which, as it happened, Alan Cranston and I had cofounded in 1957. So, if I decided to run, what it would come down to would be a pitched battle, in the Democratic primary, between me and Cranston.

To cut at least part of this story short, what happened next was that my legal advisers started calling with the answer to the question of whether or not I was eligible to run—I was. So should I? I had but ten days, until March nineteenth, to file.

Two days before the deadline, I told Bobby Kennedy and Ken O'Donnell that I was *very* close to deciding to run.

"Run only if you can win," was Bobby's typically Kennedyesque advice. Ken O'Donnell called the idea of me running for the U.S. Senate "interesting," but then added, "I don't think you've got the guts."

That wasn't quite the encouragement I'd wanted, so I made another, and most important, call. I phoned Jackie Kennedy and asked if I could drop over to her house in Georgetown that evening. I told her I needed her advice. When she heard what I wanted to do, she said enthusiastically, "I *know* you'll win. If there's some quiet way I can help, please let me know."

Bobby Kennedy surprised me by stopping by my house that same night. Over a drink, he said he didn't think I had enough time to put together a "winning organization," but he told me I could count on his help. (Five months later, he clearly outdid me in the "Carpetbaggers' Sweepstakes" by announcing his candidacy for the U.S. Senate from New York State.)

The very next day, I was having lunch at the Sans Souci in Washington (now long gone and sorely missed) when the call that I had been waiting for came through. It was from my California lawyer friend, who'd found ample precedent for my eligibility. He said, "Go for it." On my way out of the restaurant, I noticed Ken and Helen O'Donnell having lunch. I stopped by long enough to tell him, "Remember saying I didn't have the guts to run? Well, I'm on my way to tell the President I'm resigning." He looked as if he'd swallowed his wineglass.

I couldn't see LBJ right away, so while I waited, I placed a fast call to my friend Arthur Goldberg, formerly the secretary of labor and now an associate justice on the U.S. Supreme Court.

His immediate reaction was that I had been given bad legal advice. "It doesn't seem possible to me," he said quickly, "that a man who votes in Virginia can run for the Senate from California."

Thirty minutes later, while I was still waiting to see LBJ, Justice Goldberg called back. "It appears you are eligible. I've had one of my clerks look into it, but," he added, pausing for a moment, "if your case ever comes up before the Supreme Court, I'll have to disqualify myself."

I saw President Johnson at 3:30 P.M., and told him what I planned to do. I started to explain my reasons, but he cut me off, saying, "I did the same thing myself once." A hour and a half later, I gave LBJ my letter of resignation, and he gave me his acceptance of my resignation. I particularly appreciated the last two sentences, which read: "I hate to see you go. I will always be grateful for the help and devotion you have shown me—but above all, for your friendship."

Suddenly, the President pulled out his wallet. "You know I can't get mixed up in a Democratic primary in California," he said, "but I'd like to do *something* to help. What's the filing fee out there?"

"Four hundred and fifty dollars," I told him. Apparently he didn't hear quite what I'd said, for he took two one-hundred-dollar bills and a fifty out of his wallet. I thought better of correcting him, and thanked him profusely. LBJ beamed.

My decision to oppose Alan Cranston in the primary caused some consternation in the Democratic ranks; my victory (by a margin of 174,000 votes, which solidly put to rest the charge that I was a carpetbagger) caused some bitterness, the lingering effects of which would prove harmful. I could not afford to give that situation too much thought, however, for I had a U.S. Senate race to run. Accordingly, I threw myself, and my (California) family, into it with great glee and abandon.

As I wrote in an earlier account: "The Republican I would face in November was actor George Murphy, who won his party's nomination in a breeze from industrialist Leland Kaiser. But because of the 3 to 2 edge in Democratic voters in California, only two of the state's political observers gave him a chance to win. One was Murphy himself. The other was me."

A funny thing happened on the way to the election—I got to the Senate first. On August 3, Clair Engle, a great man as well as a great senator, died. Several days later, Governor Pat Brown appointed me to fill out his term.

At the time I was appointed, I was also working on such other commitments as a series of articles for *Look* on overseas reaction to American foreign policy, a task that took me to the Far East. I visited Tokyo, Manila, and Vietnam. (In fact, I was in Saigon when word reached me of Senator Engle's death.)

On August 5, after a sleepless night spent on an airplane from California (following a sleepless day in an airplane from Vietnam), I went before the United States Senate and took the oath of office.

I served in the Senate for only 148 days. But I was able, in that short amount of time, to push through an amendment to the Social Security Act that would have meant $6 million in additional benefits to elderly citizens of California. Unfortunately, it died in committee. I coauthored, with Thomas Kuchel, California's Republican senator, a regional water plan for the Pacific Southwest that is still a sound basis of negotiation for the long-standing dispute between California and Arizona over how to divide the waters of the Colorado River.

I was able to express my own great respect for Senator Engle by introducing legislation that resulted in Trinity Dam, in northern California, being renamed Engle Dam.

In my maiden speech in the Senate, I was able, with White House approval, to answer the entirely baseless charge by Senator Barry Goldwater that John F. Kennedy had deliberately provoked the Cuban missile crisis to influence the fall elections in 1962. I also fell heir to one of the traditional duties of freshmen senators—that of presiding when a quorum is not present. One night, I spent more than two hours alone with Wayne Morse in the chamber while the Oregon senator read a hundred or more letters from constituents protesting our policy in Vietnam. (As for my own views on the war, they were still being formed, as were those of most other senators. Case in point: When the Senate voted on the Tonkin Gulf Resolution, which authorized LBJ to expand the war, the tally was ninety-eight in favor and only two opposed. I was not one of them, they were Wayne Morse and Alaska's Ernest Gruening.)

One afternoon, my youngest son, Stephen, happened to be in the gallery at the same time I happened to be in the chair. Later, while we were riding the Senate subway back to my office, he said, within earshot of several other senators, "Gee, Dad, you've only been in the Senate a week and already you're running the joint!"

Earlier, my advisers and I had had to think hard, and with no time to spare, about whether or not I should accept the appointment, and we had concluded that the good (mainly the earlier seniority date, in case I won, which would mean an advantage over other newly elected Senators in committee assignments, thus benefiting my constituents) outweighed the bad (less time to campaign, and the fear, which turned out to be correct, that my opponent would revive the carpetbagger issue). So while Murphy made hay in the sunshine, I toiled in the relative dark of the Senate chamber.

In addition to all of this activity, I was on an emotional roller coaster during this period. The upcoming Democratic National Convention would be the first since 1946 without John F. Kennedy in attendance, and I did not anticipate the effect this would have on me. One of the highlights of the convention was a film entitled *A Thousand Days,* which I had planned to watch, not on the convention floor, but with Ken O'Donnell and others in Ken's motel room. I got as far as Bobby Kennedy's moving introduction and had to get up and leave, tears streaming down my cheeks. As the film was watched by thousands of delegates in the hall and millions of people on television, I walked the Atlantic City boardwalk, alone with my thoughts and memories of JFK.

I did receive a considerable amount of solace during the campaign, thanks to the charms of a woman I met. She was married to an extremely famous actor, who was conveniently out of town for weeks on end. Our affair was one that we both appreciated, in part because we knew it would last for only a relatively brief time. But being with her at the end of almost every hard day's campaigning did wonders for me. When we parted, it was as good friends, and when I read of her death many years later, I felt very sad.

In the fall, with Congress *finally* out of session, I had rushed back to California to campaign full-time. George Murphy, who was waging one of the least issue-oriented campaigns in state history, kept ducking my request for a debate, but finally, after I'd hounded and hounded him, he agreed, and we had an hour-long debate. As the saying goes, I shoulda stood in bed. Try as I might, I could never get my opponent to take a clear position on any of the issues on which we differed.

The chief one he ducked was Proposition 14, a proposed constitutional amendment that would, in effect, nullify California's fair-housing law. I opposed it, and Murphy, in an apt metaphor, given the types of movies he was famous for, danced all around it. Still, the message that went out assured those who might wish to resume discriminating in housing, or approved of such actions, that Salinger was their enemy, and Murphy, though *he* never came right out and said so, their friend.

So I debated as best I could, which was not bad, but I was up against a trained actor—a man the camera *liked*. When the debate was over, one of the technicians said to me, "You won the debate, Pierre, but George won the Oscar, and that's what counts on TV."

The campaign was not exactly a model of decorum. My sister, Anne, who lived in northern California at the time, was a great help, flying around in small planes, making speeches for me, even standing up to a barrage of rotten fruit.

As she recalls, "I came down to Los Angeles and boarded a campaign train for San Diego. On the train were Angie Dickinson and Gene Tunney, also the large gentleman who was in *Little House on the Prairie,* Dan Blocker. There was a lounge car, and also a platform to go out and stand on, like on the Presidents' trains.

"I didn't know anything about Orange County, not *anything,* so I was very unsuspecting. Well, we got to Orange, and the train stopped, and all of a sudden there were mean-faced people all over the place, carrying carpetbags, and they started throwing tomatoes and oranges and God knows what. They were *so* unkind. Pierre said, 'Sorry, but you can't go out on the platform anymore.' It's a good thing he said that, because when we got down to Oceanside, the same thing happened all over again. It was awful!"

The closer we got to the election, the more obvious it became that Proposition 14 was going to win—big. I could have taken the advice of some that I soft-pedal my opposition to it, that I didn't have to mention

Prop 14 in every speech and interview, but that would have meant denying my own history. I hadn't sweated out the historic events of Birmingham, Alabama, and Oxford, Mississippi, with John F. Kennedy so I could turn around a few years later and sell out the civil rights movement. Fair housing may not have been a moral issue to Mr. Murphy, but it sure was to me.

Consequently, when I got the news shortly before the election that ticket splitters—people for LBJ and the Republican Murphy—were *for* Proposition 14 by the staggering margin of nine to one, I knew I'd had it. A few months earlier, I'd become the youngest United States senator in history, and now I was about to become the youngest *ex*-senator!

While LBJ was trouncing Barry Goldwater in California by some 1.3 million votes, I lost to George Murphy by a difference of 216,643.

Oh, by the way, Proposition 14 passed by a margin of 2,130,713 votes. If I'd kept my mouth shut about the need for fair-housing laws, I'd have been returned to the U.S. Senate, where I might have stayed for many years, and the later chapters of my life story would have been very different. But it would not have been worth it. (For the record: In addition to opposing Prop 14 on moral grounds, I also thought it was illegal; some ten months later, the California Supreme Court overturned it on just those grounds.)

A late-night call from Robert Kennedy—who had just been elected to the Senate from the state of New York—helped ease the pain. He said, "My brother would have been proud of the way you lost."

In the final analysis, so was I.

The emotional roller coaster that hit bottom with my political loss also had a personal component. My wife, Nancy, had never liked the fast-paced life of national politics, and I sought it, perhaps even needed it. When I told her I was going to run for the Senate, she basically abandoned me, and thereafter took no part in my campaign.

Admitting that we no longer had a life together, we agreed to a divorce. There were no shouting matches, no recriminations, just regrets. My daughter, Suzanne, chose to stay with Nancy in Falls Church and finish high school. The boys would be moving back to sunny California, where their father, for the first time in his life, was going to become a businessman!

A lot of people were kind to me after my loss. One of the kindest was a man who is always ready to lend a hand to someone who is down. I'm talking about Frank Sinatra. The night of my defeat, Frank—who'd fought hard against Proposition 14, just as he has so often done for other liberal causes—called and "ordered" me down to Palm Springs for a week of R and R. In fact, he sent his Learjet to pick me up.

Among the other guests were Leo Durocher and Yul Brynner, and one night as we all sat around the pool, Sinatra asked his African-American houseman, George Jacobs, how he'd voted on Prop 14. Without missing a beat, George glanced at Brynner, who was part Mongolian, and deadpanned, "I voted yes. You think I want that Oriental living next door to me?"

On my last day as Sinatra's guest, I was sitting in the breakfast room, reading a newspaper, when a truly beautiful young woman, who couldn't have been much over twenty-one, walked through the living room, carrying what seemed to be a blanket. I felt as if I'd had a vision. Sinatra looked at me and laughed. "That's my new girlfriend. Isn't she something? Her name's Mia, Mia Farrow. She's on TV." (Later, I learned Mia was all of nineteen!)

A few short years later, I was in Europe when I got a call from Mia. She said her marriage to Sinatra was coming apart. Could I do something, say something, to help her save it? she asked. She asked me to call Frank and tell him she'd like to try again. I did, and he was not pleased at my intercession.

"Pierre," he said, "I don't need friends to work on my marital situation. I got lawyers for that." Don't we all.

CHAPTER TWELVE

THANKS TO THE kindness of Bob and Ted Kennedy, I was able to lick my election wounds in Europe. Accompanied by my son Marc, I opened the John F. Kennedy Library exhibits in Zurich, and Milan. It was a good time to be away from the United States, though the nature of the trip had a certain bittersweet flavor. It was also good to be with Marc, who, at sixteen, was an interesting boy. Smart as a whip, he was also a talented musician, with a tendency to drive himself a little too hard for a boy of his age. Nancy had been as good a second mother to him as she could be, and he had very strong feelings for her, but I know he looked forward to going back to California because it meant being closer to Renee, his real mother. I had some doubts about how that would work out, as Renee had not exactly conquered her problems with alcohol. But her escapades were certainly fewer and further between, and, as she was always a very loving mother, I knew she was anxious to see her sons back in California, even if not in the same city.

On the long flight back from Europe, I looked over at a sleeping Marc and, putting my hand gently on his arm, said a quiet prayer that everything would turn out for the best. I had not been the world's most attentive father, but, luckily, I was being given a chance to do better.

Having resigned from the Senate on December 31, 1964, giving a three-day present to my winning opponent, George Murphy, I started the year

1965 in a rather depressed state. Thanks to my early resignation, Murphy had been sworn in three days before the other new senators (a group that included Bob Kennedy). As a result, he had first choice of the available senatorial offices. He did not, however, send me a thank-you note.

Obviously, I was looking for work, and about two weeks into 1965, I got a call from Eugene Klein, who had been one of the most generous contributors to my Senate campaign. Klein was the owner and president of the National General Corporation, a company that owned 250 movie theaters across the United States. He offered me a job as vice president of National General, and after very little hesitation, I accepted.

Just as I joined the company, they were beginning to talk about expanding into the production of movies, and I came up with an idea that I thought was brilliant, if I do say so myself. I suggested that National General start making *opera* movies in countries where the story of the opera takes place. Because I had sources in the Soviet Union, I suggested that I go to Moscow to negotiate a joint agreement with the Soviets to make our first opera movie—*Boris Godunov*.

My concept for this joint operation with the Soviets was to film the opera in the Russian steppes. I submitted the following plan to the company: I would ask Leonard Bernstein, the musical director of the New York Philharmonic Orchestra, to conduct the Moscow Symphony, and then I would ask the world-renowned Peter Ustinov to direct the film. Finally, I would ask George London, the famous basso profundo, who was considered by many critics the greatest Boris in the world, to play the title role.

In addition, I planned to ask the Russians to provide the Bolshoi Ballet, the orchestra, and all the other actors and singers in the film. What's more, I would suggest we use their cameras and their cameramen. National General and the Russians would then negotiate a worldwide agreement governing distribution of the profits.

In May of 1965, I headed for Moscow, my first trip there since I'd spent two days with Nikita Khrushchev in 1962. At the company's suggestion, I was accompanied by Samuel Pisar, a National General lawyer who was based in Paris. Born in Poland, and reportedly the youngest survivor of Auschwitz, Pisar had become an American citizen as a result of a congressional resolution signed by President Kennedy. In addition to numerous other talents, Pisar spoke perfect Russian, a fact that would be a great help to our operation.

On my arrival in Moscow, I ran into someone I knew. Gordon McLendon, who owned a radio station in Texas, had befriended me during my Senate campaign. Gordon was politically conservative, but he had been intrigued by my campaign—in particular my stand against Proposition

14—and had contributed a good bit of money to the campaign. After we'd cleared customs, Gordon pulled me aside and opened one of his suitcases. It was filled with vodka bottles!

I was more than a little amused: Gordon McLendon had to be the first person in history to bring four bottles of Smirnoff vodka, which is made in the United States, *into* the Soviet Union which produces the best vodka in the world! (Years later, I learned that for some odd reason Smirnoff vodka is in great demand in Russia, and therefore highly useful as barter. Maybe Gordon knew what he was doing after all.)

We were installed in the Peking Hotel (not one of the best hotels in Moscow) with a six-day reservation. I thought our negotiations with the Soviets would take quite a while, first, because we were dealing with Russians, and, second, because the nature of the deal was so complicated. But the next day, when I went to my first meeting with the Soviet Export Film Corporation, I was stunned by the speed of the proceedings.

It took only four hours to come to a complete accord on the *Boris Godunov* project. The Soviets agreed to accept all the conditions I had proposed, and we were even able to divide the profits in a way that made us the clear winner. The Soviets would get the profits from the socialist countries, and we would get them from everywhere else. It was almost too good to be true.

With the accord negotiated, I decided to stay in Moscow for six days and try to see some of my old Russian friends.

My first call was to Mikhail Sagatelyn, the former Washington bureau chief of the Soviet news agency Tass during the Kennedy administration. I'd known for a long time that he was part of the Soviet intelligence agency, the KGB—and he also knew that I knew. (In fact, this had facilitated our relations while he covered the White House.)

Mikhail sounded genuinely happy to learn I was in Moscow, and immediately invited me to dinner with him and his wife at the Soviet Journalist Club. At about 11:00 P.M., as the dinner came to an end, Mikhail asked me to his house, a most unusual invitation for a Soviet citizen. When we got there (and I expressed my pleasure—and surprise—at seeing a framed picture of President Kennedy on his wall), his wife made and served coffee, with cakes and cognac, which she left in the living room, and then quietly slipped off to bed. As soon as she'd left, Mikhail turned to me and said, "Now let's talk about what you *really* came to Moscow to do."

Surprised by his question, I said, "Mikhail, I came here to make a deal on a film. I don't have anything to do with my government anymore. I'm not even in politics anymore. I just came to make a film deal."

Mikhail's answer provided my second surprise. "You've got your contract, haven't you?" Evidently, the Soviet government had instructed the Soviet Export Film Corporation to arrive at an accord rapidly so I could be freed for something else they wanted done.

"You know, Mikhail, here in the Soviet Union, there is the tendency to think that people are not what they seem to be. But in my case, it's simple. I came here only to negotiate a film."

Mikhail responded immediately. "How can you say that, when you came here accompanied by two such men as Pisar and McLendon? Pisar speaks Russian too well to be an ordinary lawyer in Paris. Obviously, he is CIA. As for McLendon, he is an old friend of President Johnson, and he was certainly been sent here to accomplish a mission."

I had no choice but to ask, "So what is my mission?"

"Your mission is to discuss with us how to bring an end to the Vietnam War."

I replied that nobody had given me such a mission and repeated that I had no power in the government, but Mikhail pressed on for an hour, and I finally agreed to discuss the issue.

Suddenly, I realized that I might have stumbled onto a golden opportunity. If the Soviets were really trying to negotiate an end to the Vietnam War, this could certainly interest the U.S. government.

Mikhail and I talked for an hour and a half. He wanted us to study different scenarios by which the United States and the Soviet Union might possibly bring the war to an end. Once the two superpowers agreed on a specific plan, it would be submitted to the North Vietnamese government by an intermediary, probably a Third World country, probably a socialist country.

Once we had reached the agreement, I would go to Paris and submit the solution to the embassy of the Third World country so they could intervene with Vietnam. As we closed the meeting, he said, "I've got a friend who holds a high post in the foreign ministry here. He would like to meet with you and discuss these problems. Would you have lunch with us tomorrow at the Aragui, the finest Georgian restaurant in Moscow? But you must come alone. Don't bring Pisar."

I accepted.

The next morning, I quickly contacted the U.S. ambassador, Fay Kohler. "Play the game," he told me. "Try to find out what they want."

I went to the lunch and met a man who identified himself to me only as Vassili. He never told me his patronymic. For three days, we attended meetings, and as these discussions got deeper and deeper, I sent more and more detailed messages back to Washington (through the U.S. embassy), explaining what was going on. I had the impression that the information was having an impact on the Johnson government.

In fact, on the second day of our discussions, Johnson halted all bombing of North Vietnam. To this day, I don't know whether Johnson's decision was linked to the discussions I was having. However, on the third day of our talks, there was an announcement that there would be a meeting in Vienna between U.S. Secretary of State Dean Rusk and the Soviet foreign minister, Andrey Gromyko. Again, I don't know if that announcement was linked to the talks I was having with Vassili.

Each day we had lunch and dinner, not in the Aragui itself, but in a private room on the second floor. Finally, the last day arrived.

We met in the morning to take a look at the document we had put together on the negotiation plan to be turned over to the Polish embassy in Paris. I thought it was all but finished. However, Vassili shocked me by opening the meeting with the statement that there were "a few things that need to be added to this document."

"For example?" I said. Vassili replied, "The United States has to publicly take the position that it will never invade Cuba. The United Sates must also withdraw all their troops from the Dominican Republic."

"You're crazy," I shouted. "That has nothing to do with Vietnam."

Vassili said that those conditons were "absolutely necessary."

At that moment, I understood. "Something has happened. Someone has told you to stop these negotiations—because you know that these new conditions are completely unacceptable to the United States." We talked for another half hour, but it was clear that someone higher up had given him orders to sabotage this operation.

I left Moscow and returned to Paris with Samuel Pisar. I never briefed him on these discussions.

When I got to Paris, there was an urgent message from the State Department. They wanted me to fly to Washington on the way back to Los Angeles. When my plane landed in the U.S. capital, a State Department car was waiting to take me to the office of Llewellyn Thompson, the former U.S. ambassador to Moscow and the State Department's top expert on Soviet affairs.

He said, "We were really intrigued by this story. We would very much like to know Vassili's true identity. All you said was his first name and that he has a sixteen-year-old son. So we asked the CIA to look into their files."

With that, he opened the drawer of his desk, pulled out a pile of photos, and tossed them on the desk. The first one was the right one. The man had been identified as Vassili Sitnikov, the head of the KGB's "department of disinformation."

This department's mission was to confuse the political adversaries of the Kremlin by giving them false information. It was what they had tried to do with me. I did a complete report on what had transpired in Moscow for the State Department and for Richard Helms, the head of the CIA. Poof, the story disappeared.

Two years later, I got an urgent call from Mr. Helms; he was sending someone to see me in California. Twelve hours later, a man showed up and identified himself as an agent of the CIA. He told me that Helms was going to testify at a closed hearing before the Senate Committee on Intelligence and that he planned to talk about the work of the KGB's department of disinformation. He wanted my permission to use the material I had sent him on my discussions with Sitnikov. I said, "Of course."

Later, the whole story became available during the trial of Daniel Ellsberg, who had been accused of leaking the Pentagon Papers to the *New York Times*. The Pentagon Papers were accompanied by four volumes, entitled *The Diplomatic History of the Vietnam War*, which revealed, for the first time publicly, the story of my visit to the Soviet Union in 1965. But because the trial focused on the Pentagon Papers, the story of my trip to Moscow never surfaced.

In the summer of 1965, I got a call from my friend Bob Six, the aviation pioneer who'd founded Continental Airlines almost twenty years before, asking me if I could meet him for lunch. I could and I did. At lunch, he offered me a job—vice president of international affairs for Continental. He told me Continental was filing applications with the Federal Aviation Authority (FAA) for the right to fly across the Pacific to such countries as Australia, New Zealand, Indonesia, Malaysia, Japan, China, and Korea.

I wasn't quite sure where he saw me in all of this activity, but then he said, "I'm also starting a company in Southeast Asia, calling it Continental Air Services, and when the word got out, I got a call from the CIA. They want me to set up a company for them, a legit operation, and they've asked me to deal with AID, the Agency for International Development. I need someone to negotiate with AID for me. That's where you come in."

Bob Six went on to say that the CIA owned an airline called Air America but it was widely known throughout the world that it was a CIA operation. With the Vietnam War going on, they were worried that Air America, which was carrying out operations to help the U.S. military, would be barred from Southeast Asian countries. The CIA contact asked Six to set up a subsidiary of Continental in such a way that it had no CIA investment, to take up some of the work in that area.

Also, to avoid being in negotiations or close connections with the CIA during the operation, he told Six that negotiations for activities of Continental Air Services would be done with AID.

Six wanted me to be the negotiator with AID, an organization created by the U.S. government after the Marshall Plan, to run programs of assistance to foreign countries. Six told me the headquarters of Continental Air Services would be in the capital of Laos, Vientiane. I had studied information on Laos during my White House career. I knew that the neutral government of Souvanna Phouma was having extreme difficulty with the attacks of the guerrilla group, the Pathet Lao, linked to the North Vietnamese government. Also, about forty to fifty thousand North Vietnamese were crossing the border into Laos. The reinforcement of North Vietnamese troops in South Vietnam was coming via the Ho Chi Minh Trail. I also knew that the Geneva accord of 1961 forbade foreign troops from entering Laos. The CIA had organized a covert army with the Meo, a mountain group, and it was totally financed and supplied by the U.S. government. The help to the Meo that had been provided by Air America would be turned over to the Continental Air Services.

Six told me he had the meetings at the CIA with William Colby, then the director of covert operations, later the head of the CIA. Colby told Six he needed someone with top secret government clearance to work at a high level of the new company. That's why Six had approached me. I had had top secret government clearance during my career in the White House.

I accepted the offer because it sounded like an exciting job. Almost immediately, I was off to Asia to see top transportation ministers and explain Continental's desire to fly across the Pacific. In Indonesia, I struck a deal with Garuda Airlines, the Indonesian national airline, for Continental to consult with them on technology, at a cost to Continental of about sixty thousand dollars. I also visited all the other principal Asian countries to establish contacts for Continental.

Early in my work, I headed for Vientiane to start my job with Continental Air Services. We had purchased a motel that was near to the Vientiane airport, and two rooms had been set up especially for me and for Bob Six. At the very beginning, it was clear what we were doing. Each morning, old DC–3's and C–54's took off with sacks of rice. But it was obvious that the bags were heavier than just rice and that we were parachuting military equipment to the Meo. In fact, we referred to the rice as "hard rice."

The air director in Vientiane, whom I met my first day there, was Dutch Brongersma, a man who'd had years of experience with the CIA. For example, when the U.S. government had officially refused to help the French in their desperate battle with the Vietnamese at Dien Bien Phu, the CIA had covertly organized help for the French by flying them supplies. One of the pilots of that operation was Dutch Brongersma. Also on my first trip, I made contact with Joe Mendenhallm, who had been sent to Laos to negotiate operations with Continental Air Services.

As I looked more closely into the new company, it became clear that at least 50 percent of the employees had CIA links. In addition to providing the Meo with hard rice, we also launched flights every day to survey the Ho Chi Minh Trail and report on troop movements, information that was eventually used by the U.S. Air Force to bomb the incoming North Vietnamese military.

Soon after I went to work for Continental, I was contacted by the State Department. They said that, increasingly, they were getting requests from French political leaders who wanted to go to California and other West Coast areas, but the State Department had no one there to take care of them. They asked me if I would be responsible for setting up lunches and dinners, as well as meetings, with these French political leaders. I agreed to their request, and soon French political leaders started showing up in Los Angeles.

The most interesting contact came in late 1965. It began with a call from the State Department asking if I would set things up for a visit to the West Coast by a rising young French politician who was traveling with his wife and one of his political colleagues. I had already heard of the young man (in the spring, he'd given President Charles de Gaulle a scare by forcing him into an unexpected second round of voting). I was told they hadn't yet made any hotel reservations. By this point, I had moved from my house in the Hollywood Hills to a large and beautiful residence just outside Beverly Hills, so I asked, "Would the three of them like to stay at my house?"

The State Department representative said he would check and get right back to me. An hour later, he called and said they would be delighted to stay with me. They showed up, and for three days and nights I shepherded them around town and wined and dined them. We got on famously.

Fifteen years later, both of the French politicians had risen to the heights of their profession. The friend who traveled alone became defense minister in 1981, the same year the other man became president of France. Their names are Charles Hernu and François Mitterand.

When Mitterand became President of France, I was the Paris bureau chief of ABC News. He more than showed his thanks for that visit to my home in Los Angeles: During his entire first term of office, he granted interviews only to representatives of the American Broadcasting Company. Before he left office, he granted a very specific request, thereby doing me a very great favor—but that's a story for later.

Nineteen sixty-five was an important year for me in a number of ways. It was the first year I worked solely as a businessman (thereby instantly increasing my income far beyond the possibilities of either a journalist or a public servant), the year I began to travel extensively to far-flung destinations, thus setting, unbeknownst to me, a pattern for the rest of my life, and, to save the best for last, the year I married again.

Back in the fall, while still in the midst of my race against George Murphy, I was in an elevator in Los Angeles when I heard, from a man and woman standing next to me, the familiar cadences of the French language. Parisian, I thought.

"*Quelle coincidence*," said the woman, an attractive brunette who introduced herself as Nicole Gillman and the man with her as a photographer. She went on to say she was working for the Swiss magazine *Réalités* and that her assignment was to interview me!

"I've been calling your office for three days, but they say you are too busy. I'm writing about, how do you say it, the 'comeback' of JFK's men into politics. You here in California, Robert Kennedy in New York, and Joe Tydings in Maryland."

"Good idea," I said. (Of course, given Ms. Gillman's looks, I would have offered that same assessment no matter what she'd said.) "I've got to attend a number of rallies this afternoon. Why don't you come along? You can interview me as we go." She did, firing questions at me in her rapid and excellent French.

It was a most pleasant interlude, especially for a newly single man like myself, but I chalked it up as one of those wonderful little encounters that fate sometimes grants us. So several months later when she called my hotel in Paris while Marc and I were on our way to Zurich, I began to wonder if perhaps fate didn't have something more serious in mind.

We were married in Paris on June eighteenth, the anniversary of General De Gaulle's speech to the French people in 1940 exhorting them to resist the invading Nazis ("France has lost a battle. But France has not lost the war"). The mayor of the Sixteenth Arrondissement, the section of Paris where the marriage took place, was there, and he gave a grand speech about the many fine French-American alliances, another of which occurred that day.

We began our life together in my house in the Hollywood Hills, but eventually moved to a larger home near Beverly Hills (the same one where Mitterand had stayed). In March of 1966, Nicole gave birth to our son, Gregory. Not only was it a fine year for children, it was an excellent year for wine. In fact, 1966 was one of the five great wine years of the century, so we bought two hundred bottles of the excellent French Bordeaux for Gregory, who has kept most of them to this day. Within the space of little more than a year, I had become as happy personally as I was professionally.

As I was finishing these memoirs, my son Stephen asked me if I'd mentioned a very special party that my wife and I threw shortly before we moved out of the wonderful, but rather small, house in the Hollywood Hills. I'll let him describe it.

"I was about sixteen, and we were still living in Hollywood. I was awakened one night around one o'clock in the morning by music and loud voices. I looked out my window, and there down in the little area next to the swimming pool my father was slow dancing with Elizabeth Taylor— he must have been fulfilling a lifelong fantasy. I crept out of my room and down to the landing where I could see into the living room. There, sitting side by side on the couch, were Richard Burton and Bobby Kennedy, taking turns reading lines from Shakespeare! In a corner of the room were two people I didn't know, deep in conversation and completely ignoring the others. I later found out they were Rudolf Nureyev and Margot Fonteyn."

A footnote to Stephen's story: That wonderful party lasted until 4:00 A.M. At ten the next morning, I awoke in extreme pain, suffering from what turned out to be hepatitis. Everyone who'd been at the party had to be tested (by means of a most intrusive procedure involving a tubal insertion) to make sure they had not also contracted the disease. My recovery period lasted five months—but I used the time to write my book *With Kennedy*, so it was by no means a total loss.

The next several years flew by. I enjoyed the life of a businessman, and my heavy travel schedule suited Nicole far better than it had Nancy. She often traveled with me, especially on trips to Europe. It was a good life, and I hardly missed Washington or politics at all. Or so I thought, until suddenly it was 1968 and on March thirty-first of that year, President Johnson stunned all of America, but particularly the Democratic party, by announcing that he would not run for reelection.

C H A P T E R
T H I R T E E N

"YOU KNOW, DON'T you, that somebody's going to try to kill you?"

Bobby sat cross-legged on the floor of John Frankenheimer's Malibu house. Shirtless, he'd just come from the surf, and was holding a glass of orange juice. When the question came, he was swirling the golden liquid and staring into the glass. Those of us within earshot froze, but he looked up slowly, pushed his errant forelock back into place, and began to answer.

It was Sunday, May 26, 1968, nine days before the all-important California primary. Bobby had been campaigning hard, but, knowing he needed to rest before the final push, in late May he'd called me and asked me to find a place where he could take a day off. I got in touch with the Frankenheimers, who graciously offered to move into town for a few days so that Bob and Ethel could have their beautiful Malibu beach home to themselves.

Then, Bob called again and said, "Why don't you put together a kind of a fun lunch on Sunday. Try to get some people out there who will be a little different."

So I put together a very special guest list. Most of the people were Kennedy friends and supporters from the entertainment world.

Shirley MacLaine and her brother, Warren Beatty, were there, as well as Andy Williams and his wife, Burt Bacharach and Angie Dickinson, the astronaut John Glenn and his wife, Annie, the Frankenheimers, and the French novelist Romain Gary and his wife, actress Jean Seberg (the former

Iowa schoolgirl who'd electrified the world with her portrayal of Joan of Arc). It was the outspoken Gary who'd posed the question that hung in the air like an unanswered bell.

Everyone at the party was some degree of liberal, but Jean Seberg and her husband were activists. Certainly she was, for she'd been involved with the Black Panther party, hosting fund-raisers for them at Arden, the home she and Gary shared in Los Angeles. Romain Gary, who was twenty-four years older than his wife and who'd lived in Europe before moving to Los Angeles in the early 1950s, had seen his share of radicals and revolutionaries.

He differed with his wife as to the purity of the motives of some of the people she supported. (He may also have still been smarting from the open secret of her affair with Clint Eastwood while they were making *Paint Your Wagon.*)

I guess I shouldn't have been surprised that Gary asked Bobby *the* question, for just a few weeks earlier he'd asked it of me. We'd been at the home of Paul Ziffren, the head of the Democratic party in California. The candidate was elsewhere. And this time the question was even more blunt. He'd said, "You know, of course, that your guy will be killed?"

It took me a long time to answer. "I live with that fear," I said. "We do what can be done, and that isn't much. He runs around like quicksilver."

Ziffren cut in to ask Gary why he was so certain this would happen.

"Since Jack's assassination," said Gary, "Bobby represents an irresistible temptation for the average American paranoid personality—the psycho-contagion of deeply traumatic events, with its craving for more of the same.

"And another thing, Bobby is *too much.* He is a constant challenge, a provocation for any man with a paranoid grudge who is tortured both by his desire to assert himself and by his feeling of nonexistence. Bobby is too rich, too young, too attractive, too happy, too powerful, too successful.

"He arouses in every persecuted type a deep sense of injustice. He acts on such a person the way a luxury store window display acts upon a destitute Harlem kid, or in the way the exhibition of American wealth acts upon the underdeveloped countries. Bobby is *too much.*"

These comments of Gary's flashed through my mind as I stood in Frankenheimer's living room, waiting for Kennedy to answer.

It took Bobby far less time to answer than it had taken me. Obviously, he'd thought about the possibility. All eyes were on him as he said quietly, "That's the chance I have to take."

Pressing, the writer asked him if he were taking any precautions.

Bobby said, with a shrug, "There's no way of protecting a country-stumping candidate, no way at all. You've just got to give yourself to the people—and to trust them. From then on, it's just that good old bitch, luck.

"You have to have luck on your side to be elected President of the United States. Either it's with you or it isn't. I am pretty sure there will be an attempt on my life sooner or later. Not so much for political reasons; I don't believe that. Plain nuttiness, that's all. There's plenty of that around."

Then Bobby asked Romain Gary a question. "Take De Gaulle. How many attempts on his life has he survived, exactly?"

"Six or seven, I think," said Gary.

"I told you," said Bobby with a slight laugh, "you can't make it without that good old bitch, luck."

In direct contrast to his brother in 1960, getting Bobby Kennedy to run for the presidency of the United States in 1968 was not easy. We, his supporters and advisers, had to drag him into the fray, and it was quite some time before he really got into the spirit of it. Once he did, however, once he realized he had a constituency of his own, he put his heart and soul into it and campaigned as no Kennedy has ever campaigned before or since.

Bobby Kennedy was a reluctant participant in public office. I spent a great deal of time with him in the year between his brother's assassination and his own race for the Senate in New York, and I know that he became a United States senator mainly because he needed a base from which to operate.

At that time in his life, Bob was not, in my opinion, psychologically attuned to being a candidate for public office. He did not meet people easily; he wasn't the backslapping, handshaking type. In fact, he looked upon the prospect of having to do a lot of that with real horror. We had long talks about alternatives, including the outside possibility of going back to Massachusetts and running for governor. He nixed that because Teddy was already a senator by that point, and Bobby thought that, in a way, would be unfair to his younger brother, who finally had his own thing to do in life. (Within the family, Bobby was always Teddy's biggest supporter and protector.)

As for the world of business, he wasn't interested. I think what he really wanted was to stay in government and public service, but given his well-known feud with Lyndon Johnson, it wasn't likely he'd be named to any post of significance. So, I think he came to view the Senate as the only real choice available to him.

Once he got to the Senate, he wasn't exactly wild about the place. For him, it was too archaic, too slow and inactive, and he was soon rather restless. I'd visit him in his Senate office, and sometimes we'd sit there for four or five hours talking about people and problems that had little or nothing to do, directly, with his Senate duties. In addition, he had a constant stream of foreign visitors. A number of them were people I'd arranged for him to see, people such as the French political figures Pierre Mendès-France and François Mitterand. When those people came in, Bobby got quite animated, and it was clear to me he much preferred talking to them than to people from, say, Mississippi.

He did manage, however, to use the Senate to highlight problems. For example, he became extremely interested in and involved with the problems of American Indians, almost to the point of obsession. I hate to confess that there were times, especially later in the campaign, when I'd get a little exasperated with him for talking about Indians in places there were none and hadn't been for a hundred years.

His interest was absolutely genuine, though. I recall a time early in 1968 when he visited an Indian school on a reservation in California. The people who ran the school were not expecting, not exactly interested in, an in-depth visit, but within minutes Bobby was zeroing in on the problems and making very real contact with the kids. That ability was one of his most special gifts.

During the four years after JFK's assassination, a period that included Bobby's first three years in the Senate, we had any number of visits but very few, if any, discussions about his own political future. He didn't encourage such discussions for the simple reason that he hadn't focused on the subject himself. If you began that kind of discussion, he would soon shift to another topic, like a radio signal that had drifted.

I think he just didn't know what he wanted to do. Of course, people were mentioning him as a potential presidential candidate, yet I doubt that anyone could be found who had had a serious discussion of that topic with him in those days, and that would include people who worked for him in his Senate office, like Adam Walinsky and Peter Edelman (who very much wanted him to run). I was in and out, rather than being there on a daily basis, but I knew Bobby Kennedy as well as, or better than, anyone else, and it was never my impression that he was giving any serious thought to running for President in 1968. Nonetheless, I felt he was up to the job. When I'd first met Bobby, he saw life in terms of black and white, but his years at the Justice Department and also in the Senate had really caused a broadening, an expanding, of his view of the world and its problems, and the needs of its peoples.

That did not mean the rest of us weren't thinking increasingly about him doing so, myself included. I've always been pretty good at reading political tea leaves, and as we got halfway through 1967, it was clear to me that Bobby's popularity with the American people was ascending at the same rate that LBJ's was descending. I had a second reason for thinking the time was ripe: Unlike the majority of Americans, I did not believe LBJ would run for reelection in 1968—and my very solid source was none other than the President himself.

In the four months I'd served as LBJ's press secretary, he told me over a dozen times how much he hated the White House and how much he would rather be down on his ranch. Now, the first few times he said it, I didn't believe him, but when he kept repeating it over and over again, I must say I came to believe him.

One beautiful late-summer day when Bobby and I were sitting outside his home at Hickory Hill, I said to him, "I think the time has come for you to face up to running this time." He looked at me and didn't say anything, so I went on.

"I think you've got to focus on it, and I think you have to start having some people think for you in those terms and give you their best thoughts as to what to do."

"What do you suggest?" he asked, not indicating his opinion one way or another.

"I think a meeting should be organized—but I don't think you should be there—a meeting under another guise, where we get together some of the people in whom you have confidence and let them bat it around for a couple of hours. Then I'll come back and tell you what they say."

Bobby stared out toward the Potomac River for just a few moments and then said, "That sounds like a good idea. Why don't you go ahead and organize it."

The "cover" we decided on was my scheduled visit to New York in October 1967 for the publication of the paperback version of my book *With Kennedy.* I went back to California, worked up a list, and called the people on it, all of whom agreed to come to my suite at the Regency Hotel (where my publisher had put me).

I did pretty well at listing Bobby's most trusted advisers, for the only name he added was that of Fred Dutton, the California lawyer who'd worked in the JFK White House and at the State Department. The participants were Kenny O'Donnell, Chuck Daley, Ivan Nestigen, William vanden Huevel, Dick Goodwin, Arthur Schlesinger, Jr., Theodore Sorensen, and I.

Then, the day before the meeting, Bobby began to think maybe he should be there himself.

"No," I said quickly, knowing I was reflecting the opinion of the others. "If you showed up, it would be sure to leak out. This way, at least we'll have a chance of keeping it out of the media."

"All right," he said, "but suppose I send a few other people, anyway. How about Steve [Smith], Tom Johnston, Joe Dolan, and Teddy?"

"Fine," I said.

They all showed up at the Regency on the day appointed, and while we did have a division of opinion, it is accurate to state, as later (*leaked*) accounts did, that the general consensus was against his running. At that time, the most articulate proponents of his entering the race were Dick Goodwin and Arthur Schlesinger. The two Teds, Kennedy and Sorensen, were adamantly against his running, on the basis that it would be better if he waited until 1972. As they pointed out, an incumbent President had never been defeated at convention. Also opposed, though to a lesser degree, was Kenny O'Donnell (who I think felt that way because he was sure Bobby wouldn't run).

As the one who had called the meeting, I didn't say much either way, but probably the others suspected I wanted to see him go for it. If they did, they would have been correct. At one point in the meeting, I said something that surprised everyone else: I said, for the first time in public, that Lyndon Johnson would not run for the presidency in 1968. While I did not overtly urge Bobby's candidacy, I maintained that we should think in terms of what the situation would be if and when LBJ declined to run for reelection. I should add that no one at the meeting accepted my theory, but, as I mentioned earlier, I had it straight from LBJ himself.

A month later, we had another, even larger meeting, which was pretty much of a shouting match. After that, Bob decided it was counterproductive to have such large meetings, especially as he was now beginning to participate. In fact, at one point Bobby looked across the table at Fred Dutton, who had been very cautious, almost tentative, in his comments, and said heatedly, "This country can't stand another four years of Lyndon Johnson. It's not a question of my political future—it's a question of the country's. And the country can't stand another four years of this man."

He was very tough on that point, and I remember walking away from that meeting saying to myself, *he's going to run; he's going to run!*

Kennedy was certainly on target. Across the country, college students were rioting, and in the ghettos there was more and more talk of violent resistance—and this was *before* the horrible shocks of the Tet offensive and the murder of Dr. Martin Luther King, Jr.

On Christmas Day, 1967, I met Bobby in Sun Valley. From that day until the sixth of January, I was with him almost continuously. Then, after a break of several days, he came to California and stayed at my house for four straight days. During that time, we carried on a near nonstop dialogue on the subject of whether or not he should run for the presidency.

What emerged from these lengthy conversations was that he was very seriously thinking of running. What held him back, however, was the question of what this would do to Eugene McCarthy, his predecessor in the antiwar movement. In fact, he and Gene McCarthy had discussed what effect Bobby's entry into the race would have on McCarthy's political future.

What Bobby kept saying to me, in various ways, was, "Give me a good excuse for running; tell me why I've got to run." I feared my answer—"You owe it to the country to run because you're the only man who can possibly win"—was too broad, but I was trying to throw back at him what he'd said to Fred Dutton about the country not being able to stand another four years of LBJ. Finally, he agreed that this was the central point, but he was still vacillating.

I don't mean to suggest that Bob Kennedy was holed up at my house and not talking to anyone else. Just the opposite was true. He was taking all sorts of calls and listening to all sorts of counsel. Still, he was vacillating. There was one meeting, however, in Los Angeles, that seemed to have a major impact.

I'd organized a breakfast with a group of Rand Corporation people who were experts on Vietnam. One after another laid out all the mistakes that the Johnson administration had been making in Vietnam, and it added up to a real horror story. All the people were bright, able people, and I could see that the meeting, which ran much longer than we had anticipated—something like three hours—was disturbing Bobby greatly.

They were spelling out errors in military strategy, explaining why the pacification program was not working, and both generally and specifically painting a very pessimistic picture. He kept asking question after question, probing, trying to absorb everything these smart people were telling him about Vietnam. He was totally engrossed, impressed by the caliber of the information and depressed by its character.

Even these skilled experts had not been able to predict the stunning event that took place on January 31, 1968, an event that would be known in the bleak history of our involvement in Vietnam as the Tet offensive.

Nine days later, a still shaken Bobby Kennedy told a crowd in Chicago, "Half a million American soldiers, with seven hundred thousand Vietnamese allies, with total command of the air, total command of the sea, backed by huge resources and the most modern weapons, are unable to secure even a single city from the attacks of an enemy whose total strength is about two hundred and fifty thousand."

Eugene McCarthy was already up in New Hampshire, ringing door-bells and shaking hands in preparation for a primary that quite a few of us had been urging Bob Kennedy to enter. At one point, I told him that the word was McCarthy would get 40 percent of the vote. When he didn't believe me, I called Bill Dunfey, an old Kennedy hand from the 1960 campaign who was now working for LBJ. Bill verified the probable accuracy of the rumor.

One evening just days before the primary, I was in Bobby's apartment in New York when he pulled a letter out of his pocket and handed it to me. It had been written in Ireland by Bobby's friend, the writer Pete Hamill. In the letter, Pete said he understood Bobby's decision not to run, but then he went on, in marvelously effective prose, to list the reasons why he thought he should have.

Hamill's letter said:

> I wanted to remind you that in Watts I didn't see pictures of Malcolm X or Ron Karenga on the walls. I saw pictures of JFK. That is your capital in the most cynical sense; it is your obligation in another, the obligation of staying true to whatever it was that put those pictures on those walls. I don't think we can afford five summers of blood. . . .
>
> Again, forgive the tone of this letter, Bob. But it's not about five cent cigars and chickens in every pot. It's about the country. I don't want to sound like someone telling someone that he should mount the white horse; or that he should destroy his career. I also realize that if you had decided to run, you would face some filthy politics, and there are plenty of people in the country who resent you or dislike you.
>
> With all of that, I still think the move would have been worth making, and I'm sorry you decided not to make it.

The letter was a relatively recent one, but it already looked old and creased. Obviously, Bobby had been reading and rereading it, and showing it to others to read. I prayed its message would get through.

On March 16, 1968, Robert Francis Kennedy announced his candidacy for the presidency of the United States.

On April 4, 1968, Dr. Martin Luther King, Jr., was shot and killed in Memphis. Bobby had just arrived in Indiana, only a half hour after the shooting, and was scheduled to speak at a rally in a rough ghetto area when

I reached him with the news. Despite much advice to the contrary from people on the scene, Bobby kept that engagement—and gave what was perhaps the best impromptu speech of his life.

"Martin Luther King dedicated his life to love and to justice for his fellow human beings, and he died because of that effort," he told the restless but eventually rapt crowd.

In this difficult day, in this difficult time for the United States, it is perhaps well to ask what kind of a nation we are and what direction we want to move in. For those of you who are black—considering the evidence there evidently is that there were white people who were responsible—you can be filled with bitterness, with hatred, and with a desire for revenge. We can move in that direction as a country, in great polarization—black people amongst black, white people amongst white, filled with hatred toward another. Or we can make an effort, as Martin Luther King did, to understand and to comprehend, and to replace that violence, that stain of bloodshed that has spread across our land, with an effort to understand with compassion and love.

For those of you who are black and are tempted to be filled with hatred and distrust at the injustice of such an act, against all white people, I can only say that I feel in my own heart the same kind of feeling. I had a member of my family killed, but he was killed by a white man. But we have to make an effort in the United States, we have to make an effort to understand, to go beyond these rather difficult times.

My favorite poet was Aeschylus. He wrote: "In our sleep, pain which cannot forget falls drop by drop upon the heart until, in our own despair, against our will, comes wisdom through the awful grace of God."

What we need in the United States is not division; what we need in the United States is not hatred; what we need in the United States is not violence or lawlessness, but love and wisdom, and compassion toward one another, and a feeling of justice towards those who still suffer within our country, be they white or black. . . .

We've had difficult times in the past. We will have difficult times in the future. It is not the end of violence; it is not the end of lawlessness; it is not the end of disorder.

But the vast majority of white people and the vast majority

of black people in this country want to live together, want to improve the quality of our life, and want justice for all human beings who abide in our land.

Let us dedicate ourselves to what the Greeks wrote so many years ago: to tame the savageness of man and to make gentle the life of this world. Let us dedicate ourselves to that, and say a prayer for our country and for our people.

In the few short days that followed the Saturday lunch at the Frankenheimers' house on the beach at Malibu, the lunch at which Romain Gary asked Bobby if he wasn't afraid someone would try and kill him, the campaign in California intensified. Bobby Kennedy rose to each occasion, one after another, with a passion that surprised even me. He was in a tough race, but he was acting more like a winner. It was wonderful to see.

I try to keep an even keel, emotionally speaking, as a campaign winds down to its conclusion, but as the California primary day neared, I found myself increasingly caught up in the excitement of what I, too, felt was going to be an important victory. Bobby Kennedy's enthusiasm was contagious.

One of the main reasons for his strong push in California, aside from the state's huge number of electoral votes, was the fact that his loss to Eugene McCarthy in Oregon was the first time any Kennedy had lost an election, either a primary or a general election (except, as Arthur Schlesinger, Jr., likes to point out, for the Harvard Board of Overseers). For a normal politician, if there is such an animal, such a loss would have been bad enough, but for a Kennedy, and especially this Kennedy, it was terrible. As a result, he felt he simply *had* to win in California. And the rest of us on his team felt the same way.

One of the most frightening miscues of my entire political career occurred in that effort. I was on my way to Oregon and then California, four days before the Oregon primary. I rarely handled funds, but on this occasion Bobby's campaign headquarters in Washington asked me to deliver fifty thousand dollars in cash to my cohorts in the West. I put the money into one of my suitcases, and, as I'd recently been having a lot of back problems, checked all of them through to Oregon.

I flew from Washington, D.C., to Portland by way of St. Louis, and when I arrived at Portland, one of the suitcases was missing. It was the one with the money. Oh my God, I said to myself, don't tell me somebody knew that there was fifty thousand dollars in that suitcase and stole it!

As soon as I got to the Benson Hotel in Portland, I called the airlines and told them they had to find that bag. I didn't tell them why they had to find it, just that it was important.

Shortly after two in the morning, there was a knock on my hotel room door. "Mr. Salinger?" said an airline representative. "We have something for you." It was the bag.

My immediate thought was, I may have the bag, but there's no lock on it, so the money has to be gone. I jerked the bag open, and there, to my total surprise and immense relief, was the fifty thousand dollars. Back in my White House days, I had occasionally been referred to in print as "Lucky Pierre," a nickname I had never liked. For once, however, it was entirely apt.

One of the problems with a candidate like Bob Kennedy, and his brother Jack before him, was that, given the Kennedys' personal or family wealth, people assumed they didn't need contributions. Of course this wasn't true, and from time to time most of us on the upper levels of the campaign pitched in to try to raise funds. This was particularly true in the case of the California primary, where it fell to me to ask for a contribution from none other than Howard Hughes, the reclusive billionaire.

We'd had a meeting in the office of Bobby's brother-in-law Steve Smith to discuss money, and I'd said I thought Hughes was approachable, so I got the assignment. I knew Hughes's right-hand man, Robert Mahue, quite well, so I called and made an appointment with him. We talked for about an hour.

My pitch was that we needed money for the campaign, and I said that while we recognized Mr. Hughes was in the unique position of not needing a President of the United States for *anything*—he could get along quite well without one—he probably did need a President who had the imagination that Robert Kennedy had and who could understand some of Hughes's concepts.

Mahue listened patiently, and when I'd finished, he said he would present my request, as I'd explained it, to Mr. Hughes.

I thanked him and left. The next morning, I got a call from Mahue, who said Mr. Hughes had agreed to give Kennedy $25,000 and that I could pick up the check in Las Vegas on June 3, the day before the California primary. As things turned out, I wasn't able to get there on that date, and then, after that time, I guess you could say we no longer needed the money.

Bobby spent Tuesday, June 4, the day of the primary, at the Frankenheimers' beach house in Malibu with Ethel and six of their ten children. (She was pregnant with their eleventh; daughter Rory would be born in December.) At 6:30, John Frankenheimer drove him to the Ambassador Hotel, where I had been all day. By then, Bobby already knew that the early projections were giving him 49 percent, a lead of some six or seven points over McCarthy.

There was a huge crowd milling about in one of the hotel's main halls, anxiously waiting for the candidate to appear and make a victory speech, but he was not yet ready to do that, and he went up to the suite instead. Not long after 9:00 P.M., George McGovern called from South Dakota, where the polls had just closed, to say Bobby had won big, getting more votes than the two area candidates, Humphrey and McCarthy, combined.

When the first solid good news came in regarding California, I went upstairs to the suite to tell Bobby and to suggest it was time to go down to the ballroom. No, he said, he would wait a bit longer. We were sitting there talking when the phone rang, and it was Chicago's Mayor, Richard Daley. He was calling to make it official—he would now publicly support Robert F. Kennedy as the Democratic candidate for President in 1968. Bobby and I exchanged a look that we both knew meant only one thing— he had the nomination.

I went down to the pressroom, a floor below the main hall, where we had a fervid bunch of loyalists toiling away. Although I didn't mention the call from Mayor Daley, I did tell them, officially, that we'd won both South Dakota and California. They knew immediately what this meant, and they got even more excited. I went to a phone and called Bobby and suggested this was the right time to come down to the hall.

When he walked in, accompanied by Mrs. Cesar Chavez and a mountain of muscle in the form of Rafer Johnson and Roosevelt Grier, the Olympic champion and the pro football player, plus Ethel and a handful of their children, the room went wild. It took him quite some time to get them to quiet down enough for him to begin speaking.

"Here is California," he said, after joking with the crowd for a few moments, "the most urban state of any of the states of our union, South Dakota the most rural of any of the states of our union. We were able to win them both. I think we can end the divisions within the United States. . . . "

He said he felt we could work with the McCarthy people, whom he asked to join, not fight, us, and he praised the senator for having begun "this great [antiwar] movement."

Then he went on, growing more impassioned. "What I think is quite clear is that we can work together in the last analysis, and that what has been going on within the United States over a period of the last three years—the division, the violence, the disenchantment with our society, the divisions, whether it's between blacks and whites, between the poor and the more affluent, between age groups or on the war in Vietnam—is that we can start to work together. We are a great country, an unselfish country, and a compassionate country." Then, to resounding cheers, he said, "I intend to make that my basis for running."

While Bobby spoke, I was standing in a throng of journalists on the other side of the podium from where he was to make his exit. I began to think about the plans for the rest of the evening. I was hosting a big victory party at The Factory, a new Los Angeles discotheque of which I was a part owner, along with Paul Newman, Peter Lawford, and the night's entertainment-to-be, Sammy Davis, Jr., as well as several others.

Kennedy stepped down, waving as he did so, and then shook some hands before starting off to the left. I started to move in the same direction, but it was slow going.

I could see that the crowd between him and the far exit was massive. Apparently, he and the phalanx of people around him, Grier and Johnson and Pete Hamill—the writer whose letter had such an impact on Bobby—and several others, could see that, too, for they stopped and then deliberately moved to the left and toward the doors that led to the kitchen. I altered my course, following them. Bobby had barely passed through the swinging doors and entered the kitchen—where a young madman named Sirhan Sirhan was waiting for him—when I heard the shots.

I have no idea how long it took me to fight my way through to where he lay, on his back, on the kitchen floor. My immediate thought on seeing him was that he was dead.

Within minutes, there was an ambulance at the loading dock off the kitchen, and Bobby was taken to Central Receiving Hospital, where he was examined and worked on for about two hours. Then he was taken to Good Samaritan, where they had larger facilities.

My wife had joined me by this point, and we ran into the street to hail a cab, forgetting we were in Los Angeles, not New York, but there were no cabs to be found. There was, however, a motorcyclist there. We hurriedly talked him into taking *both* of us on the back of his motorcycle to the second hospital. Once we got there, we went right up to the room where Ethel Kennedy was beginning a terrible vigil that would last almost through the night, and where she was eventually joined by Jackie Kennedy and Coretta Scott King.

I was fielding most of the calls, and a recurrent one was from Senator Gene McCarthy, who wanted to talk to Ethel. But Ethel did not want to talk with him. He said he'd be right there. When he arrived, I asked Dick Goodwin, the speechwriter and strategist who'd worked for the McCarthy campaign prior to opting for Bobby, to join us. When McCarthy arrived, we went into a private room and talked for about fifteen minutes.

We had a hard message for Gene McCarthy, so recently our opponent.

We told him that in light of what had just happened, the best thing for everyone concerned would be for McCarthy to fly to Washington as soon as possible, meet with Lyndon Johnson, and convince him that he should change his mind and run for reelection.

"It's our only hope of winning," we said, then added, with as much kindness as we could muster under the circumstances, "You can't get the nomination, and Hubert can't win the race for President."

To his credit, Gene McCarthy said he could see the logic to what we were saying, and he promised us he would think about it. Of course, he never did it.

Sometime during the morning of the day Bobby died, I got a phone call from Robert Mahue. He said, "Mr. Hughes wants you to know the twenty-five-thousand-dollar check is as good today as it was yesterday. You may pick it up anytime."

Several weeks earlier, during the Oregon primary, I'd had a conversation with one of our campaign workers; it would haunt me for years. And then, when I'd finally forgotten it, I received a letter that brought it all rushing back to mind.

In Portland, at the Benson Hotel, as I was going over election-night arrangements with two aides, Bill Gruver and Jim McManus, it struck me that this would be a good thing to do for the California primary, as well. I told McManus I wanted him to go to Los Angeles to check out the election-night setup at the Ambassador Hotel.

"Sure," he said, "but I'd like your permission to make one change in our standard election-night procedure."

"What is it?" I asked.

"I want to keep him out of the kitchen," McManus said. "I know that's been our usual getaway route, but I keep remembering him in that tiny kitchen at the Sheraton-Lincoln Hotel in Indianapolis with all that hot grease, boiling water, and slippery floors. He could get hurt in some foolish accident just because we've routed him through a dangerous place simply out of campaign habit."

McManus's suggestion made a whole lot of sense. "Do it," I said.

As it turned out, it was Gruver who made the trip to Los Angeles. When he got back, he told McManus it would be no problem to implement his idea. In fact, he said, by doing so, the candidate could visit not one but two public rooms that would be jammed with celebrants. By using a stairwell from the floor below, Bobby could bypass the kitchen, go first to the Embassy Room, and then back down the same stairwell to the other public room.

"From there," said Gruver, "he can hook around through an outside hallway to the elevators and go up one floor. When the doors open, he'll be looking at the Colonial Room, which we'll have set up for the briefing."

As Gruver talked, McManus ripped off a piece of a brown sandwich bag and drew a rough map of Gruver's plan. Early the next morning, McManus brought the map to me. Knowing the senator and Ethel were still in their suite, I took the map from Jim and motioned him to come with me. However, when we got up there, they were in the middle of a meeting. Bobby signaled for me to join them.

"Thanks for your help, Jim," I said. "I'll show it to him at some point today."

That point never came, unfortunately, and that night I stopped by McManus's room to talk about the schedule. I pulled the map from my pocket, shook my head, and put it on Jim's desk. Jim crumpled it up and tossed it in the wastebasket.

From there, I stayed with the candidate, and McManus went to New York City to work on setting up the national press operation at the head-quarters in Manhattan. That was where he was when I reached him in his hotel room at 4:30 on the morning of June 5 to tell him that Bobby Kennedy had been assassinated.

A stunned Jim McManus asked me one question, "Where did it happen?"

"The kitchen," I said.

"What the hell was he doing in the kitchen?" McManus shouted at me over the long distance line.

All I could say was, "I don't know."

In the spring of 1994, as I was gathering material for this book, I received a letter from Jim McManus. It was the first time I'd heard from him in years. As it happened, he had retired from the newspaper business (to which he'd returned after Bobby Kennedy's death) and was also writing his memoirs. He wanted me to verify the facts I've just outlined. He had it exactly right.

At the end of his letter, Jim McManus, a kind man, wrote, "I recall very clearly the pain in your voice that night, and, even today, I wince a bit inwardly to recall it for you."

Another person with a clear memory of those days is my former secretary Betty Duffy. A highly skilled executive secretary, Betty worked at Continental Airlines for Bob Six and other executive-level people, but as soon as I saw how good she was, I commandeered her. Later, she went to work for Bobby's campaign, on both the East and the West coasts.

In September 1994, she talked with John Greenya about those days.

"The first time I met the senator was in California a few weeks before the primary. A bunch of campaign people had gone up to his suite to watch the news, and I went along. I walked in the room, and there he was, sitting on the bed, wearing his pajamas, his hands around his knees, all scrunched up. My first thought was, He's so *little*!

"Just then, Angie Novello, his personal secretary, who was so devoted that she actually mothered him, came in the room. When she saw how he was dressed, she said, 'Senator! You're in your pajamas! Where is your robe?'

"I remember going into her room in the hotel once and seeing Bobby Kennedy's socks and underwear and handkerchiefs spread out all over the balcony to dry. She'd hand-washed them! What a lovely lady."

Betty has a good memory for the humorous anecdote ("I kept after Pierre to get me one of the little plastic admittance cards for The Factory, 'cause I'd seen that all the good-looking young girls seemed to have one. He kept saying I didn't need one, that everybody knew me, but I finally said that I just wanted one. So he said he'd get me one, but then added, 'Those cards are for the hookers' ") and an even better one for the dramatic events. This is part of her recollection of the night Bobby died.

"Pierre and I were manning the press table, about forty, fifty feet away from the ballroom, and everything was going so great. It seemed to me it was something like 10:00 or 10:30 when the results were announced, and Pierre was so excited. We were jumping around and hugging each other and dancing around, and everybody was shouting, 'We're going to win; we're going to win,' and 'It's off to Chicago!' And I thought, Oh my God, I can't believe this is happening to me, little old Betty from Rhode Island. But then it happened."

"It," of course, was the shooting. Betty continued: "There was a little anteroom that was off the hallway where the pantry was where he was shot, and Duff, my husband, who was a guest that night, was kitty-corner over there. It wasn't a very big room. I didn't even realize it until later, but Duff said I had to get up on the table to get away from everybody. It was just chaos. Everybody was screaming and running toward the shots, Pierre included. I was on *two* phones at the same time, had two phones to my ears, trying to get a hold of different people.

"Then Pierre called me and told me to try to reach Senator Ted Kennedy, who was in San Francisco, and also Jackie, who, as I recall, was in Colorado. Oh, one of the very first calls was to circumvent the two doctors, the two neurosurgeons, who were heading to the Central Receiving Hospital, where he was first brought, but by then he had been transferred to Good Samaritan. Pierre wanted me to track them down and tell them where to go. Somehow, through the chaos, I did all this. Pierre and I were still functioning, though I didn't know where he was a lot of the time because he ran off so quickly saying, 'Stay with all this stuff'—all the material that was still there from the election. He thought enough to think of *that*.

"Next thing I knew, he was calling from the hospital—he and Nicole having gotten there on the famous motorcycle ride. No, *that's* when he told me 'Stay there with all the stuff. Stay put. I'll be in touch. We don't know anything more now.'

"Things calmed down a bit at that point, but I still remember how Pierre had looked at the time of the shooting. He went *white*, his face was just *chalk*."

About that time, I called Betty from the hospital again and asked if she had any way of getting there, as I needed her to spell the other secretaries, who'd been working nonstop. She replied that her husband was still there and could drive her. I should have told her what to expect.

She remembered: "When I got out to the street, there were *lines* of people, and they had klieg lights and ropes all along the streets to the hospital. I thought, God, this is like a Hollywood production. What's going on here? It was like so unreal.

"I got to the hospital . . . and Pierre was just devastated. He was very close to Bobby, having met him before he met Jack. He was going through a bad time, a really bad time.

"In the morning, when I went down for the last of the many press conferences held throughout the long night, I ran into . . . oh gosh, one of the really big TV journalists, and he said, 'Betty, you look like you need a drink,' and he gave me a big scotch—in the middle of the morning. What a mistake! I took a swig of it and I was sick—I had to run."

Later that morning, we had to make arrangements for a plane for the press, to take Bobby's body back to the East Coast for his funeral, and, of course, all the press wanted to be in the front lines at the funeral Mass to see the most and to get the best shots. Betty recalls that it was at about this time that I lost it.

"The journalists were all screaming at one another, all of them wanting the first place for their cameras, and that's the only time I ever saw Pierre—who was so upset and so tired and upset with *everybody*—get angry. He became unglued! He screamed at one of the journalists, 'You can't always have it all your way.' And he swore at him, in front of everybody. That's the only time I ever saw him do that. He was *never* like that. He got along real well with the press."

Betty has one other memory of my behavior during that time, but it was not one I knew she had.

"I don't know how Pierre would feel about my telling this, but I remember that at one point, in the hospital, I couldn't find him when he was needed. I said, 'Where's Pierre?' but nobody knew. So I went looking around for him, up on that private floor of the hospital, and I found him in what was like a pantry area, in the semidark, and he was all curled up on a counter there, all curled up, and he was crying.

"I didn't know at that point if I was more upset for him or . . . because I knew how close he was to Bobby and how he felt, and then after having lost Jack, and I thought, *This can't be.* . . . This was the point when the reality of the situation finally hit me.

"I don't think Pierre knew I was there, and when I saw him there like that, I thought, *He needs to be alone,* and I walked away."

One last tragic note: In 1979, several years after she and Romain Gary had divorced, Jean Seberg took her own life. The next year, Gary shot himself to death.

In 1970, in his nonfiction book *White Dog,* Gary had written:

> I hadn't realized to what extent that last month with Jean in America had shattered my nerves. I feel a permanent tension in my shoulders, arms, and hands, a physical emptiness that yearns to be filled, like some last echo of the tremendous physical craving of adolescence. I try to soothe myself by closing my eyes and remembering all the Nazis I killed during the war. I only succeed in wiping out people.
>
> Camus said: "You condemn to the shooting squad a guilty man, but you always shoot an innocent one." That old dilemma again: love for the beast and a hatred of beastliness.

C H A P T E R
F O U R T E E N

THREE WEEKS AFTER Bob Kennedy was assassinated, I plunged into another political operation that I had not seriously assessed in advance. The Democratic convention was coming up and most of the delegates who had been elected to represent Robert Kennedy were angry and frustrated about his death and did not want to go to the convention, either to vote for Gene McCarthy or Hubert Humphrey, the two other candidates. I had discussions with Frank Mankiewicz, who had been Bobby's press secretary, and we decided it was vital to get the Kennedy people to the 1968 convention and that the only way to do so was to talk another politician into entering the race. Our selling point was that even though he would have no chance of winning the nomination, we believed this candidate could have a very good chance of winning the nomination in 1972. So, sacrificial in '68, successful in '72.

We finally concentrated on Senator George McGovern, a liberal democrat from North Dakota. McGovern was a highly intelligent man, and while seen by some politicians as *too* liberal, he was a strong campaigner. Frank and I flew to Washington and had a meeting with McGovern to try to talk him into running. McGovern was for the idea from the beginning, but he insisted that both Mankiewicz and I give our promise that we would help run his campaign in 1972. We both agreed, and McGovern announced his candidacy.

The convention in Chicago was a mess, with massive demonstrations going on in the parks outside the hotels where the delegates were staying. At the convention, Senator Abe Ribicoff of Connecticut and I were named as the floor managers for the campaign. When the convention opened, rumors started to flow across the convention floor. Delegates from Louisiana, Texas, and other states contacted me and said they did not want either Gene McCarthy or Hubert Humphrey to win the nomination. They said that McGovern had entered the race too late and that the only person who could defeat Richard Nixon, then seen as the sure Republican candidate, would be Senator Ted Kennedy. I was not against that idea, given all the links I had with the Kennedy family. I knew Ted Kennedy was in Chicago, but I could not reach him, so I contacted Steve Smith and asked him to talk to Teddy and see if he would run. About twelve hours later, Steve came back to me and said that Teddy did not want to run.

The convention then proceded normally. Hubert Humphrey easily got the nomination, but McGovern picked up a lot of the Bobby Kennedy votes. One of the important points of the convention was a debate on a resolution to oppose Lyndon Johnson's policy on Vietnam. A lot of delegates were against the Vietnam War and wanted it to come to a close. I was chosen as the delegate to open the argument for adopting the resolution. But in the end, the resolution was defeated.

Just after Humphrey was nominated, Larry O'Brien and a few others went to see Humphrey and told him that if he was going to win the election, he had to resign as vice president. Humphrey declined, and for the first part of the campaign, he backed Johnson on his policy. But later, he made an important shift toward the anti-Vietnam policy, and that shift almost won him the election. In the end, he lost to Nixon by only a half million votes, and most experts believe that if the election had lasted another forty-eight hours, Hubert Humphrey would have won.

Right after the convention, still completely shattered by Bobby's assassination, which rekindled the painful memories of John Kennedy's, I decided to leave the United States and move to France. My idea was to stay there for a year or perhaps slightly more and then to return to the United States. However, a series of events transpired that, in fact, kept me in Europe, except for one brief (nine-month) period, for twenty-five years.

In the fall of 1971, McGovern contacted me and asked me to start working on his campaign. He told me to take a tour of the United States and talk to leading political journalists and explain to them how McGovern was going to win the Democratic nomination in 1972. (It was a difficult assignment because at the time McGovern had the support of only 1 percent of the American people.)

My most interesting visit was to Chicago, where I had lunch with John Driesky, political editor of the *Chicago Daily News*. I spelled out for him how the primaries were going to work and exactly how McGovern was going to win the nomination. I said McGovern would lose early primaries in New Hampshire and Florida but would make a strong comeback after winning the Wisconsin primary, and would then go on to victory. The next day, Driesky wrote a column saying that the former press secretary of President John Kennedy, having lost his American ties and his understanding of American politics, was now spreading foolish information.

When McGovern won the nomination in 1972, that same editor wrote a very generous column apologizing to me and telling his readers I had been 100 percent right in my assessment.

In 1972, I spent most of the year in the United States, working on the McGovern campaign with Frank Mankiewicz and a young man named Gary Hart. About a month before the convention, when I was on a trip with McGovern, we had a long discussion about how we would handle the campaign after he was nominated. He offered me the post of chairman of the Democratic party.

I told McGovern I was delighted to accept it but that I would just run the Democratic party during the campaign and resign afterward. McGovern agreed. About three days before the convention, however, McGovern contacted me and told me that he had decided a woman should be chairman of the party. He had selected a lady from Colorado, Jean Westwood. He asked me to accept the post of vice-chairman and to run the entire public-relations operation during the campaign. I was unhappy at his decision to go back on his promise to me to head the party, but I agreed to take the vice-chairman's job, feeling that I could make an important contribution to his campaign from that post. I was stunned by what happened next.

When McGovern won the nomination, we immediately went into a meeting to choose the vice presidential candidate. My feeling was that Ted Kennedy, who had gone through the Chappaquiddick affair, would be a good candidate. (It would have been an advantage for Kennedy, because even if McGovern lost, all the attacks that would be made on him by the media on Chappaquiddick would evaporate if he later decided to run for President.) McGovern agreed and asked me to call Teddy. But Teddy immediately refused, saying he had no interest in running for vice president. We finally settled on Senator Thomas Eagleton, from Missouri, and he won the nomination unopposed at the convention.

The day after the convention, the Democratic party met to elect the chairman and vice-chairman. McGovern opened the session by nominating Westwood for chairman. His motion was seconded, and she was immediately voted into power. McGovern then got up and nominated me for vice-chairman. But this time, there was a different reaction. Another delegate got up and nominated someone else for the job. What usually happens at these convention meetings is that the presidential candidate then steps up and says he would rather have the person he nominated. McGovern, however, said nothing.

This gutless behavior made me extremely angry. I went up to the podium and pulled out of the race. I walked out of the meeting, went to the airport, and flew to Hyannis Port, where I had been invited to stay at the home of Ethel Kennedy. I had been on my feet so long during the convention, running the floor-management job, that I was exhausted and my legs had gone numb. I went to bed and slept for twenty-four hours.

When I finally got up, Ethel told me I was getting urgent calls from George McGovern. I decided to call him. He told me he was extremely sorry for the way he had handled the Democratic convention and apologized. He then went on to say he had an important operation for me to carry out and wanted me to come to Washington to get the information. I told him I would but that I would remain in Hyannis Port for about a week to rest up from the convention.

When I went to Washington, I learned he wanted me to go back to Paris and enter into negotiations with the Vietnamese delegation. McGovern had been invited to Hanoi and was interested in going. But he wanted me to make a deal with the Vietnamese that would guarantee him the release of a number of American POWs if he went to Hanoi. I was not very optimistic that such a deal could be made, but I agreed to get involved in the meetings.

McGovern told me that the talks had to be very secret and I agreed to say nothing about what I was doing. I flew back to Paris and set up the meetings. They went on for nearly a week, but in the end, the Vietnamese would not guarantee any release of POWs if McGovern went to Hanoi. I decided to fly back to the United States to report to McGovern.

As soon as I landed at Kennedy Airport, I was confronted by journalists and told that they had heard I was negotiating with the Vietnamese. I refused to answer the questions, but I could not figure out how the press had learned the nature of my meetings.

When I got to the hotel, I discovered that McGovern had put out a statement saying he had not asked me to have any negotiations with the Vietnamese. He was putting the whole operation on my back.

I called Fred Dutton, one of McGovern's top assistants, and told him that if McGovern didn't correct his statement, I would put out one that told the truth. McGovern then released a second statement, admitting he had asked me to talk to the Vietnamese. I was named cochairman of the National Citizens Committee for McGovern, and during the rest of the campaign, I crisscrossed the country, giving almost five hundred speeches on his behalf.

Perhaps it seems strange that I would still go to bat for McGovern despite his *double* betrayal, but I had made a pledge in 1968 (as had Frank Mankiewicz) that if McGovern would agree to run in that splintered-party year, we would do our damnedest to campaign for him in 1972. A promise is a promise, and both Frank and I kept ours.

News of the Watergate affair had broken just before McGovern's nomination, and in an early press conference in Cleveland, I got specifics as to the names of those who had planned the operation, including John Mitchell, the first attorney general of the Nixon administration. McGovern called me and told me he didn't want to use the Watergate issue in the campaign. The result was that the Watergate affair did not become nationally important until after McGovern lost the election in November.

The day of the election, I flew back to Paris. I was again exhausted—but this time it was more than just postconvention loser blues. I had become very unhappy with politics, so unhappy that I decided I would never again play a role in either the Democratic party or any campaign—not ever. However, twenty-five years later, George McGovern and I are once again friends.

While I was resting in Paris, I was contacted by Jean-Jacques Servan-Schreiber, the owner of the French weekly news magazine *L'Express,* and he asked if I was interested in joining his staff. I had a meeting with the editor, Philippe Grumbach, and we immediately worked out a contract that called for me to start work just after New Year's, 1973.

As an editor of *L'Express,* I was specifically appointed to cover American affairs, including the Watergate scandal. In addition, I was to travel abroad with U.S. Presidents to countries such as Iran, India, Saudi Arabia, Jordan, Syria, and China. I had returned to my first love, journalism, but this time I had a much, much larger canvas.

During the early days of my work at *L'Express,* Aristotle Onassis's son was killed in a helicopter crash. I immediately sent off a telegram offering my condolences. I had met Onassis several times in the past, both before and after his marriage to JFK's widow.

I was one of the first people to learn that Jackie was going to marry Aristotle Onassis. I heard the news from Jackie's brother-in-law, Prince Radziwill, at a dinner party at his country place outside London. The prince urged me to keep the information to myself, and I did so.

A few weeks later, I got a call from Steve Smith, de facto Kennedy family spokesman. He said, "Something very important is happening. You've got to come to New York and see me."

"What is it?" I asked.

"We've been hearing rumors that Jackie is going to marry Ari Onassis."

"Those aren't rumors," I said, "it's true."

There was a brief silence, and then Steve Smith said, "Oh, shit."

I went to New York and met with Smith. "The family's very upset about this," he said. "Among other things, the media coverage is going to *be huge*. We were wondering if you could make sure that she gets married in Greece."

What an assignment!

I thought about it all the way back to Paris, and quickly came to the conclusion that as much as I liked and admired the various members of the Kennedy family, my first loyalty was to Jackie. That same night I sat down and wrote her a long letter, just opening my heart to her in friendship. I said I believed she had the unlimited right to marry anyone she wanted to marry, and that she shouldn't think, even for a second, that she was somehow obligated by history to be the widow of John F. Kennedy forever.

I told her that as far as I was concerned she was a totally independent person who had a right to do whatever she wanted in life. This decision was hers and hers alone to make. I wrote that for whatever it might be worth to her I fully supported her right to make that decision. I closed my letter by saying, as diplomatically as I could, that given the Kennedy family's attitude toward her marrying Onassis perhaps the wiser course would be for her to have the wedding in Greece.

Frankly, I no longer recall whether or not my suggestion had anything to do with her eventual decision. Certainly, the Kennedy family was pressing hard for the nuptials *not* to be in the United States. All that mattered was that Jacqueline Bouvier Kennedy had the right—and the need—to marry someone who could guarantee her *and her children* safe passage through the rest of life.

One final, very important point. No one should forget that this wedding took place in October of 1968, which was only four months after Bobby's death, the second Kennedy assassination in less than five years. Bobby and Jackie had become extremely close after John's death, and I know how hard his death was for her to take. I also know that it drove her fear for the lives of her own children to the point of paranoia, if paranoia was even possible under the horrible circumstances that prevailed in 1968. It was not paranoia to fear for the safety of Caroline and John.

I still had a vivid memory of Jackie having appeared in the doorway to my White House office two days after her husband had been killed. She looked almost ghostly as she sat down and began to talk. "Pierre," she said, softly, "I have nothing else to do in life but help my children deal with this terrible problem, the effect of their father's assassination, to bring them up well, and see that they become decent, caring, and intelligent people. I have to make sure they survive."

As things turned out, I did not attend the wedding because of a long-standing business obligation. However, the next time I saw Jackie she thanked me for my letter, and then added, her hand on my arm, "But most of all for your support."

For years people speculated about the possibility of Jackie writing her autobiography, but I was not one of them. I'd always known how very private she was, and how much she treasured that privacy. To have written about her own charmed yet tragic life would have been the height of inconsistency. I believe Jackie herself said it best in 1981 when she told an interviewer, "I want to live my life, not record it."

Forty-eight hours after young Onassis's death, I was at home in Paris when the phone rang late at night. I immediately recognized that familiar breathy voice as Jackie's.

"Pierre, I have a very big favor to ask of you. I hope so much you'll say yes."

"Of course," I said. "What is it?"

"Ari is very low in spirits. Alexander's death has just devastated him. I've convinced him to take some time off, for a cruise, but he needs someone else to be with him, another man. Could you and Nicole free up your schedule right away for ten days? Ari has always liked you, and I think it could be very good for him to have you there. But you'd have to meet us at Orly the day after tomorrow. Please say you can do it!"

Without any hesitation, I said, "We'll be there." (Of course, seeing as I'd only been at my new job one week, that took a little doing, but my editor was most accommodating.)

Two days later, we met Jackie and Ari and one other couple, both Americans, at Orly Airport in Paris, and from there we all boarded an Olympic Airlines jet bound for Dakar, Senegal, where we were to board the *Christina*, Onassis's fabulous yacht, which he'd named after his only daughter.

The trip started well, thanks to a most humorous scene that took place in the airport at Dakar while we were waiting for our luggage so that we could go through customs.

My former wife Nicole remembers it better than I do: "We were taken to the VIP lounge in the airport and while we were there some

members of the Senegal government in Dakar came up to welcome Mr.
and Mrs. Onassis, and us, and one man presented Mrs. Onassis with a
bouquet of flowers. (I noticed something rather touching, which was that
Pierre had suddenly reverted to his role as press secretary to the President
and therefore working for the First Lady.)

"Obviously, this member of the Senegalese government was so happy
to meet Mrs.—to him, I'm sure, she was still Mrs. Kennedy—and so he
was very nervous. At least we thought that was why he was so nervous.
At one point, suddenly, he grabbed the flowers from Mrs. Kennedy's lap,
took the bouquet away, said good-bye very, very quickly, and raced out
of the room. He ran toward a plane that was landing.

"What had happened was that he was at the airport to welcome
the prime minister of some other African country, Zambia or Nigeria,
and when he heard that Jacqueline Kennedy Onassis was landing at the
airport, he couldn't resist meeting her. So he took the bouquet of flowers
meant for the prime minister and made a little side trip to give them to
her. Then, when he saw the prime minister's plane landing . . . well, he
realized what he had done, and, in a panic, he grabbed the flowers back
and fled.

"We all laughed a lot, but most of all Jackie. She had a fabulous sense
of humor. Also, she had a great—how do you say—*complicité*—she was
on the same wave length—with Pierre."

I knew that Nicole and probably also Jackie would have loved to
have had a look around Dakar, a lovely old city, but that was not to be,
as Ari apparently wanted to get on his boat and out to sea as soon as
possible. So we raced through the city, and we were soon aboard the *Christina,* a three-hundred-foot-long vessel that was just this side of opulent.
Nicole has always been a better observer of such things than I am, so, once
again, I'll defer to her recollections.

"It was a very lovely boat, very low on the ocean. It was very pleasant
because it had—I don't know how you call it—the back part of the boat,
where we would spend most of the day. It was a very grand boat, with a
beautiful drawing room with leather bound books and sofas, and a painting
by El Greco. Most Greek shipowners had El Grecos, and his was above
the fireplace in a very formal drawing room, but we hardly ever sat there.
We sat instead outside in the back of the boat. There were big navy blue
cushions, and a little swimming pool made of mosaic tile that represented
a scene from the Knossos Palace in Crete. The boat was *incredible.* There
was a huge staff, and everything you could possibly want. It was like being
outside of time, out of this world.

"It was all very poignant, very moving. Here was this man—I always compared him to an olive tree, whatever those trees are that can take frost and heat but never move—a nice solid man. He was very much from the Middle East. He was born in Smyrna, Turkey, and he was very much from Greece, from that part of the Mediterranean. He had loved that son of his, and it was so tragic, but he never discussed it. He had a lot of dignity. Maybe he discussed it with Pierre late at night. That I don't know, for sure, but I doubt it.

Onassis was a man who loved to walk, to walk and talk, and he was the kind of man who doesn't go to sleep at night—he talks and talks and loves to discuss. I think that must be a Greek specialty. To talk and argue and develop a conversation with somebody is quite an art. And Pierre was *perfect for this,* because Pierre also loved to talk—and especially with somebody like Onassis, somebody interesting—and develop arguments and defend them, and then listen to the other's arguments—to conduct the art of conversation. That went on very late at night between Pierre and Onassis. It was very pleasant—quite lovely, really.

"Jackie had brought along many books to read. She loved to read, but Onassis didn't read much—or at all, I think. He learned everything from talking. He knew many, many things. He was incredibly cultured, but not in a literary way. He was special. The two of them, he and Jackie, got along very well, at least they did at that time. They did not have much in common, but she was obviously fascinated by him. And he was by her.

"The point of the trip was to cheer him up, and I think we did that. His mood improved. Of course, he was a man who was very badly wounded. You could *feel* he was, but he didn't show it. The trip was a distraction for him, and it was good for him to have somebody like Pierre along. He loved Pierre. They always argued about Roosevelt, and all sorts of subjects from American history, present and near past. They went on for hours and hours, pacing up and down the deck, talking and arguing."

Ari Onassis did love to argue and to talk politics. I recall, some months later, when we were visiting them on Skorpios, their island, John Kennedy, Jr., by then a smart and handsome youth, saying to me at breakfast, "How late did you two stay up last night arguing about Roosevelt?"

Staying up late was Ari's style, not mine. He had a command center on the boat, a room filled with all the latest equipment, especially radio equipment, and he would go there in the wee small hours to keep in touch with the parts of his far-flung empire. Then he'd sleep very late, often not joining the rest of us until we were having lunch.

After lunch, when I would light up a cigar, Onassis would smile and say, in reference to a late friend of his who had been on board many times, "Ah, you're doing your Churchill thing."

Ari could be most generous. For example, when the cruise was over, he had one of his private planes fly Nicole and me back to Paris.

Both Nicole and I felt the trip was efficacious. As she recalls it, "Jackie Onassis was very thoughtful and protective of Ari, and her idea of inviting Pierre was perfect."

That isn't the word I'd use, but I would agree that the trip did seem to help. Some years later, when I learned of Onassis's death, I was genuinely saddened.

One of the many things that so impressed me about Jackie Kennedy was her unwavering insistence that her two children grow up with as full—and as realistic—a sense of their father as possible. To that end, she would ask people who had been close to him to share their memories of him with Caroline and John. The first time she asked me to do so was when we were on the *Christina*, the trip shortly after the death of Onassis's son.

At that time the children were still young—fourteen and eleven, respectively—and I could only sketch the broader outlines of what had been *such* a special life. But I made certain to stress their father's wonderful sense of humor and his love of life—and especially of them. Without going into detail about his numerous injuries and bouts of illness, I pointed out that even though he often had reason to be sad, he was usually the person who cheered up all the others in the room. I have few memories of that first session, except for a clear picture of those two innocent, beguiling faces turned up to me and listening with rapt attention.

There were several later sessions, especially amidst the almost fantasylike privacy of Skorpios, Onassis's private island. During those talks, which both Caroline and John would increasingly interrupt with questions, I talked about JFK's love of history, and in particular his passion for reading. They laughed when I mentioned that it wasn't safe to leave anything that looked interesting on one's desk in the White House for fear their father would stroll by and make off with it; I think they'd already heard that from other adults who'd known and loved him.

One of my main concerns was to avoid, perhaps even to counteract, what I had come to view as the *Camelotization* of their father and his time as President of the United States. Having seen Caroline and John many times over the years since then, and having watched them grow into interesting, responsible adults, I was always pleased to see that their view of their historically important father was kept in a healthy perspective, that of the loving children of a man they understood had been a human being, not a myth. Again, the credit goes to Jackie.

* * *

In July of 1975, I got a call from a good friend in Mexico, Fausto Zapata Loredo, spokesman for then President Luis Echevaria Alvarez. Fausto said that President Echevaria, who was near the end of his term, was about to begin a thirty-country world tour and wanted to invite me to accompany him. However, the trip was to last for three months, and it was not possible for me to leave *L'Express*, where I'd just started to work, for that long.

I asked Fausto to read me the list of the countries the president was going to visit, and when he said Cuba, I said, "Stop right there!"

Having lived through the debacle of the Bay of Pigs and the Cuban missile crisis, and knowing that no one from the Kennedy administration had been in Cuba since then, I was excited at the prospect. Making it doubly intriguing was the fact that in 1975 Americans were still barred from going to Cuba. However, if I was to be part of a Mexican delegation, there would be no problem. I told Fausto I could make the Cuban part of the trip. Fine, he said.

Fausto told me to meet the Mexican delegation in Trinidad on August 14. I decided to take a two-week vacation in Venezuela first and then fly to Trinidad. In Venezuela, I spent most of the time with a family who were my friends. One of the daughters spoke both Spanish and English, so I asked her if she would like to go to Havana as my interpreter. She accepted.

I arrived in Trinidad on the fourteenth. The Mexican delegation, including President Echevaria, had arrived the night before, and all of them wore special Mexican shirts called guayaberas. Obviously, I did not have one, but President Echevaria not only insisted I get one, he also sent a government plane back to Mexico to fetch one for me! It arrived the next day.

On the morning of the seventeenth, we flew to Havana, and we were able to go directly to the city without having to go through passport control. Each of the delegates was assigned a person from the Cuban Foreign Ministry to help them during the trip. (I soon got the impression they all worked for Cuban intelligence.)

For the first four days, we traveled all over Cuba, and it was clear that the Castro government had made important progress on such subjects as education and health care. Cuba remained a poor country, but it was not the kind of poverty that existed in many other Latin American countries. It was also clear that the Castro government was tough. There were over ten thousand political prisoners in Cuban jails, an indication that Castro continued to repress any opposition to his Communist regime.

All during the trip, I kept pressing Fausto Zapata to ask President Echevaria to set up a private meeting for me with Fidel Castro. I wanted to meet the leader and talk with him about the relationship between the

United States and Cuba during the Kennedy administration. My answer came on the next-to-last day we were in Cuba: Castro would receive me (and Scotty Reston of the *New York Times*) the next day.

The evening before the meeting, Castro threw a bash, a giant and lavish party for Echevaria, in a building called Protocol House Number 5, once the palace of the Batista-era millionaire Gomez Mena. The palace was elegant, with marble floors, toilets the size of monuments, and a magnificent garden with a huge swimming pool. Literally hundreds of tables covered with food, drink, and glorious flowers had been set up on the lawn. Despite the fact that austerity was the rule in Cuba, I had a feeling this house and its gardens had seldom looked better.

When Castro arrived—in a new Soviet limousine—the party peaked, of course. I was introduced, as was Reston, and the Cuban premier graciously told us that he was looking forward to our meeting the next day.

It was in the late morning of August 21 that Reston and I went to a grand villa left over from the previous administration and now used by Castro for face-to-face meetings. I was accompanied by my interpreter, but when we got to the room where we were to meet Castro, we discovered that he, too, had brought an interpreter, another woman.

The meeting went on for three and a half hours and was utterly fascinating. (Before it began, however, Castro, with a big smile on his bearded face, gave me a handful of *cohibas*, the Cuban cigar made only for him.) Castro spoke softly, clearly, and frequently with humor, always exhibiting strong confidence in the future of his Communist revolution. At the same time, one got the impression that Fidel Castro had become more realistic and more pragmatic.

At one point, he said, "The United States has finally had to accept me, because the CIA failed to eliminate me."

It was true. The CIA had mounted many plots to assassinate Castro, but none had succeeded.

We discussed the Bay of Pigs and the Cuban missile crisis for a long time. Castro said he understood why the United States had had to impose sanctions on Cuba after the Bay of Pigs, adding that JFK had been seen as failing in his effort to overthrow him and had therefore had to do something tough. Yet at the same time, and to my surprise, Castro kept saying he had great admiration for Kennedy.

"If Nixon had won the election in 1960, I am sure that the U.S. Marines would have come into Cuba during the Bay of Pigs and it would have been a dirt war."

He said he was extremely sad that Kennedy had been assassinated. "Relations between Cuba and the United States would probably have been renewed under the Kennedy administration. He had sent me a trial balloon just before he was killed."

Actually, that was also true. About four days before the assassination, Kennedy met with a French journalist, Jean Daniel, who at that time worked for *L'Express.* Daniel was on his way to Cuba after his meeting with Kennedy, and the President gave him a private message to give to Castro. The message indicated that he was ready to start negotiating with Cuba for the reestablishment of diplomatic relations between the United States and Cuba.

Castro said, "Daniel was sitting in my office when the telephone rang and I learned that Kennedy had been assassinated."

During our meeting, Castro asked me as many questions as I asked him. He was curious about internal U.S. politics. He wanted to know whether Senator Ted Kennedy would be a candidate for President in 1976. And he wanted an appraisal of President Gerald Ford, who at that point had been in office, following Nixon's resignation, for about a year.

Several hours before we had met Castro, the United States had partially reduced the sanctions against Cuba.

"That was a reasonable decision for the American government to take," Castro said. "We must normalize the relations between our two countries. Lots of things have changed. We are moving toward détente between the East and West. The Vietnam War is over. We must take account of the new conditions that are now existing in the world."

Castro puffed on his cigar. "And we, too, have changed. We have awakened."

At that moment, something fascinating occurred. James Reston turned to Castro and asked, "Would you mind if I put on a different hat?"

Castro smiled. "What kind of hat?"

Reston said he wanted to put on a diplomatic hat because he had been given a message for Castro by Secretary of State Henry Kissinger.

"The message is that the United States would like to open negotiations to reestablish relations between the United States and Cuba." I about dropped.

Castro replied immediately. "Those kind of negotiations are impossible without the United States lifting sanctions first."

It was Reston's turn to smile. "That is exactly how Secretary Kissinger said you would reply. But what about if we have pre-negotiation talks?"

Castro agreed. After thirty minutes of discussion, the two men finally came to the conclusion that the pre-negotiation talks would take place in Madrid and that they would be between U.S. and Cuban ambassadors.

Part of the discussion would focus on reparation payments from Cuba to the U.S. companies, such as ITT, Standard Oil, Bacardi, and the Hilton Hotels, that had been taken over after the 1959 revolution. In agreeing to discuss these issues, Castro said that Cuba also had indemnification claims against the United States.

"We claim damage and interest for the problems you have caused us in fourteen years of boycott."

Castro said the Cuban claims would be about $2 billion—which was exactly the same sum the U.S. companies were asking from Cuba. Castro also mentioned that the accord reached after the Spanish-American War in 1898, which allowed the United States to have access to the military base at Guantánamo Bay in Cuba until 2001, should be brought to an end earlier.

Castro was still frustrated that the resolution of the Cuban missile crisis had been negotiated solely between the United States and the Soviet Union. He felt that if Cuba had taken part in the negotiations, they might have convinced the United States to pull out of Guantánamo Bay in return for the Soviets taking their missiles out of Cuba.

I walked out of the meeting surprised at what Reston had done for Kissinger, but also surprised by Castro's reaction.

It seemed that the Ford administration was seriously moving in the direction of normalizing relations with Cuba. But in the months that followed, it became clear that it would not work.

First, Castro sent thirty thousand Cuban troops to Angola to fight with the Communist-led government against the opposition forces, which were strongly supported by the U.S. government. Second, there was a conference in Havana on the independence of Puerto Rico, something that also angered the Americans.

As I write this book, twenty years later, those very same sanctions against Cuba still exist. In fact, during the early months of President Clinton's administration, the sanctions were stepped up. But while the sanctions exist, while Cuba has gone into a deep economic crisis because of the end of the Cold War and the termination of its longtime financial relations with the Soviet Union, Fidel Castro also still exists.

That should not be surprising, however. Most leaders gather strength under sanctions—Saddam Hussein, Colonel Gadhafi, Castro. Sanctions are not the way you topple them. If we had been imposing sanctions on the Soviet Union and the Eastern European Communist nations, the Cold War would never have ended.

C H A P T E R
F I F T E E N

"I DON'T MEAN to be rude," I said, "but I have to tell you I think *A.M. America* is the most boring morning show on television."

Scowling, my dinner companion replied, "You don't say."

But indeed I had, and, what's more, he had to know I was right. ABC, which had few top news correspondents, was dead last in the ratings.

It was October of 1975, and I was at a dinner party in the New York apartment of Steve and Jean Kennedy Smith. The guest who had to bear the brunt of my criticism was Roone Arledge, then president of ABC Sports. It was the first time we'd met, and we had a lengthy conversation, during the course of which I suggested they let me do a weekly half-hour segment from Europe, presenting interesting personalities from France and England.

To my surprise, Arledge said, "That's interesting. Let me discuss it with the news division and get back to you."

I heard nothing for weeks and so figured it was a lost cause, but then one day in early November, I got a call from Roone Arledge's assistant, who stunned me by asking, "How would you like to work for ABC Sports at the Winter Games in Innsbruck in February?"

"What?" I said, "I don't know anything about winter sports. I've never even been on skis in my life!"

"We don't want you doing skiing," he said. "We want you doing fun and games around the Games."

"Okay, I'm interested," I said.

"Meet me in Munich tomorrow morning," he told me. "We'll do an on-camera test by making a five- or six-minute feature on the history of Innsbruck."

As soon as I'd hung up, I called my friend the Austrian ambassador to France and asked if he had an expert on Innsbruck within the embassy. He said he did, so I raced over there and consulted for three hours with a wonderful gentleman who seemed to know everything there was to know about the place. By the time I left, I was well prepared for my new assignment.

Early the next day, I flew to Munich, met Arledge's assistant, and we drove to Innsbruck, where we spent the rest of the day filming historic sites, with me providing (instant) expert on-camera commentary. Although I'd never done that before, it went well. At least I thought it did, but I worried when weeks passed and I had no word from the man who'd said he'd get right back to me with the results of my "test."

On Christmas Eve, just as Nicole and Gregory and I were beginning to open our presents, the phone rang at our country home in the Loire Valley.

"You've got the job," said Arledge's assistant. "I need all your sizes."

"What for?" I asked.

"So I can assemble your Innsbruck Games uniforms!"

When I got to Innsbruck, I discovered that the man I had beaten out for the job was none other than Peter Jennings, who later became America's most-honored and, in my opinion, best news anchor. Poor Peter— he was in Innsbruck for *A.M. America*, which would be seen by 1 million people, whereas my audience, on ABC Sports, was certain to exceed 50 million.

In addition to reporting on Austrian foods and wines, I also did a piece on a club in the mountains where all the members, men and women alike, swam naked together. Another piece had me being coached by one of the top skiers in the world. When the lesson was over, he flew off down the mountain.

I stood there, gazing out at the beautiful scenery and the inviting ski run directly in front of me. The camera remained on my face, at which point a beautiful Swiss miss skied up to me.

"How about going down the hill and having a drink with me?" I said in my suavest manner.

She said yes, then started off, as did I—only to fall flat on my face. The camera kept rolling, and I managed to turn my head around, face the camera, and ad-lib, "Back to you, Jim McKay."

The Innsbruck assignment worked out so well that Roone Arledge asked me to cover the Olympic Games in Montreal that summer.

The ABC assignments, as interesting as they were, remained part-time work. I was still with *L'Express,* to which I returned following the Games in Montreal. All that changed the following summer, that of 1977.

Arledge took me to dinner in Paris and confided that he was about to be named president of ABC News. He felt the news division was very weak (I resisted the urge to say, I told you so) and said he was going to name some new network correspondents. Did I, he asked, want to be one of the first? I did, and we worked out a deal. I would do an occasional piece for ABC, but I would stay with *L'Express.* The magazine had no objections, because I was only obligated to write one article a week for them.

The arrangement seemed ideal, which is probably why, before long, it all fell apart.

The seeds for my leaving *L'Express* had been sown in 1975. At a lunch that year, Sir James Goldsmith, whom I had known for some years and come gradually to regard as a friend, shocked me by saying that if Teddy Kennedy became President of the United States, he, James Goldsmith, would go to the United States and assassinate him.

Obviously, he didn't mean it literally, but having lived through the assassination of two other Kennedys, I erupted in anger at the poor taste of his remarks. I stormed out of the lunch, telling Goldsmith I would never speak to him again. And for several years, I did not.

In 1978, James Goldsmith bought *L'Express.* Seeing as I had not spoken to him for over two years, I figured my days there were certainly at an end. However, shortly after he'd bought the magazine, I went to London to cover the Group of Seven or G7 Summit, and apparently Goldsmith was aware of my assignment, because I got a call from his secretary inviting me to dinner at his magnificent house in London. There were four of us, Sir James, myself, and two lovely ladies he rather peremptorily dismissed immediately after dinner (by sending them upstairs to watch one of David Frost's interviews with former President Richard Nixon).

We went into the living room, where he provided cognac and cigars and began a lengthy apology for what he'd said at lunch. We talked for over two hours, mostly about the future of *L'Express,* and I left thinking the breach had been repaired and that now things were going well.

However, when I got back to Paris, I learned that none of my articles had run. I went to Goldsmith and told him I was resigning.

"No, no," he said. "I am not your problem. Your problem is the editor. But I am naming a new editor in September. His name is Jean François Revel, and I am sure you will have no problems with him."

I was delighted at the news, for Jean François Revel was a good friend of mine, and a man I greatly admired. I told Sir James I would stay, but I informed him I was about to begin a three-month leave of absence to finish writing a book about Carlos Andrés Pérez Rodríguez, who was stepping down as president of Venezuela.

I went to Venezuela and finished the book, and to my surprise, I learned that Goldsmith had continued to pay my salary for the months I was absent from his magazine.

When I got back to Paris, I went in to see Revel, who greeted me warmly and told me of his plans to name me editor of the international edition of *L'Express* and to give me a weekly column. I walked out of the office a happy man.

Five days later, I got a call from an excited Jean François Revel. "Come right over to the office. Something bad is happening."

When I got there, he explained that Goldsmith had just instituted a new policy. No one who worked for *L'Express* could work for another news organization—such as ABC. With that, he handed me a letter. Without reading it, I knew what it said.

Under French law, when a new editor takes over a magazine or newspaper, any of the magazine or newspaper's journalists can resign, saying they don't want to work with the new editor, and, under this law, they have to be paid as if they were retiring. I could tell from the look on Jean François Revel's face that this was not his doing; it was the work of Sir James Goldsmith. I accepted the letter and left.

Goldsmith had made a costly error. If he'd accepted my offer to resign, the law would not have covered me, and he would have saved tens of thousands of his beloved dollars. *C'est la vie!*

I now turned to television journalism with a passion. At first, there was frustration on two fronts. One was my own, and it involved the difficulty of switching over—mentally, for the most part—from reporting a story in two to three thousand words to doing so on television in three to five hundred. (I'd been used to traveling the world with just a notebook and then phoning in or dictating the story to an editor. Now I was traveling with a producer, a cameraman, a soundman, and five hundred pounds of equipment.)

The second frustration was that a number of my new colleagues at ABC had either forgotten or had never known that I'd been a newspaper and magazine journalist. They thought Roone Arledge had gone out and hired a well-known former presidential press secretary and was trying to pass him off as a news correspondent. I was going to have to prove myself all over again.

In 1979, while those frustrations were still operative, Arledge solved the problem with a single stroke by naming me ABC News' Paris bureau chief. He was banking on the fact that my high-level contacts throughout France and the rest of Europe would prove to be valuable. He was dead right. I was very happy with my new job, and soon after I'd taken it, two things happened that launched me into television like a rocket.

On August 27, 1979, one of England's most respected figures, Lord Mountbatten, was killed by the Irish Republican Army, or IRA. ABC's *World News Tonight,* a highly respected show, asked me to do a three-part series on the IRA—which meant talking to people who were IRA members or were close to those who were. We dared not talk to the militant wing of the party, so when we arrived in Belfast, we made contact with some leaders of the political group Sinn Fein.

The next morning, my producer and I and a French television crew were picked up by a van and driven to a house where we were placed in a room and told to wait. A short while later, I looked out the window and saw the place was being surrounded by British tanks. Almost immediately, there was a shout, and we were told to go downstairs and begin filming the interview, which we did. Whereupon, the doors burst open and *everyone*—the Sinn Fein leaders and the ABC team, led by one Pierre Salinger—was arrested and taken to the main prison in Belfast. I was stripped of all my possessions, including my belt, and put into a small, windowless cell. The charge? Dealing with terrorists.

The experience was hair-raising, but we were finally released about one in the morning (but not the Sinn Fein members; they were held for three days). The news of our arrest had spread, and we were met outside the prison by scores of reporters, including a team from ABC News. I had managed to get back our tape of the beginning of the interview, which showed the British troops breaking in to arrest us. Roone Arledge loved it. When I got back to the hotel, there was a telegram from him: PIERRE, YOUR GETTING ARRESTED WAS A SMASH HIT FOR ABC NEWS.

The second big breakthrough in my television career began just a few months later, on November 4, 1979, when hard-line Iranian nationalists took sixty-six Americans, almost all of them diplomats at our embassy in Teheran, hostage.

One night in early December 1979, I was asleep in my home in Paris when the phone rang at 3:00 A.M. It was the ABC evening news desk in New York.

"Pierre," said John Herrick, the night editor, "the Iranians are about to release thirteen or fourteen of the hostages. You've got to charter a plane and go to Frankfurt to cover their arrival."

"Wait a minute," I said, beginning to wake up, "I can't fly out of Paris. There's a huge strike by the air-traffic controllers, and not one plane has left here in ten days."

"That's your problem," said Herrick firmly, then hung up.

For the next several minutes, I sat on the side of my bed, trying to figure out what to do. *C'est la guerre,* I thought. I've nothing to lose by trying. I picked up the phone and called the tower at Le Bourget Airport, the one all the charters leave from, and after identifying myself, I asked if the controllers' union had a twenty-four-hour control center. The man said yes and gave me its number.

"This is Pierre Salinger of ABC News," I said. "Some fourteen American hostages are about to be freed and sent to Frankfurt. This is a highly important story for the Americans. Can you issue permission for *one* charter to fly out of France so I can go there and cover the story?"

"Hold the line, please," said the man on the other end. I could hear some discussion going on in the background, and then he came back on the line. "Permission granted."

Amazed that my plan had worked, I thanked him and hung up. I quickly arranged for the charter and organized a crew. We drove hurriedly to Le Bourget, tumbled into a plane, and as its engines were warming up, the pilot radioed the tower for permission to take off.

The tower's response was instantaneous and incredulous:

"*Etes-vous fou? Vous ne pouvez pas partir. Il y a une grève,*" he said, wondering if we were crazy, asking to take off in the middle of an air controllers' strike.

I sank into an instant depression. Apparently, my plan had not worked. No one in the plane said anything for thirty seconds, but then we heard again from the tower.

"*Pardon,*" he said, "*Est-ce que c'est l'avion de Pierre Salinger?*" ("Is this Pierre Salinger's plane?")

"*Oui,*" said the pilot immediately.

"*Il a le droit de partir,*" the voice crackled back over the radio. We had just been cleared for takeoff.

We arrived at the Frankfurt airport minutes before the plane carrying the hostages, and we were able to cover the event. I had managed a major coup for ABC News.

My work on the hostage crisis, which began with that trip to Frankfurt, was the most exciting and important coverage of my entire television career.

I am not very introspective. Perhaps I should be, given the fact that I was raised as a Roman Catholic and spent so much time in Catholic schools, including my last year of college after World War II at the University of San Francisco, a Jesuit school. I think it would be accurate to say that I do not wear my emotions on my sleeve, and I admit that I was once described by my own son Stephen as an "emotional ostrich." I have no real defense to offer, other than to say that were I a more openly emotional person, I might have had an even harder time dealing with the number of deaths that have befallen people who were close to me. Recently, my mother told a friend who suggested the possibility that I seemed to "hold back" emotionally that to do otherwise "doesn't pay."

I used to agree with that attitude, but I have to say that as I grow older, I'm not so sure.

All of this is in preface to the fact in 1977, and at a time when everything in my life—job, marriage, family—seemed to be going splendidly, tragedy struck once again.

It was February 9, 1977, and my wife and I had gone up to Paris from our lovely château in the Loire Valley to attend a performance of Beethoven's Ninth by the Orchestre du Paris and its chorus, with Daniel Barenboim conducting. The orchestra was in glorious "voice" that night, and after the performance, we went backstage to visit Maestro Barenboim, who had invited us.

We got home about eleven, and there was an urgent message for me to call my daughter, Suzanne, no matter what the hour.

Filled with dread, I placed the call.

"Daddy," said Suzanne, who was in Washington, "I have to tell you this straight out. Marc is dead. He committed suicide."

"Oh my God."

"And, Daddy, he jumped off—I'm so very sorry, but I have to tell you this, too—off the Golden Gate Bridge."

It is no coincidence that the Mass card Marc's mother, Renee, and I chose for him, the firstborn of our three children, bears a picture of St. Francis, that gentlest of saints. It carries this prayer, which is attributed to St. Francis:

> Lord, make me an instrument of your peace.
> Where there is hatred . . . let me sow love.
> Where there is injury . . . pardon.
> Where there is doubt . . . faith.
> Where there is despair . . . hope.
> Where there is darkness . . . light.
> Where there is sadness . . . joy.
> O Divine Master, grant that I may not so much seek
> To be consoled . . . as to console,

To be understood . . . as to understand,
To be loved . . . as to love,
                    for
It is in giving . . . that we receive,
It is in pardoning, that we are pardoned,
It is in dying . . . that we are born
    to eternal life.

That was Marc—a giver of faith, hope, light, joy, consolation, and love—when he was healthy. But when he was depressed—and in the last several years of Marc's almost thirty years on earth, his depression was clinical and acute—he was most of the other things—doubt, despair, darkness, and, for certain, sadness.

One of the first calls of condolence, in the middle of the night, was from Ted Kennedy. He knew a lot about what I was going through. He offered to do anything he could to help, but I thanked him and said that "thank God" my family on the West Coast would take care of things until I could get there. After a quick call to TWA, I was off.

On the flight back to the States, I thought long and hard about my oh-so-talented and oh-so-troubled son. It's a shame to rely on a cliché, but it is nonetheless true that like so very many young people his age—children of the sixties, secondary casualties of assassinations and the war in Vietnam (whether they served or not) and darlings of the media for the simple fact of being young—Marc was still trying to find himself. The tragedy was that he got lost in the finding. A talented musician, he was also an excellent writer and a fine poet. But he was *so* hard on himself.

And, to be frank about it, like so many other young people of that time, he had smoked a lot of marijuana, *a lot*. I think that was a factor. In 1975, Marc had what, for lack of a better term, was a nervous breakdown. He had been hospitalized for a time and then lived in a halfway house. I had thought he was getting better, as did the rest of the family. To this day, I don't know if we were all just wrong or if some other event intervened to tip the scale away from recovery.

I had so many memories of Marc. Among the most vivid were two from the White House years. My oldest son idolized JFK, and not from afar. I remember how proud he was the times he caddied for the President (I have a marvelous picture of him doing that). I remember also how upset Jackie and the President were when *Look* magazine published photos of the Kennedy children that had obviously been taken *inside* the grounds of the presidential retreat at Camp David. I was about to scream at the press for a gross violation of the rules when I learned that the culprit was none other than my son Marc, who was then ten years old. Stanley Tretick, that most enterprising and talented of photographers (perhaps most famous for his shot of John-John playing under the desk in the Oval Office while his father, in suit and tie, sat working away at the desk) had given Marc a tiny camera, showed him how to use it, and then how to smuggle it out when he was done snapping candid shots of Caroline and John.

To outlive one's own child is a terrible thing, but to do so because your child has taken his or her own life is horrible. As the plane crossed the Atlantic, I had hours and hours to think about what had just happened—and to try and figure out why. Someone who knew us both very well later observed that Marc was "trying to find his own personality *against* his father, not *along with*." What was *my* responsibility for my son's death, if any? Trying to answer that has been, and remains, a question for the rest of my life.

That airplane flight was the longest of my life.

The letters of consolation that poured in—almost half of them in French—were from the great and the near great, the known and the unknown. Except for just a few, I will not mention names, but I want to quote briefly from the letters of several people who knew him well. They described him accurately, and they may even shed some light on why he did what he did at the end of a life that for so long seemed to hold such great and wonderful promise.

Now married and a mother, a girl Marc had known while growing up in northern Virginia while I worked in the White House wrote:

> . . . I was saddened—deeply—but I must say not shocked at the news, as I suddenly recalled something Marc had told me the night after President Kennedy's assassination—which was that he'd almost driven off Columbia Pike into the Lake Barcroft Dam the day before. I'm afraid something very special went out of Marc's life that day, as indeed it did out of all of our lives—but as Marc had a rather privileged position and truly worshipped the President, I am afraid he never recovered. By the way, I don't know what Marc was doing driving at age fifteen, but as I recall, you were out of town!
>
> I have many good memories of the fun Marc and I and our friends had during our teens—it seemed like we were always dancing or singing or swimming or sailing—I remember

Marc as a Boy Scout asking me to dance at a Boy Scout–Girl Scout dance—I was thrilled, of course—having had a "secret crush" on him, and he was a very good dancer. From that dance to the ones we shared at Lyndon Johnson's Inaugural Ball, Marc was very special to me and to the rest of my family. He used to come over to our house often after school and drink cocoa, and sometimes stayed for supper and to play our piano (my father had a Steinway and enjoyed hearing Marc play on it). Of course you moved to California soon after that and the last time Marc and I got together was when you very kindly conveyed my message to him that my family was vacationing at Disneyland, where Marc came to meet us—bringing me a darling stuffed animal which my baby daughter, Rebecca, was playing with as I began this letter.

My father died suddenly that next winter and Marc immediately wrote me a special delivery letter to express his sympathy and concern. That meant so much to all of us. . . .

I know it sometimes helps to talk, and I'd be happy to talk with you anytime about Marc. He was a very big part of my life. . . . I think it took a great deal of courage for Marc to act as he did, and I'm sure he is now enjoying a well-deserved and peaceful afterlife. I like to think of him and my father taking turns playing the piano for each other in their heaven.

If there was a theme running through the messages, it was that somehow we had to find something positive in what had happened. One man with whom I'd served in the U.S. Senate included this Biblical verse: "We are afflicted in every way, but not crushed; perplexed, but not driven to despair; persecuted, but not forsaken; struck down, but not destroyed." He hoped I'd find some solace in that verse. I tried.

A woman who'd been new to politics when she met a young Marc Salinger wrote, on February 10, the day the news reached the media: "Many years ago, in my first job, I spent a few months in Atlantic City working for the Dem. National Committee at the convention. Mark [*sic*] was about 16 and he slept on our floor for the duration of the convention. Last night I looked through some old photographs and found a picture of us in the midst of the convention activity—it appeared in the New York Times. After [a friend's] accident Mark sent me a lovely note—something I'll always remember. I'll cherish the meaning of that warm and compassionate young boy."

Another letter was from a young woman Marc had been closer to than any other. I found her letter a great kindness. She wrote:

Dear Pierre,

I am writing to you for a few reasons. One is to say how sorry I am for what has happened. It is something that is difficult to grasp, and more painful and difficult to accept and to live with. I loved your son, and his love and warmth and intelligence and care have changed my life. No one has ever loved me or given to me as Marc did. The time I spent with Marc was the most enriching, growth-promoting period of my life. I believe what happened is that Marc experienced another breakdown, loaded with delusions and distortions which led him to his death. It all makes one feel so angry and so helpless that such things can have such effects.

I want to share with you the positive feelings Marc expressed towards you. He loved you very deeply and spoke of you with the greatest warmth and pride. He conveyed a great family sense, love, and enthusiasm.

He was a beautiful man, and I am so thankful for his having touched my life. I will live always with his memory and with the transformations that came from his presence and his love.

> *My fondest feelings and*
> *deepest sympathy . . .*

Three people with the same last name who were all too well acquainted with death also took time to write. John F. Kennedy's mother, Rose, sent a beautiful note:

Dear Pierre,

I have just read of the passing of your beloved son and I want to send you my fervent prayers, my heartfelt sympathy and deep affection.

We must be resigned to the fact that we shall never be able to understand the ways of Almighty God—the crosses which He sends us, the sacrifices which He demands of us. We must have faith in His plans for our salvation and for the salvation of our loved ones, and we leave our lives here and our future to His inscrutable Providence.

I shall pray for you, dear Pierre, that God may bring you solace and peace.

Ethel Kennedy sent a handwritten letter:

Dear Pierre,

All my love and thought and prayers are with you and Nicole, Stephen and Suzanne, and, most especially, for Marc.

The depth of your loss is, of course, immeasurable—and would be unbearable if it weren't for the tremendous consolation that comes with the certain knowledge that the same Gracious God who gave Marc the gift of life can also give him new life—Life that will now be everlasting and full of love and joy.

You know that Jack and Bobby were there to welcome him into the unspeakable and inconceivable joys of Paradise. . . .

A touching letter that came from another Kennedy was also handwritten. On a single sheet of U.S. Senate stationery, it read, in its entirety: "Dear Pierre, Life is precious yet it is so very tenuous. We all try to be strong but we are but frail and vulnerable. Sometimes a parent's love is not enough. Yet it is all we can give. Marc is beyond pain and suffering now. I am so very sorry Pierre. Ted."

Marc and I exchanged many letters over the years, and his were a delight to receive. They were warm and witty, and often affectionately irreverent. As an adult, he was an excellent correspondent, yet I find that when I want to think about him, to remember him, I go back to a much earlier letter. In a fine cursive hand, for a nine-year-old, it says:

Dear Daddy,

Friday afternoon I went to the Symphony. I heard Overture, leonore No, 1 by Beethoven and Mother Goose by Ravel and Concerto for Percussion and small Orchestra by Milhaud Mr Kohloff played the Percussion.
I heard Symphony no. 1 in c minor by Brhams.
Yesterday Jerry taught me how to play golf.

love Marc
X X X X X X X X X X X X X X X X X X X X X X X X

Life, of course, went on. I continued to work for ABC. In fact, I shocked my wife by attending a long-planned business luncheon meeting on the same day I returned from Marc's funeral. It was the only way I could go on. Perhaps I did not know how to do otherwise.

The weekend after my Frankfurt coup, I returned to Paris. On December 1, I was sitting at home when I received a phone call from a French lawyer whom I had never met. He said his name was François Cheron and that he had important things to talk to me about regarding the hostage crisis. I told him to come to the house the next morning.

Cheron arrived around 11:00 A.M., and words began to tumble out of him. He started by telling me he was with a law firm in Paris that had represented three key Iranians when they lived in Paris: Abolhassan Bani-Sadr, who had become president of Iran when the Khomeini regime took over almost a year before; Sadegh Ghotbzadeh, who was now the foreign minister; and the Ayatollah Khomeini, who had come to Paris in 1978.

Cheron said his principal partner was Christian Bourget, who had high contacts in Iran. Cheron said he had been in Rome nine days earlier and had had dinner with an old friend, an Italian lawyer named Dario Piga. Piga had told Bourget that an old friend of his, Giulio Andreotti, at that time a former Italian prime minister (some years later, he was back in that job), had been asked by the U.S. government if he knew any responsible people who had contacts with the new revolutionary government of Iran.

Piga, knowing Cheron's contacts, had asked him whether he was willing to meet with Andreotti.

Cheron told me he flew back to Paris to consult with his partners and then called Piga to say he was ready to talk to Andreotti. An hour later, Andreotti called Cheron and asked him if he would be willing to contact the Iranian government on behalf of the United States. After the call, Cheron said, they had contacted Bani-Sadr and Ghotbzadeh and had had a very positive response that they were ready to talk to the Americans through lawyers they knew well and trusted.

Over the next twenty-four hours, he told me, he contacted Andreotti and told him the Iranians were ready to talk. He was invited to dinner in Rome, but when he arrived, he was stunned by what Andreotti told him. "I'm sorry I bothered you and had you come down here, because I've gotten a call from the American embassy thanking me for my services and informing me they are no longer needed."

Cheron said that put him in a difficult situation. "I alerted Bani-Sadr and Ghotbzadeh that the Americans want to have contact with them, and now I have no contact. But I have Bani-Sadr and Ghotbzadeh, who have things they want to say to the Americans. What do I do? I need to make contact with the Americans. That's what I want you to do."

Making contacts with governments is not a journalistic responsibility, but I was impressed with the contacts Cheron had with Iran, and of course I was concerned about the hostages. I decided it was important for me to intervene.

"Where will you be in an hour?" I asked.

"I'm going directly home," he answered.

"Okay, stay there. In one hour, you'll get a phone call."

As soon as Cheron left, I called Arthur Hartman, the U.S. ambassador to France, a man I knew well and greatly admired.

I told him of my meeting with Cheron: "It sounds to me like these people could be an extremely valuable contact to the American government in dealing with the Iranians. It's unfortunate that this channel has been dropped, and I think we should pick it up immediately. There ought to be some reaction from the American government today, so that these men know that they are back on the track." Hartman said he would look into the matter immediately.

Before long, I received a call from Warren Zimmerman, the political counselor at the American embassy. "How do I contact Cheron?" he asked.

At seven o'clock that evening, Cheron called me. "You've done it. I've had a two-and-a-half-hour meeting with Zimmerman, and I've already given him some of the thoughts of Bani-Sadr and Ghotbzadeh."

The back-channel negotiations were under way.

Before Cheron hung up, I asked him whether he and his partners would keep me briefed on what was going on. I told him that I would not broadcast the information until after the hostages were freed. He agreed immediately and then set up a meeting the next day with his partner, Christian Bourget.

This led me into more than a year of following closely what was going on behind the scenes. When I'd told Roone Arledge I'd established these contacts, I'd said I thought I should stay on the story even if we didn't broadcast the information. I pointed out that putting out this information might endanger the hostages or halt the possibility of their release. Roone agreed, and we kept the entire operation covert.

I also discovered that an important Egyptian, the former assistant to President Nasser, Mohammed Heikal, was involved in back-channel talks with the Iranians for the United States. Also of importance was the work of Hector Villalon. I flew to Cairo to interview Heikal, and that night I had a dinner with some top Egyptian officials. They told me that President Sadat, who had made a deal with the Israelis, was highly popular around the world but was extremely hated in his own country and would not survive very long. That was in November 1980. I sent a memo to Roone Arledge that said, "Get ABC on the alert. Sadat is going to lose power in 1981." My prediction turned out to be accurate—he was assassinated just months later.

On January 20, 1981, within minutes of the inauguration of Ronald Reagan, the hostages were released. Two days later, using the information I'd been gathering and saving for all those many months, we went on the air with a three-hour documentary that went behind the scenes of the hostage situation.

It was a critical and a dramatic success. Many newspaper people observed (in print) that it was the first time a television network had scooped the country's leading newspapers. The show, which I'd entitled "America Held Hostage," was so successful that Roone Arledge had us upgrade it for a second performance a week later.

As proud as I was, and am, of that program, I will always remember it with a lingering sense of frustration. "America Held Hostage" won 24 Emmys for ABC News, but despite the fact I'd anchored the show and done all the reporting, someone forgot to include my name on the list of people responsible for the show, and I was therefore ineligible. I have won three Emmys since then, of which I am also very proud, but each time I was fortunate enough to get one, it reminded me that I did not win one for the best show I ever did.

CHAPTER
SIXTEEN

"EACH MAN HAS two fatherlands—his country and France." So wrote Thomas Jefferson, third President of the United States and our second ambassador to France. In my case, that statement happens to be the literal truth, though perhaps I should amend it to read two motherlands, because it is the native land of my mother, not my father.

My first two visits to the country that has played such an important role in my life were separated by thirty-six years. The first, as I wrote earlier, was made when I was but six months old; my mother had returned to France to get her own mother and bring her back to the United States to live with us, and as I hardly weighed more than a small piece of luggage, I was taken along. While I've no memory of that initial trip, I have always enjoyed knowing that I encountered my second father-motherland at so tender an age.

The next time I saw Paris, or any other part of France, I was the press secretary to the President of the United States. On that April 1961 trip, there was, of course, a whole cadre of us. I was part of an advance team that was setting up JFK's first foreign trip and his meeting with Charles de Gaulle. When it came time for my first press conference, I had an ace up my sleeve:

"*Bonsoir, messieurs et madames. Comme vous le savais, le Président Kennedy vas rencontrer avec le Président de Gaulle.*" To the amazement of the French press, I conducted the entire conference in their native language. Having grown up in a household where French was spoken as often as English—and sometimes more often; my grandmother steadfastly refused to learn to speak English—I had no trouble doing so. It was grand fun to watch the initial reactions of my interrogators.

My third trip was a month later, when JFK had his actual meeting with De Gaulle. (Kennedy won thunderous applause at the end of the trip when he said, "I am the man who accompanied Jacqueline Kennedy to Paris." Well, I was the man who accompanied him!) Very quickly, I fell in love not just with Paris but with every part of the country I saw, and that same summer, 1961, when I was able to get a few days of vacation time, I headed straight back to France.

I visited Feche l'Eglise, the small village in the east where both my mother and my grandfather had been born. Walking around the village, I struck up a conversation with an elderly gentleman who had actually known my grandfather, Pierre Bietry. He insisted on putting together a party for me that very night. It was a great party and a marvelous welcome "home."

On those trips, and the few I made in the next five years, I began to get a certain feel for France. First of all, it was quickly apparent that *culture* means something very different in France than it does in the United States. What's more, it was equally apparent that the citizens of each country had little understanding of one another's worlds other than a few superficialities. This was true despite the fact that we shared several centuries of friendship and a considerable amount of history, beginning in our Colonial days and continuing through two world wars and right up to the present day. It seemed to me even then that perhaps there was a role for me to play in helping these great, longtime friends get to know and understand one another better. In a sense, it might even be a role I was born to play. For that reason, among many others, each time I went to France in the almost five years between the two Kennedy assassinations, I found the country increasingly *sympathique*.

In 1968, Bobby's death left me about as sad and soul-weary as I'd ever been, so I decided I had to leave the United States. There was no debate as to where I'd go—it was always Paris.

In addition to my strong and growing love for the country, my then wife was a French citizen, a fact that would further facilitate our daily lives there. Nonetheless, many friends warned me that I would regret the move. They claimed it would be impossible for an American "to penetrate French cultural society."

When I asked what they meant by that, they said, "Tourists from

France are regularly invited into American homes, but the reverse is not true. The French never invite American tourists into their homes. This isn't to say that the French hate Americans, just that it isn't done."

Well, I thought, we'll have to see about that. For one thing, I would not exactly be going as a tourist, for I planned to stay at least two years. Plus, neither my wife nor I would have a language barrier to worry about.

Rarely was a prediction as far off the mark as that of my American friends. From the moment I arrived in Paris, I was welcomed with open arms. I knew the French had admired the late Kennedys, but I hadn't realized it went so far beyond just admiration. As a man who had been close to both slain Kennedys, I became, from the moment I landed on French soil, the channel into which they could release their pent-up love for John and Bobby Kennedy. I'd never seen anything like it, nor have I since. Suddenly, without any period of adjustment, I was being sought out by people from all walks of French life and society—politicians, journalists, artists, actors, even restaurant chefs and, to my great delight, producers of wine!

I thought I'd stay in France for two years; I ended up staying twenty-five.

In the process, I became the best-known American in France. I'm sorry if that sounds immodest, but it happens to be true (though it has a lot more to do with my association with the Kennedys than with my own accomplishments).

After I'd been in Paris for a few years, I began to be what I, in my own days as a journalist, would have called good copy. There was a steady stream of interviews. By December 1975, one paper had said, "The best-known American living in France is no ambassador or film star but a bulky cigar-chomping journalist. Pierre Salinger has become 'Mr. America' in France." Later that same year, the *Los Angeles Times*, interviewing me at the Cannes Film Festival, was highly complimentary in an article entitled, "Columnist Pierre Salinger: Our Man in Paris."

Interest in this transplanted American continued at a fairly steady pace. In 1976, when I went to work for ABC doing color commentary at the Innsbruck Games, the *Philadelphia Bulletin* sent a reporter over to interview me.

She wrote, "To those Americans sitting at home in the dreary month of February, wishing they could take a nice trip somewhere, Salinger is their man. He is taking them on a trip, and they don't have to go through customs."

She also wrote something that caused me a little ribbing from friends back home: "He and his wife and son live in an apartment in Paris, on the

Rue de Rivoli, overlooking the Louvre, and they have a house in the country, near Tours, 130 miles outside of Paris, an early 18th century manor house on 27 acres.

" 'How could I have a better life?' said Salinger. 'Three or four days a week, I go home for lunch, and have a nap before I come back to work. Weekends we go to the country and I read and write and walk and nourish my soul.' " Well, it was true.

As much as I appreciated that very flattering article (which was entitled "Innsbruck Means Another Fun Job in the Lucky Life of Lucky Pierre"), it appeared in only one paper. The next year, my reputation was wonderfully enhanced by the wide dissemination given an article written by John Florescu, a young reporter with the Associated Press. It was a great help to me, in that it told many, many readers where I was and what I was doing.

John Florescu told me recently that my giving him the interview turned out to be a big help to *his* career with the AP. "It got me tenure," he said. Apparently, he didn't need it, for he left AP. Today, Florescu is co-executive producer of "Talking with David Frost," as well as Sir David's main man in America.

One of the most startling facts of my life in Paris was that I was recognized on the street far more often there than I was in the United States, a very strange feeling for an American. I did not kid myself that they were treating me as some sort of celebrity because I was writing a column for *L'Express* or giving lectures or appearing on television, though those were positive accomplishments in their own right. People were making a fuss over me because of their strong feelings for John and Robert Kennedy, not to mention Jackie, Rose, Ethel, and all the rest. My calling card was my association with the Kennedys, for the French loved the Kennedys. I knew that my "rise," for lack of a better word, in France was a kind of accident.

Nonetheless, I had a living to make—and an ego of my own to feed—not to mention a few things I wanted to forget. As a result, I threw myself into my work, and because an increasing amount of it was done on television, I became even more well known and more often recognized in public by perfect strangers.

I wrote and spoke about politics a great deal. When Richard Nixon became inextricably enmeshed in Watergate the French hungered for someone to explain it to them. I was their man. They simply could not believe that Nixon, a man they admired for his toughness and his foreign-policy accomplishments, could be brought down by something as unimportant as covering up a politically inspired "third-rate burglary." I'm not sure I ever got the French (and other Europeans) to see that the

American people simply will not countenance being lied to by their own President.

I found it interesting that although I went back to the United States quite frequently, every few months at least, living away gave me some perspective. Despite the horror of the two Kennedy deaths, I began to become somewhat optimistic about my native land, because I came to see that for us the tough part was over. I felt that the period from November 1963 to August 1974 (the death of JFK to the resignation of Richard Nixon) marked a great turning point in American life. It was a period of national cleansing. Also, I felt that when we finally ended our tragic involvement in Vietnam, all sorts of relationships, both at home and abroad, could and would only improve.

In general, I rarely looked back at my old life in American politics with any longing. But in 1976, when Jimmy Carter's election brought a Democrat back to the White House for the first time in eight years, I thought I spotted a chance to grab hold of a lifelong dream. I thought it was a good idea, but as it turned out, it was good old-fashioned hubris going before a fall.

Realizing that I'd never completely recovered from the fact that President Kennedy's death meant he would not be able to keep his promise to name me the U.S. ambassador to France during his second term, I contacted Mr. Carter and applied for the job. Oh, it wasn't just my idea; a number of people high up in (or close to) his administration had urged me to do so, or suggested my name, or both.

In any event, I wrote to the President-elect and spelled out what I thought were my impeccable credentials. Then I sat back and waited . . . and waited . . . and waited. But nothing came—no phone call, no letter, and definitely no appointment. I licked my self-inflicted wounds and "turned another page."

While I saw (and interviewed) Jimmy Carter many times in the next few years, and have many times since, I never spoke to him about this matter. Finally, a year ago in St. Petersburg, when we were both part of the same conference, I screwed up my courage and, mentioning my letter, asked why he'd never responded to it.

"What letter?" said the former President. "I never got any letter from you. Why, if I had, I surely would have named you ambassador to France!"

Of course, when Bill Clinton was elected, I went for the third strike. But he had already made an important choice in Pamela Harriman. Thus ended my final hope that I could cap my career by returning to public service and playing an important role in the relationship between the land of my birth and that of my mother, the land that's been America's great friend for as long as there has been a United States of America.

* * *

All of this is not to say that I became less American and more French, or that I blindly approved of anything and everything French. One thing I thoroughly *disapproved* of was the way Parisians drove! I could never understand why they drove so fast and so recklessly. I had a car myself, however, and I was determined to drive it, so I abandoned my years of safe driving and became as much of a madman behind the wheel as your average Parisian.

Soon I was flying around corners, blasting down boulevards, honking my horn (with its odd squeak) and gesticulating with one finger when someone cut me off or beat me to a parking space. The only real difference between me and the native-born drivers was that in my case, driving that way was simply a survival tactic. With them, it was a way of life.

Another difference, though not an unpleasant one, was the attitude toward work and toward one's employer. I had always been used to a relatively long workday, even after leaving the White House (where the hours were simply ridiculous). Thus, I was quite surprised to see French businessmen taking two- to three-hour lunches—after which, some of them would then go to see their mistresses for an hour or two before returning to the office!

Much of the work I did for ABC was heavy-duty reporting of international crises, especially later in my time with the network. But earlier, I had a lot of fun doing feature pieces and interviews. The best part of these assignments was that they always added something to my knowledge and understanding of France and her people.

Undoubtedly, the most fun was *Dining in France,* a series of television programs that featured the nation's leading chefs and their specialties. The half-hour shows, which were shown in both France and the United States, were not, however, cooking shows. People didn't tune in to learn how to prepare a specific dish; rather, they saw and heard extremely knowledgeable people talk charmingly about their passion for eating and drinking well, which just happened to involve the glorious food and wine culture of France. (The show was very popular; the U.S. version was rebroadcast eight times.)

One of my favorite shows was entitled simply "Bread and Cheese," and I took the viewers through bakeries in and around Paris and to farms outside the city where the farmers made cheese in exactly the same way it had been made for centuries. (In the introduction to that show, I mentioned, "De Gaulle once said, 'How can you govern a country with three hundred and sixty-five different cheeses?' but Churchill turned it around on him by saying, 'How can a country with three hundred and sixty-five different cheeses ever fail?' ")

Another lovely episode was called "Markets and Products." Anyone who has been to Paris and walked around the glorious open markets with their cornucopialike offerings of the freshest in vegetables and fruits can never forget the marvelous sights, sounds, and, of course, aromas. On this show, we also visited the giant market at Rungis, which supplies all the others, and which any Parisian chef worth his sauce visits each working day before the sun is up. If he doesn't, his restaurant will suffer. At Rungis, they also sell meat, poultry, fish—you name it, they have it—and they throw nothing away. At Rungis, the customer sees not only bins of tripe and sweetbreads but also barrels of eyes and hooves. Looking down from the top of the racks are row upon row of the now-eyeless skulls. A trip through Rungis is not for the faint of stomach.

Another of my favorite shows took me—and Poppy, who had entered my life by that point—to Alsace, one of the loveliest regions in all of France and the home of my absolute favorite restaurant, Auberge de l'Ill, named after the picturesque river that flows through the town. Jean Pierre Haeberlin is the general manager, and his brother Paul and Paul's son Marc are the chefs. Auberge de l'Ill was awarded its third Michelin star over twenty years ago. Alsace is also the home of my favorite vineyard, the house of Hugel. The families who run the restaurant and the winery have been friends for generations.

After our lunch at Auberge de l'Ill—a huge steak cooked in butter in an open pan for twenty to twenty-five minutes and served with a bone-marrow sauce—we were joined by the Gerards, a father-and-son team who sell some of the best Cuban cigars in the world. As we had just finished the dessert course, their timing was perfect.

The son was carrying two large bundles of giant cigars, at least double coronas, which he said were over five years old. He fired mine up with what appeared to be a miniature blowtorch (obviously, lighting a cigar of this magnitude is no job for a mere match). As he performed this ritualistic task, he waxed almost poetic about his product.

"A cigar is all philosophy. Why? Because it allows you to appreciate the meal you've just had. As you smoke it, the cigar taste forms on your palate and takes over. It's not like smoking a cigarette. That's a *nervous* gesture that has nothing to do with the philosophy of a cigar."

The atmosphere soon became wonderfully mellow, and I decided to share with the group one of my favorite cigar stories of all time, and one which I had decided against putting in my book *With Kennedy*. (This is the first time I've told this story in print.)

"It was in 1961, after the Bay of Pigs," I began, "and I was working for President Kennedy. He called me one night and said, 'I need a lot of cigars.' I said, 'How many, Mr. President?' and he said, 'About a thousand.' At that time, he smoked a cigar called a Petit Upman.

" 'Tomorrow morning,' he said. 'Call all your friends who have cigars and just get me as many as you can.'

"The next morning when I got to the office at eight o'clock, my phone was already ringing. It was JFK, and he said, 'I've got to see you right away.' I ran into his office, and he said, 'How did you do on the cigars last night?'

" 'Mr. President,' I said, 'I was very successful. I got eleven hundred.'

"He smiled, and then he opened his desk and pulled out a decree banning all Cuban products from the United States.

" 'Good!' he said. 'Now that I have enough cigars to last for a while, I can sign this!' "

Before leaving Alsace, we paid a visit to the Hugel vineyards. Jean Hugel greeted us at the door of his castellated office-showroom; he was holding a bottle of wine from 1865. "Since this bottle was produced—before the Franco-Prussian War—there have been four generations of Haeberlins and four generations of Hugels."

When Mr. Hugel talked about his vines, he was at least as poetic as Gerard *fils* had been in talking about his cigars.

"We are always thankful when nature gives us a great vintage, but the vine is a Mediterranean weed which grows, and should grow, where nothing else grows. The vine wants to suffer, and so we help it to suffer." (Later, on the show, we would use his words over pictures of his workers, all middle-aged Alsatian women, bending and tying the vines so that they were not free to grow "as they wished.")

"As all good wine growers know," he continued in his charmingly accented English, "you should not make life too easy for the vine. A vine which suffers has a chance to give you something great—like an artist or a painter or a musician. When they suffered, and had a difficult life, they became great artists. So it is for vines, and wines."

I showed Jean Hugel again at the end of the episode. He stood on a hillside, overlooking the beautiful rolling countryside where his family had lived for centuries, despite the many wars that have been fought in the region.

"We have our roots here in the soil of Alsace. The Haeberlins, the Hugels—we all love where we live. You would think, having all these problems, we would like to go somewhere else. But"—he smiled—"we are a bit stupid here. We do the same thing for three hundred and fifty years, and the Haeberlins have cooked for over a hundred years. And we are always happy when a new generation is able to take over and continue the same business with the same enthusiasm as we do it."

Smiling a broad Gallic smile, he concluded, "That's our life. We are *born* here and we will *die* here." From the look on his face, you could tell that was just fine with him.

My work for ABC also took me to beautiful places to talk with beautiful people. One of my subjects was Grace Kelly, the Hollywood movie star who married Prince Rainier of Monaco. When I scheduled the interview, however, I had no idea one part of it would turn out to be prophetic.

The princess quickly lived up to her advance billing as one of the most intelligent, as well as most beautiful, women in Hollywood. We had a solid interview, with some interesting comments from her about the media, especially those she charmingly referred to as the "intrusive media." Eventually, I got a signal from my cameraman that we were about out of tape, and with that, a question popped into my mind. It seemed a good way to tie the interview together.

"I know it's much too early in your life to ask you this question, but I'm sure at some point somebody's going to ask it. How would you like to be remembered?"

Smiling her lovely smile, Grace Kelly said, "Oh, I suppose I think mostly in terms of my children and their children—how they will remember me. I would like to be remembered as trying to do my job well, as being understanding and kind."

"Are there any things about your career," I asked, "that you'd like to have remembered? They'll be remembered, anyway."

"Well, I don't know," she said, "I don't feel as though I achieved enough in my career to stand out more than many other people. I was very lucky in my career, and I loved it, but I don't think I was accomplished enough as an actor to be remembered for that particularly.

"No, I'd like to be remembered as a decent human being, and a caring one."

I had one more question. "If you had another life, what would you like to do with that life? Have you ever thought of that?"

The smile got even bigger. "Oh, there are lots of things." She laughed and shook her hair. "If I have to be reincarnated, I think I'd like to come back as one of my dogs. They have a very happy, nice life, and an easy one."

Prince Rainier, Grace Kelly's husband, is fond of classic autombiles and has quite a collection. One day a few weeks after our interview, she was driving a fine old Mercedes-Benz around one of Monaco's many curving mountain roads when something went wrong with the car and Princess Grace plunged to her death.

Our interview had been her last.

* * *

One of the biggest surprises in my professional life came in France in 1972 when I was invited to be a member of the jury of the prestigious Cannes Film Festival.

My entire "film experience" consisted of one attempt to produce a movie version of an opera and one acting job in a film. The former was the aforementioned, stillborn *Boris Godunov,* and the latter was my role as the American consul at the U.S. embassy in Paris in *The Marseille Contract,* an action film that starred Anthony Quinn, James Mason, and Michael Caine. (With the single exception of an episode of the television show *Batman,* in which I played a lawyer named Lucky Pierre, there has been no further demand for my acting services.)

I was excited by the invitation to join the Cannes jury for several reasons, not the least of which was that I was a great admirer of Jeanne Moreau, the brilliant French actress who was jury chairman. I had another surprise in store for me. The people who run the festival pick the chairman and the jury members, all of whom then get together and choose a vice-chairman—who turned out to be me!

I was stunned by my selection but managed to catch my breath and begin the work, which turned out to be fascinating. We saw two movies a day for almost two weeks and then gathered together to pick the big winner. We chose an Algerian film that went into an immediate decline and was never seen outside of France. The organizers of the Cannes Festival were not just upset with us over this choice; they were downright angry.

I thought I'd never be asked to judge a film again, but not long after that, I was asked to be one of a group of advisers who were to plan the creation of the Deauville Film Festival, which now takes place annually in Normandy during the first weeks of September. As the Deauville features only American films, it came under heavy attack by Jack Lang, whom Mitterand named as his minister of culture after François's election as president in 1981. Lang's beef was that France was hosting an American film festival, but the United States was not reciprocating. But that problem abated soon after Ruda Dauphin, an important person associated with the Deauville Film Festival, created an annual French film festival in Sarasota, Florida.

While it amounted to only a minuscule percentage of my life's work, I have to say that I thoroughly enjoyed all of my film-related efforts. (And, just like a real actor, I'm still hoping that the phone will ring again.)

A decade later I got to serve on another prestigious jury, this time a literary panel.

"When I dream of afterlife in Heaven," the famous American writer

Ernest Hemingway once wrote, "the action always takes place in the Paris Ritz." Indeed, the Ritz Hotel played a big part in Hemingway's life and in his work. In fact, he claimed to have liberated it personally when the Allies retook Paris in 1944; if he wasn't actually the first to step into the foyer of this magnificent edifice on that grand occasion, he certainly was with the initial group of American troops to do so.

Hemingway's love for the Ritz was one of the first things that popped into my mind in 1984 when Mohammed Al-Fayed, who had bought the hotel several years earlier, asked me for a suggestion on how to memorialize *and* publicize his hotel. "Why not give a prize for the best novel of the year? Call it the Hemingway Ritz Prize, or the Ritz-Hemingway Prize. And, if you can, make it a *big* prize.

Al-Fayed loved the idea. And he knew just the man to go to for the *big* part, his friend the Sultan of Brunei, His Majesty Sir Muda Hassanal Bolkiah, who promptly put up enough money to fund the new organization and its annual prize of $50,000.

"You," said the sultan, looking at me, "will be the president of the jury."

We quickly assembled an excellent jury. Among its members were the poet and novelist James Dickey, writers William Styron and Lady Antonia Fraser, and the excellent Peruvian novelist Mario Vargas Llosa. Just before our first meeting broke up, I had a thought: "We've got some very good writers on this jury. Perhaps we should say that if a panel member is nominated, he or she would step down from the jury." Everyone thought that was a good idea, and my suggestion was adopted.

On December 21, 1984, we sent letters to more than five hundred critics, writers, scholars, reviewers, and others, announcing the "Ritz Paris Hemingway Award," and asking them to nominate three books for best novel of the year. Six weeks later, the nominations having flooded in for what was an extremely generous prize for a work of fiction, our international literary consultants met in Boston and chose three finalists. One was *The Unbearable Lightness of Being*, by Milan Kundera, another Yevgeny Yevtushenko's *Wild Berries*, and—*The War of the End of the World* by Mario Vargas Llosa, who promptly quit the jury.

On March 28, the jury, having carefully read the three final selections, met in Paris and made its choice. The winner was *The War of the End of the World*, by Vargas Llosa, the great Peruvian novelist (and former jury member).

The next night we threw a monster bash in the ballroom of the Ritz to announce the award, which was presented in stages by a number of different people. I gave him the $50,000 check, flanked by a number of Hemingways, including granddaughters Margaux and Mariel, but his eyes truly lit up when he saw that the golden quill, the symbol of the award, was to be presented by the stunning French actress Catherine Deneuve. Stunning was a good word to describe the whole event.

Indeed, Llosa stunned all of us, and the world, a week later when he gave his entire award to the orphans of Peru's guerrilla warfare zones. "By doing this," he said, "I want to make public my solidarity with the innocent victims of the homicidal violence and pay homage to those who quietly and nobly work to alleviate the pain of Peru's disinherited."

We gave the award for a couple of years after that, until (I suspect) the sultan found a different use for the money. We made several other writers very happy, but no one looked as happy as did Mario Vargas Llosa on the night of March 29, 1985, because, at that moment, he alone knew the very special use to which he would put his prize money.

When American Presidents and other world leaders came to Europe during my Paris (and later my London) years, I covered them. And when world leaders fell ill and seemed close to death, I covered that, too.

At about the same time as the hostage crisis in Iran, Marshal Tito, the Communist leader of Yugoslavia for so many years, lay dying. ABC sent me to his country on what became a deathwatch. I was in and out of Yugoslavia for four months while he hung on. As these were still the days of communism's stranglehold on Eastern Europe, visitors from the West, and especially those from the United States, were constantly under the surveillance of intelligence agencies. Nonetheless, I didn't have the feeling that Big Brother was watching me. I was wrong.

The week before Tito died, I got a call from ABC Radio. They wanted me to do a ten-minute analysis of the consequences of Tito's impending death. They said they would hold whatever I came up with until his actual passing.

I studied the country as thoroughly as time would permit and then wrote and taped the piece. New York wanted it right away, so I went down to the desk at the Intercontinental Hotel and asked them to photocopy the text for me, which they did while I waited.

At seven the next morning, I was awakened by a phone call from a woman who said she was with the Ministry of Information.

"What are you doing today, Mr. Salinger?" she asked.

"The only thing on my schedule is the noon press briefing on Comrade Tito's health."

"Very good," she said. "I will send a car for you at nine this morning. The acting president wants to see you."

I did as I was told, and soon I found myself in the middle of a heated discussion that lasted for two hours. Obviously, the acting president had been given a copy of what the hotel staff had photocopied. And he had not liked what he'd read.

I had written that following Tito's death, the government he had organized would not function well at all. In fact, I predicted that the yearly change in the presidency, which was mandated by Tito's plan, would result in near chaos, that the country would be split apart and there would be ethnic violence.

The acting president disagreed wholly—and vocally—with my analysis. He said his country would be stable.

As things turned out—though it took a decade for it all to happen—he was wrong and I was right. In 1991, the whole country exploded, and the result was disaster.

While living in France, I also got back to the writing of books. The first (since *With Kennedy*), which was quite easy, was *Je Suis un Americain.* That was the result of a long interview with my friend Philippe Labro, a fine journalist who now runs one of the most important radio stations in Paris. Unfortunately for the vast majority of my American friends, that book was printed in French and never translated into English.

The second book grew out of my work in 1976 commemorating the American Bicentennial, the two hundredth anniversary of U.S. independence. France Inter, a radio station, asked me to do a daily fifteen-minute broadcast—to run from February 16 to May 14—on the four-hundred-year link between France and North America. A true labor of love, my research for the series produced a thick pile of scripts that began to resemble a manuscript. The result: *La France et le Nouveau Monde,* or, *France and the New World.* It began with the same quote from Thomas Jefferson with which I began this chapter, that each man has two father-lands.

I must have taken this Jeffersonian declaration to heart, because my book won a prize given by the French government for the best book written in French on the two hundredth anniversary of American independence.

Yet another book came about, but only after a high degree of difficulty. That it appeared at all is an object lesson in the importance of contacts. In late November 1983, I went to the University of San Francisco, from which I'd graduated, to spend a week with students and to tell them about the career of President Kennedy. It was a very positive way to commemorate a very negative event.

I had come over alone and was staying in a nice hotel. Each night, upon my return, there would be a slew of messages from a man named Bob Cameron. As I knew no one by that name, I did not return the calls until later in the week. We set up a time to meet at my hotel. When Mr. Cameron arrived, he was loaded down with books, all of them his, and all of them similar. Among their titles were *Above San Francisco, Above Washington,* and *Above London.* They were combinations of text and superb aerial photos that had been taken from a helicopter by Cameron, who had worked as a civilian photographer for the War Department during World War II.

"Mr. Salinger," he said, wasting no time getting to the point, "I want your help in setting up *Above Paris.*"

"Oh," I said, "that would be quite a difficult undertaking. Paris bars all helicopter flights except for the police and the military. But I suppose I could try to get permission for you."

Six weeks later, I was able to get a meeting with the *préfet de Paris,* the municipal official who had the power to grant helicopter overflights. I had brought along copies of Bob Cameron's other books, all of which are magnificent, and I could see the *préfet* was impressed and was probably already visualizing, just as I had on first leafing through these grand volumes, how his unique city would look from above.

Finally, he shook his head. I had told Cameron that getting permission would be difficult; the word the *préfet* used was *complicated.* But he did not say no.

Months passed with no word. In April, Cameron came over to Paris, eager to press his suit. He started to take aerial photos *outside* of Paris, especially areas where there were spectacular châteaux like Versailles.

At the beginning of May, we finally heard from the *préfet.* "You may fly a helicopter over Paris for one hour."

"At what height?"

"You may go no lower than six hundred meters."

Cameron was extremely disappointed. To get the marvelous shots of the other cities in his series, he'd routinely gone as low as two hundred meters.

"It's impossible," he said, thoroughly dejected. "That's the end of the book."

I convinced him to use the hour, rather than to give it up. He agreed to do so, but then it rained for almost ten straight days. Finally, festooned with cameras and lenses, he went up for one hour, took forty pictures, and came down.

Again he said that was the end of the book.

A few days later, he showed me the developed shots.

I said, "Put these together in a layout similar to what you have in mind for the finished book and get it back to me. I'm having lunch on June third with someone who might be able to help."

"Who is it?" Cameron asked.

"No point in telling you who it is," I said. "Let's just say he's an important man."

The *faux* book arrived on June 2, and several days later I took it along with me my lunch, which was wonderful. After lunch, we retired to a sitting room for cognac and a cigar.

My companion glanced toward the table where I had strategically placed the book.

"What's that?" he said, neatly taking the bait.

"Have a look."

He did, and moments later proclaimed, "This is wonderful!"

"Yes it is," I said, "but we can't get the rights to do it the way it should really be done."

My luncheon companion pushed a button. Seconds later, an aide came in and said, "Yes, Mr. President?"

Showing the model to the aide, François Mitterand said, "Arrange for them to do all the flying they want to do over Paris so they can put out this book."

Above Paris, by Robert Cameron and Pierre Salinger (I wrote the text), came out in 1985, and it sold over 400,000 copies.

President Mitterand, who years earlier had been a guest in my home in Los Angeles, was later attacked for allowing American, rather than French, photographers to do this important book. In true French fashion, he disdained to answer their complaints.

Some years later, in another volume, Cameron recalled, "There were many frustrating days in Paris, but finally, I made some of the best photographs I ever have, and, in my prints, I got the beautiful soft French light Monet and other Impressionists celebrated."

Throughout my years in France, I labored to disabuse the citizens of that country and of the United States of certain fundamental misconceptions each group held about the other. As I mentioned earlier, the French were mystified by the Watergate scandal. Next to John Kennedy, Richard Nixon was the U.S. President most highly respected by the French people (and by most Europeans, for that matter). They loved his foreign policy, so when Watergate broke and the historic drama was played out, the French could not understand why the Americans wanted Nixon out of office. That was the only time during all my years of living in France that I got scores of negative letters, all telling me how stupid it was for the United States to get rid of Richard Nixon.

The Europeans also definitely did not like the American electoral system. A two-year term for a U.S. representative seemed ridiculous to them, as did a four-year presidential term. They thought the election lasted too long and that it was far too costly. Nor did they like paid political advertising, something that barely exists in Europe. I have to say that the longer I stayed in Europe and watched their elections, the more I agreed with them.

As for the misperceptions of the Americans, they continued to insist on thinking of France only as the home of superb food and wine, good clothing designers, and beautiful women. In my lectures back in the States, I would stress that France was swiftly becoming one of the world leaders in high technology, using as examples the Concorde, the TGV, the fastest and best trains in the world, and the smart card, that banking and credit instrument then unknown in the United States, as well as the Minitel, the French telephone company's amazing computer system. When it came to advanced technology, France was way ahead, but it was not receiving proper credit. Interestingly, bringing that word to the world community would become, a few years down the road, another of my jobs—but that gets us ahead of the story.

By the time I'd lived in France for over a decade, from all outward ap-pearances, I had it made. I lived, as mentioned earlier, in a beautiful and roomy apartment on one of the best streets in Paris (the Rue de Rivoli) and spent weekends in an eight-bedroom castle set on twenty-seven acres in the countryside, where it was not uncommon for the French president, who also had a country place nearby, to drop in when out for a bike ride. I had a charming wife and a lovely child, and I should have been content to remain within that gorgeous tableau forever. But, typically, I was not.

C H A P T E R
S E V E N T E E N

WHEN I FIRST heard Aristotle Onassis quote the old Greek proverb that marriage is the only evil men pray for, I accused him of being overly cynical. He just laughed. Some years later, when I ran across George Bernard Shaw's line that it is very unwise for people in love to marry, I realized that I almost agreed with him. Of course, by then I was in my mid-fifties and had married three times. (In case anyone wonders, being multimarried does not necessarily make you better at it, or at least it didn't in my case.) All of this is in preface to saying that in 1981 my wife and I separated. Had our fourteen-year-old son been older, we would probably have divorced right away, simply because we both recognized that despite the respect and admiration we still had for each other, we clearly had what some legal jurisdictions refer to as "irreconcilable differences." Divorce would come later, but as we entered the 1980s—and I reported on the Reagan era from afar—we both remained in Paris, and we lived much the same lives, but separately. I, too, began to become cynical about the institution of marriage.

In November 1983, I met an incredible woman who changed all that. She also changed my life.

She was also named Nicole—Nicole Beauvillain de Menthon—and she was about to become the communications director for Guy Laroche, the famous designer. Earlier, she had been a journalist, and had worked for *Time* magazine and NBC before getting into communications and public relations with the huge French firm of L'Oreal. (Coincidentally, she had filmed me in the distant past. It was in Chicago, at the famous 1968 Democratic convention, with all the demonstrations and rioting. I had left the convention to talk to some of the protestors in the park, and Nicole had been part of the NBC team filming those hectic events.)

Guy Laroche had asked Nicole to set up some meetings for him with certain journalists, and mine was one of the names on her list. Throughout the month of November, she had been trying, without success, to reach me, but my office had to keep putting her off because I was traveling internationally. Finally, my secretary was able to call Nicole's office and leave the message that I would be available for a luncheon meeting on either Wednesday, November 30, or Thursday, December 1. A few minutes later, a happy Nicole called back to say that she and Laroche could make it on the thirtieth.

"I'm sorry," said my secretary, "but in the time between my call and your call back, I booked a lunch for Mr. Salinger on that day with someone else."

"No!" said an exasperated Nicole. "How could you do that? You must tell me who it is and where they are to eat."

Though quite able, my secretary was no match for Nicole de Menthon, and she soon revealed I was to have lunch with Jonathan Randal, a correspondent for the *Washington Post*. Nicole knew Randal, and so she quickly got his agreement that she and Guy Laroche could join us at lunch, as well as Palais du Trocadéro, the name of the Chinese restaurant across from the ABC bureau.

She and Laroche were already there when I walked in on the appointed day. I was stunned by her beauty. Nicole had darkish blond hair and a lovely figure, and she dressed with that special flair and smartness that only French women seem able to achieve. I thought she had a Bardot-like quality—but Bardot on her best behavior. I don't know what Mr. Laroche thought of my manners, but I spent most of the lunch talking with Nicole. We spoke mostly in French, yet I noticed that her English was quite good, and charmingly accented; she was kind enough not to say too much about my French. I thought we made a lovely couple.

I pursued her relentlessly, madly, offering to marry her dozens of times. She kept refusing, mainly for the hard-to-argue-with reason that, while legally separated, we both still had spouses. I backed off from the proposals, but I did get Nicole to agree to live with me. In March 1985, we began to cohabit in a tiny apartment on the Rue Faustin Helie.

Nineteen eighty-three, the year I met "Nicole 2," as my kids quickly dubbed Nicole de Menthon (Nicole Gillman Salinger being "Nicole 1"), I had been with ABC for five years. That year, the network named me its chief foreign correspondent, and five years later, I moved to London with that same title and the added one of senior editor, Europe. Nicole moved with me, but she was not happy. London is simply not Paris. I don't know how else to put it.

One night, back home after we'd spent the evening in a French restaurant in the heart of London, drinking a lot of Beaujolais nouveau with friends, Nicole said, totally out of the blue, and in English, "I'm drunk, and I can't stand this city! If I don't get married with you, I won't survive it!"

As I recall, my excitement was so great that I proposed on the spot. Nicole remembers otherwise, claiming I didn't respond to *her* proposal for two days and that she had to repeat it. Frankly, it doesn't matter whose version is correct, only that we agreed. In June 1989, we were married in London, at a warm and wonderful celebration that reunited some of the most important people in my life. Thus began what has been, in truth, the happiest period of my life.

Oh, I should add that just as I was finishing this book, Nicole Beauvillain de Menthon Salinger decided that she'd had enough of the confusion brought on by the fact that I had married, in succession, two French women with the same first name. Henceforth, she is to be known as "Poppy." So be it.

I will always remember January 31, 1989. It was an historic day in my life.

There was light snow, but the weather was mild—the mildest winter Moscow has lived through in more than a century. I left the office of ABC News and headed for the Mezhdunarodnaya Hotel, where I had a rendezvous for lunch with three old friends. Accompanying me was Irina Rachkovskaya, a talented Soviet woman who works for ABC News in Moscow.

In the spring and summer of 1961, I had first met the three friends I was now going to see: Alexei Adzhubei, the son-in-law of Soviet leader Nikita Khrushchev and at the time the editor of *Izvestia;* Mikhail Kharlamov, Nikita Khrushchev's spokesman; and Georgi Bolshakov, officially editor of a Soviet magazine in the United States, but actually a KGB agent. Bolshakov became a vital back channel between Khrushchev and President John Kennedy.

Kharlamov had come to New York in September 1961 with Foreign Minister Andrey Gromyko and had brought a private message to me for President Kennedy from Nikita Khrushchev. Bolshakov had met with me in the Carlyle Hotel several weeks later and handed me a twenty-six-page private letter from Khrushchev to Kennedy. Four days later, I had passed him a letter from Kennedy to the Soviet leader. Until Georgi left the States in December 1962, we had acted as intermediaries, carrying letters back and forth—a total of forty-four when Kennedy died in 1963. I had seen Kharlamov and Adzhubei in Moscow in May 1962, and during that period of the Cold War, we had developed friendly relations, based on candid talk and the desire of all of us to see U.S.-Soviet relations improve and the Cold War come to an end.

From the time Khrushchev was thrown out of power in October 1964, until November 1987 I did not see Adzhubei. He had been fired from his job as editor of *Izvestia* at the same time Khrushchev was ousted, and he had not been permitted to work for twenty years. On many visits to Moscow, I had tried to see him but had always failed. But in November of 1987, on assignment for ABC News in Moscow before the December summit in Washington between Mikhail Gorbachev and Ronald Reagan, I finally had a reunion with Alexei.

I had not seen Georgi Bolshakov since he had left the United States in December 1962. We had had our first reunion only days earlier, when we both attended a conference in Moscow on the Cuban missile crisis—a meeting that included Americans, Soviets, and Cubans, all of whom had participated in that event in 1962. And I was about to see Mikhail Kharlamov for the first time since May 1962, when I had come to Moscow for what turned into my meeting with Khrushchev. The four of us had not been together since July 1961.

When we reached the hotel, Georgi Bolshakov was standing there. He had aged and grown fat and he had a problem with his right leg. But his character and sense of humor had not changed. We hugged each other and Georgi told me that Alexei couldn't make it to lunch because he was caught up in his new work as one of the editors of *Soviet Union,* a well-respected Soviet magazine. But Georgi said that as soon as lunch was over, we would go to Alexei's apartment and meet up with him.

Georgi was also a little concerned because Mikhail Kharlamov hadn't arrived, but twenty minutes later, Mikhail walked up, a classic fur hat on his head. I had not seen him for almost twenty-seven years, but I recognized him immediately. His face had not changed at all, and he had not aged as much as Georgi had. We also hugged and then walked into the hotel and then into the Sakura, a Japanese restaurant that is considered the finest and most expensive in Moscow. We were led to a private room I had reserved. We took our shoes off before entering the room and then sat around a typical low Japanese table, our feet folded beneath us.

A lovely Russian girl with a face that gave us the impression she had a Tatar background came into the room to take the orders. We asked for a classic Japanese meal with sake (and, the Russians being Russians, vodka, as well) and started to talk.

Kharlamov still remembered vividly his arrival in Washington and our limo drive to my house, which he called my "country dacha."

He said, "I remember the phone ringing in the car and you answering and saying, 'Yes, yes, yes, yes' all the time. Then we got to your house and you gave us all sports shirts and bathing suits and we went down to the lake. It was very dirty, but we went swimming anyway, and then took a shower and came out of the house, to find you cooking chicken on a barbecue." Kharlamov also remembered that my son Stephen had played the popular Russian song "Moscow Nights" on his violin.

Talking about U.S.-Soviet relations, Kharlamov recalled being in Paris in 1960 when a meeting took place between President Dwight Eisenhower, Prime Minister Harold Macmillan, President Charles de Gaulle, and Premier Nikita Khrushchev. The U-2 spy plane had just been shot down over the Soviet Union. Khrushchev was furious. Kharlamov said he was in the room next to where the meeting was taking place with James Hagerty, Eisenhower's press secretary, and the press representatives of the two other leaders. He heard Eisenhower talking to Secretary of State Christian Herter. "This problem can be solved if I apologize to Khrushchev," the President said. "Never," Herter retorted. "Never apologize to Khrushchev."

Kharlamov said an apology would have eased U.S.-Soviet relations before Kennedy became President in January 1961.

Then, Kharlamov recalled the meeting he and Adzhubei had had with Kennedy the morning after the dinner at my home on Lake Barcroft. I was not present. "We were talking about U.S.-Soviet relations, and I said to him, 'Mr. President, we must advance relations between our two countries. You seem to be in favor of that. Why are you not moving faster?'

"And the President answered by saying: 'You don't understand this country. If I move too fast on U.S.-Soviet relations, I'll either be thrown into an insane asylum or be killed.' "

Georgi Bolshakov popped up with another memory. At the end of August 1962, he had been summoned to the White House to see President Kennedy. For over a year at that point, and in addition to the letters that went back and forth between Kennedy and Khrushchev, Georgi had been the most important back channel between the two world leaders.

Bolshakov recalled being ushered into the President's office by Robert Kennedy on August 31. "Hello, Georgi," the President said. "Look here, I know you are off to Moscow for a vacation. That's good. I'd like you to do me a favor and communicate to Premier Khrushchev the following message: Llewellyn Thompson, our ambassador in Moscow, informs me that Khrushchev is concerned about our planes flying low over

Soviet ships bound for Cuba. Tell him I've ordered these flyovers to stop today."

Bolshakov paused in our conversation and then started quoting Kennedy again. " 'I believe that the outlook for American-Soviet relations is good. I am profoundly convinced of that. To my mind, the signing of a treaty banning nuclear tests will be the next milestone along the road to their improvement. The signing of such a treaty could spare our children and grandchildren the threat of war. Tell Khrushchev I hope to be seeing him again in the near future.' " Bolshakov said the President concluded his conversation with a broad smile.

Robert Kennedy had not spoken during the entire meeting, but, according to Bolshakov, when they stopped outside the President's office, Bobby exploded: "Goddamn it, Georgi, doesn't Premier Khrushchev realize the President's position? Doesn't the premier know that the President has enemies as well as friends? Believe me, my brother really means what he says about American-Soviet relations. But every step he takes to meet Premier Khrushchev halfway costs my brother a lot of effort. If the premier just took the trouble to be, for a moment at least, in the President's shoes, he would understand him. In a gust of blind hate, his enemies may go to any length, including killing him."

Bolshakov said that when he reported this quote from Robert to Khrushchev at his vacation home in Pitsunda, on the Black Sea, the Soviet leader reacted negatively. "They can't mean it. Is he the President or isn't he? If he is a strong President, he has no one to fear. He has full powers of government, and his brother is attorney general in the bargain."

As we went through the splendid Japanese meal, sipping away at our sake and our vodka, Kharlamov kept coming up with memories. He told another story that gave a wonderful insight into Khrushchev's mind-set at that time.

Kharlamov had taken the prominent American journalist and columnist Walter Lippmann to Pitsunda to meet with Khrushchev. The first night, Khrushchev took him to the banks of the Black Sea. He pointed across the water. "You know what's over there. U.S. Jupiter missiles on Turkish soil. And they are aimed directly at us. How can we do business with the United States under those conditions?"

Khrushchev was unaware that President Kennedy had already ordered those missiles removed but that the plan had been delayed because the Turkish government objected. The Jupiter missiles were finally taken out of Turkey after the Cuban missile crisis. The American government believed it was not part of the deal made to take the Soviet missiles out of Cuba. The Soviets still think it *was* part of the deal.

The next morning, Kharlamov was summoned to Khrushchev's

house. The Soviet leader was in a rage. "Why can't I get Moscow Radio? I have tried five frequencies and there is terrible noise on all of them that prevents me from hearing any news." As the head of Soviet radio and television, Kharlamov was embarrassed, but he said he didn't know the answer to the question. He called one of his deputies in Moscow, who told him that the KGB had ordered jamming of so many foreign radios that it was spilling over onto Soviet radio. Kharlamov said Khrushchev became so angry when he learned the news that he immediately ordered all radio jamming stopped. Kharlamov said the order not to jam was not rescinded until Khrushchev was ousted from power.

The lunch ended, and we got into my Intourist-rented Volga car and headed for Alexei Adzhubei's apartment on Gorky Street. As I said earlier, I had not seen Alexei from 1964 to 1987. At our reunion, we had talked for hours about Khrushchev and particularly about comparisons between Khrushchev and Mikhail Gorbachev. Adzhubei had told me his father-in-law was thrown out of power because "he was a victim of the Soviet past." He found Gorbachev in a stronger position, although still faced with rigid opposition. Then Alexei agreed to be interviewed by me on camera for a piece I was doing for ABC News. It had proved to me that there really was a policy of *glasnost.*

But now we were heading for his apartment, which I had never seen. Georgi Bolshakov led us into the building. It was still snowing lightly. We rang the doorbell, and Alexei, dressed in relaxed fashion in a sports shirt, opened the door. He had set a tableful of food and drink. It concerned me a little because we had just arrived from a massive lunch, and one should never refuse food in the Soviet Union (because it is so hard to get). Alexei introduced me to his son, Nikita, now thirty-six years old and a professor of history. He also took me to a back room to introduce me to Nikita's eight-year-old daughter, who was lying in bed with a slight flu.

Then we sat around the table and started to talk. Georgi, Alexei, and Mikhail all poured themselves some scotch, and I took a glass of red Georgian wine. I wanted to know how they felt about being thrown out of their jobs when Khrushchev was ousted from power. Alexei's response was surprising. "I think it was normal. I think when a new leader takes over, he has the right to have his own people. What I don't like is all those people out there who have kept their jobs—from the time of Khrushchev, to Brezhnev, to Andropov, to Chernenko, and on to Gorbachev."

I had just finished attending a three-day conference on the Cuban missile crisis. It had been an extraordinary meeting, with such high-level attendees as Andrey Gromyko, the former foreign minister and president of the Soviet Union; Anatoly Dobrynin, for many years the Soviet ambassador to the United States; Robert McNamara, the former U.S. defense secretary; and Jorge Risquet, a leading member of the Cuban Communist party politburo and a close friend of Fidel Castro.

I brought up the most controversial subject that had come up at the conference. Sergei Khrushchev, the Soviet leader's son, had told some American participants during a private lunch at the conference that Fidel Castro had sent a cable to Khrushchev at the height of the crisis, asking him to fire the missiles at the United States to prevent an American invasion of Cuba.

Adzhubei shook his head. "Sergei didn't know anything his father did. I don't believe that for a minute."

He went on to say that he had visited Cuba several times after the crisis and had come away convinced that the Cubans did indeed want the missiles fired at the United States but that they had never communicated that message to the Soviet leadership.

"I remember well," said Alexei. "During the Cuban crisis, I was a member of the central committee. Every two hours, I had to go there to read the messages and reports. I never saw anything indicating Castro had asked for the missiles to be launched."

Then Alexei laughed. "You remember the dacha outside Moscow where we had dinner and where you lived for two days in May 1962 when you met Khrushchev? That was the same place where Khrushchev and the politburo were meeting all the time during the Cuban missile crisis!"

Alexei announced he had just finished writing a book and was about to sign a contract with Little, Brown for its publication in the United States. He said he thought the book would help Americans understand the evolution in the Soviet Union from the departure of Khrushchev to the arrival of Gorbachev. I told Alexei I was very interested in his book and would be glad to write the preface. He was very happy at this suggestion and immediately accepted my offer.

Dark had fallen on Moscow and I had to get back to my office. Alexei asked me to stay just a few more minutes. He wanted to read us part of a chapter from his book. He went over to his desk and picked up the manuscript, leafing through it to find the pages he wanted to read. Then he started, with Irina doing the translation. The chapter was about his reaction to the death of John Kennedy.

As Alexei Adzhubei read on, Georgi began to weep. Soon, Irina and I were also crying.

What he read was very touching. It showed that despite the hostility of the Cold War, there had been some strong friendships created between Americans and Russians that had not gone away. For me, it was especially moving, since all four of us had not been together since the summer of 1961.

As I left, I told them that I had gotten orders from New York to stay in Moscow. Our ABC News Moscow correspondent, Jim Laurie, had gone to Kabul, the capital of Afghanistan, and we had no journalist in Moscow. I had moved out of the All Trade Union Center, where I had been housed by the Soviet government during the Cuban missile crisis conference. I was now staying in the Sovietskya Hotel, in a fabulous suite with a bedroom, living room, and dining room. There was even a piano in the suite. I asked them if they could come to the Sovietskya on Thursday night for dinner in my suite. They all agreed immediately. Alexei said he would bring his wife, Rada, Khrushchev's daughter, whom I had also not seen in twenty-seven years.

On Thursday, February 2, Irina called the Sovietskya and arranged the dinner. At 7:30 P.M., a woman showed up in my suite; she was pushing a cart heavily laden with food. There was caviar, ham, cheese, fish, and bread. She set the table in the dining room. Earlier in the day, I had gone to what the Russians call a "hard currency" store and bought some vodka and some scotch. Irina went by car to pick up the Adzhubeis, and Kharlamov came by subway. They all arrived in my room promptly at 8:00 P.M.

Alexei was stunned by the suite. "How much are you paying for this?" he asked me.

"One hundred and sixty *rubles* [$257] a night," I replied.

"Wow!" he shouted. "Next time you come to Moscow, you stay at my house."

We were joined for dinner by a woman named Yulus, whom I'd not met before. Rada, whose English had improved dramatically since I'd seen her last, said Yulus was her niece. She was the daughter of Khrushchev's son who'd been killed in World War II.

After I'd passed out drinks, we all sat down in the living room. Alexei and Georgi wanted to know about the Kennedy family. How was Jackie? How were Caroline and John? I said they were well, that I'd seen them all in Martha's Vineyard the previous summer and that I'd heard John speak at the Democratic National Convention. I mentioned that Caroline now had a little girl of her own.

"When she gets old enough," said Alexei, "she should visit the Soviet Union."

Then Alexei started telling the universal story—where he was and what he was doing when John Kennedy was killed.

"I was in Paris, attending a concert given by the Soviet Military Orchestra. Someone came up to me and handed me a note saying Kennedy was dead. I was stunned. I wanted to get the message to the conductor. I got out of my seat, and it took him a while to realize I was standing below him. He leaned over, and I gave him the message. He stopped the orchestra immediately, but just a few moments later, they started playing the Mozart Requiem."

Rada said that she had not been with Alexei, but at a dinner party back in Moscow at the home of Oleg Troyanovsky, the Soviet ambassador to the United Nations, when she heard the news. She said that everybody around the table had started to cry.

I had asked Chris Jumpelt, a producer in ABC News' Frankfurt bureau (who was on part-time duty in Moscow) to bring a TV crew to the hotel. They arrived around 8:15. I asked my Russian friends if they had any objection to being filmed. They all said they thought filming our reunion was a marvelous idea, so we continued to talk in the living room, then moved into the dining room as the crew shot around us for about half an hour.

Alexei brought up our July 1961 debate on NBC, recalling that as he and I left the studio, each one of us was handed an envelope containing two thousand dollars in cash. I had told him, he reminded me, that according to White House rules I could not keep the money and that I had said I was donating it to my alma mater, the University of San Francisco. He then revealed that he and Mikhail had debated for *hours* over what to do with the money. The next day, Alexei had contacted a powerful member of the politburo, whose first reaction was surprise that they hadn't already spent the money. He had ordered them to deposit it in the State Bank. Even that seemingly simple task turned out to be complicated, according to Adzhubei: "We had to make three separate trips to the bank," he said, "before they would accept it for deposit into the State Bank."

The dinner went on, warmly, until 11:00 P.M. The Soviet serving lady reappeared several more times, first with chicken Kiev and then, finally, with Soviet ice cream, which is always of very high quality.

The talk flowed as freely as the wine, and we were definitely in another time, wondering out loud about how things would be in the present day if John Kennedy had not been killed and if Nikita Khrushchev had not been ousted from power. There was a slight argument between Alexei and Mikhail. The former was convinced that if Kennedy had not been killed, Khrushchev would have remained in power. (That was always my theory, too.) But Mikhail said Kennedy's death had no link to Khrushchev's fall from power. He called it an "internal political matter, with no connection to Soviet foreign policy."

One thing we all did agree on, however, was that if both Kennedy and Khrushchev had remained in power, Soviet-American relations would have improved much more rapidly and that there probably would have been an agreement between the two leaders that would have significantly slowed down the nuclear arms race.

On that point, Alexei said, "We were close to success."

At the conclusion of the dinner, we linked arms around one another and around the table. The two historic meetings were over, but we exchanged invitations to see one another again as soon as possible. Prior to this dinner, on my visits to Moscow I had often felt lost, but, having restored my links with friends made a quarter century ago, I knew I'd never feel lost in Moscow again. To get that feeling at the age of sixty-three is, to me, remarkable. The night had been a memorable event.

Since then, all three of my Russian friends have died.

CHAPTER
EIGHTEEN

IN 1990, I had been a journalist of one type or another at one time or another for the better part of forty-seven years. Three years later, I would make a career move, but in that period of time in between, I would cover and report on two of the biggest stories of my life. Both involved death—one in an act of war, the other an act of terrorism—and in each one, the finger of blame was pointed in the wrong direction.

It was late in the evening of August 27, 1990, and the Gulf crisis had been raging for twenty-five days. I had just come home from a delightful dinner with Art Buchwald at the Le Caprice restaurant in London when the phone rang next to my bed. It was the president of ABC News, Roone Arledge. He wanted me to go to Iraq, obviously the key player in this international drama, because he felt our contacts there weren't what they should be.

When Iraq invaded Kuwait on August 2, I had just started my vacation. We were on the island of Nantucket, off the coast of Massachusetts. Although I was not summoned back to my office in London, I had gone right to work from Nantucket, spending many hours each day keeping in contact with my Middle East sources, trying to contribute to ABC's coverage. In fact, I made several broadcasts from the island and broke the story that the Iraqis were going to be taking foreign prisoners.

I had been back in London for a little more than a week when Mr.

Arledge's next call came. I must say that when I hung up, I had mixed feelings. I was not enthusiastic about going to Baghdad.

Some of the terrorist groups I'd covered now had important links with the Iraqi government. My concern stemmed from the fact that American and other foreign males were being held as hostages in Iraq (the Iraqis called them "guests"). In addition, there were recurring rumors that journalists might be added to the list of those not allowed to leave Baghdad.

The next morning, however, when I arrived at the office, I decided to send a telex to the deputy foreign minister, Nizar Hamdoun, asking formal permission to come into the country. Earlier in the year, through a friend in London, Odeh Aburdene, an American of Lebanese origin, I had met and had a long dinner with Nizar Hamdoun. We got along very well, and I was extremely impressed with his intelligence and the candor of his views on various problems between Iraq and Kuwait.

When I sent the telex, I did not expect a response from Hamdoun for a few days, for I sensed he was heavily involved in the events that were taking place. But two hours later, a return telex came from Hamdoun, warmly inviting me to Baghdad and telling me that a visa was available at the Iraqi embassy in London. By early afternoon, I had the visa and a ticket to fly to Amman, Jordan, the next day, on Royal Jordanian Airlines.

I called Odeh Aburdene to tell him how quickly Nizar Hamdoun had replied and how grateful I was to him for having introduced me to Hamdoun. Aburdene was happy I was going to Baghdad. But he suggested I take, as a consultant, a woman named Mary Elizabeth King. She had run the U.S.-Iraq Business Council and had excellent contacts in Baghdad. ABC management in New York quickly approved the idea, and after talking to Ms. King for the first time, I arranged for her to fly to London overnight and then go on to Amman to meet me. I would soon find out how effective she was, and not only in Iraq.

On August 29, I flew to Amman in the early evening. The weather was warm and pleasant. I went directly to the Intercontinental Hotel, which has always been my base in Amman, and spent the evening in the new office that ABC News had set up in that hotel at the start of the crisis. I also discovered that Mary King had already arranged important meetings for the next evening with the Jordanian foreign minister, Marwan al Quasam, and with the former Jordanian foreign minister, now chairman of the parliament's foreign policy committee, Senator Taher Nasri.

The next morning, I went to see Randa Habib, the head of the Agence France Presse in Amman and also a consultant to ABC News. Few journalists have her special insight into the Middle East problem, and I was looking forward to getting a briefing that would help me on my trip to

Baghdad. My judgment was right. Randa's briefing was factual and fascinating.

One of the things I learned was that as early as February, Jordan's King Hussein had understood that the situation was hardening between Iraq and Kuwait and had made an important four-day trip to the principal Gulf states to try to mediate the dispute. But even more importantly, Randa had done special research on the history of relations between Iraq and Kuwait, starting in 1913, when the British unilaterally drew a line between the two countries, cutting Iraq off from access to the Persian Gulf. Looking at those historical documents, one could begin to understand the Iraqi mind-set, which was that in their view Kuwait had never been an independent nation, but always a part of Iraq.

At 6:30 P.M., Mary King having arrived, we were at the house of the foreign minister, Marwan al Quasam, who briefed me on all the events that had taken place since the outbreak of the crisis. I was amazed at his details and had no doubt he was giving me a true picture of the events. When I walked out of his home two and a half hours later, I was fully convinced that in the first four days after the Iraqi invasion of Kuwait, the issue could have been solved by the Arab nations had not the United States intervened with certain Arab nations to prevent the holding of a mini-summit in Jeddah, Saudi Arabia, on Saturday, August 4, or Sunday, August 5.

Mary King and I then drove over to the home of Senator Taher Masri. It was supposed to be a relatively short meeting, but it turned into a wonderful Arabic dinner. Masri said Jordan's King Hussein had convinced Saddam Hussein to pull out of Kuwait if they could solve the Iraqi-Kuwait problems at the Jeddah mini-summit. But now, he went on, with the Americans deployed in Saudi Arabia, it had become their problem to solve the crisis.

Masri also mentioned another element—one I'd never heard before—that may have pushed Saddam into the invasion. He said that Turkey's move on Iraq's supply of water had been a crucial element in the chronology. As a result of Turkish hydroelectric projects implemented in 1990, in Iraq, the Euphrates River, which originates in Turkey and flows through Syria before reaching Iraq, had fallen by one-third in 1990. Masri said this would have made Saddam Hussein feel geographically vulnerable, making an outlet to the Persian Gulf more crucial for him.

We touched down in Baghdad at 3:00 P.M. the next day. When we walked out of the overcrowded plane, there was a representative from the protocol office of the foreign ministry waiting for us. He helped us get through passport and customs control rapidly, and our driver took us to the Sheraton.

Never having been in Baghdad before, I was struck first by the overpowering heat. But I was also struck by the city's calm. It certainly did not feel like being in a city enveloped in a crisis that was about to erupt into a war.

As we drove into town, there was no doubt who was Iraq's leader. On every block, there were large paintings of photos of Saddam Hussein. His presence in the city was massive.

Later, when Mary and I had dinner at the hotel, I was surprised by the good quality of the food. The only shock was the price of a bottle of 1986 Italian wine—$150!

At eight o'clock the next morning, we arrived at the foreign ministry. Nizar Hamdoun was in a meeting, but he let us know he would see us as soon as possible. In the meantime, he sent us up to see Dr. S'Dun Zubaidi, the English interpreter for Saddam Hussein since the beginning of the Gulf crisis. He opened his conversation by bitterly criticizing the ABC's *Prime Time Live*, because he felt one of its anchors, Diane Sawyer, who had been sent to Baghdad to interview Saddam Hussein in June, had shortchanged Hussein in her interview. Dr. Zubaidi said, "We gave her one hundred and ninety-five minutes of interview and she only put eleven minutes on the air."

He was particularly vexed about the exclusion of the final question that Diane Sawyer had asked Saddam Hussein: Did he have a direct question for the American people? Dr. Zubaidi said the Iraqi president's answer was the most important of the entire interview, but the show had discarded it. As I worked for ABC News, I was embarrassed by his remarks, although I had already heard that the Iraqis were unhappy with the Sawyer interview. But Dr. Zubaidi calmed things down by saying that he had made ten copies of the show, which had been sent to him, and had distributed them to friends throughout Baghdad. "Most of them liked the show," he told us.

Then he launched into a major attack on Egypt's president, Hosni Mubarak. "He is a liar. He lied twice." Dr. Zubaidi said Saddam Hussein had seen Mubarak in Baghdad on July 24. He had told him: "As long as the meetings between our countries are not finished, I am not going to use force. I am not going to use force until I have exhausted negotiations. But don't tell the Kuwaitis this. Don't give the Kuwaitis hope; it will make them arrogant." He said that Mubarak went right to Kuwait and told them that Saddam Hussein was not going to use force, without mentioning the negotiations.

A few minutes later, we were ushered into Nizar Hamdoun's office. It was large and very well furnished. Up against one of the walls, there was a large TV set on which Hamdoun constantly watched CNN. I immediately began to pitch one of my subjects, my desire to get an interview with Saddam Hussein for our evening anchor, Peter Jennings. But Hamdoun had an idea of his own—a definitely novel one.

He wondered if it would be possible to set up a TV debate between Saddam Hussein and President George Bush.

I told him I thought there was little or no chance this would take place. I said that in light of President Bush's views on the invasion of Kuwait, he was not likely to agree to any conversations with the Iraqi president. Indeed, George Bush was refusing even to talk to Saddam Hussein. But Hamdoun asked me to look into the matter anyway and see what I could develop.

Our next interview was with Iran's deputy prime minister, Dr. Sadoun Hammadi. After discussing several introductory but still important points, we then got into a crucial issue, the Jeddah summit earlier in the month.

Hammadi was a member of the three-man Iraqi delegation that had gone to Jeddah. He had been accompanied by Attef Ibrahim and Ali Hassan el Majid. "We were trying," he said, "to explain that the Kuwaiti government was conspiring against Iraq through oil policy. When we went to the Jeddah meeting, we were expecting the Kuwaitis to have a solution. The Iraqi position was known."

The emir of Kuwait's refusal to attend the meeting angered Saddam Hussein and instigated *his* decision not to go, either. The head of the Iraqi delegation was Ibrahim, who soon after arriving asked for a private meeting with the crown prince and prime minister of Kuwait, Sheik Saad al Sabah, with the expectation that the Kuwaitis had brought a plan to Jeddah.

"We were arguing that the Kuwaitis were following an oil policy to bring an end to our government," Hammadi continued. "They were conspiring with the United States and the United Arab Emirates to lower the price of oil. There was another private meeting, and still nothing happened."

Dr. Hammadi said the meeting continued throughout dinner and then concluded late at night.

The next morning, Hammadi got a call from the undersecretary of the foreign ministry of Kuwait. He wanted the two countries to issue a joint statement saying that the Jeddah talks had made progress. Hammadi contacted the delegation leader, Ibrahim, who told him coldly, "We can't do that, because it didn't happen."

Hammadi then recontacted the Kuwait foreign ministry undersecretary and told him that each country was free to issue a communiqué of their own.

Dr. Hammadi said the Iraqi delegation then left Jeddah and made a short stop in the Saudi Arabian religious city of Mecca. When the delegation returned to Baghdad, at approximately 4:00 P.M. on August 1, Ibrahim went directly to report to Saddam Hussein. It was then, according to Hammadi, that Saddam Hussein made the final decision to invade Kuwait.

Before we left Dr. Hammadi, I asked him what he thought would happen if war broke out. His answer was precise.

"An American attack on Iraq would be in two parts, an air attack and a ground attack. The United States has supremacy in its air force. The United States is going to inflict damages on us. Despite [that] we will fight to the maximum. We're doing everything to outweigh the United States' technology in the air force. But the Iraqi air force is not decisive. It is the ground forces. I assure you the United States can never win the battle. We are determined. We are united. We have a ground force that would not make the battle a picnic."

Hammadi was half-right.

We had talked for two hours. I asked Dr. Hammadi if he was willing to repeat some of the things he had told me on camera. And several hours later, I returned to his office to do a television interview, sections of which were later broadcast in a special program entitled "A Line in the Sand," which ABC News aired on September 11.

A 8:00 P.M., Mary and I went to see Nizar Hamdoun a second time. We again discussed the possibility of a television debate between Saddam Hussein and George Bush. And then Nizar handed me an envelope.

He said, "Inside are two Arabic documents you will find interesting. One is the minutes of the meeting on July twenty-fifth between Saddam Hussein and April Glaspie, the U.S. ambassador to Iraq. The other are the minutes of a meeting on August sixth between Saddam Hussein and the American charge d'affaires, Joseph Wilson."

I was surprised—but quite pleased—to receive the documents. They fit perfectly into my investigation of the sequence of events that had eventually led up to the Iraqi invasion of Kuwait.

Based on those minutes, and on many other sources, including some highly placed members of the PLO, what follows is a capsulized narrative of what transpired between the Bush administration and Saddam Hussein.

On the second day of April, after Hussein had given a saber-rattling speech to his army officers (he said, among other things, "By God, if the Israelis try anything against us, we'll see to it that half their country is destroyed by fire.... Whoever threatens us with atomic bombs will be exterminated with chemical weapons"), some people at the U.S. Department of State paid attention. One of them, John Kelly, the assistant secretary of state for Middle Eastern affairs, was alarmed at how belligerent the Iraqi leader sounded.

Yet, ironically, only two months earlier, Kelly had met with Hussein and praised him highly as an important mediating force in that volatile part of the world.

This speech did not strike John Kelly as that of a mediator, so he immediately went to the office of a colleague who had the ear of Secretary of State James Baker. Within minutes, they had come up with a plan for economic sanctions, which they took upstairs to the secretary's office. They apprised him of the situation and urged him to act swiftly and unambiguously.

The threefold sanctions were: to refuse Iraq funds from the Export-Import Bank; to cancel the Community Credit Program; and to take steps to stop Iraq from bringing into the country "material with a potential military use."

A week later, Baker having interceded, they had President Bush's support for the plan. But there was opposition from the federal bureaucracy (especially the Commerce Department) and an insufficient political push from Jim Baker (who was too busy with a variety of problems, such as German unification and the Bush-Gorbachev summit). Therefore, Saddam Hussein did not receive an official warning from the United States.

Indeed, the Iraqi leader received quite a different message several days later from a group of U.S. senators then in Baghdad, a group that included Republican senators Bob Dole (then the Senate minority leader) and Alan Simpson.

When Hussein said, "I'm aware that a massive campaign has been launched against us by the United States and Europe," Dole responded by saying, "Such a campaign certainly doesn't come from President Bush. He told us only yesterday that he was quite against it." And Simpson added, "There's no problem between you and the American government or the American people. Your only problem is with our press, who are arrogant and hard to please."

Knowing that Saddam had been very angry about a February broadcast on the Voice of America (VOA) attacking him, Dole in effect apologized for the program.

"Let me point out to you," he said, "that twelve hours ago President Bush told me that he and his government were hoping to improve relations with Iraq. I can assure you that President Bush will oppose sanctions. He could even veto any such decision, unless a provocative act should occur."

Up until then, the American ambassador, April Glaspie, had said nothing, but hers was the last line of the meeting: "As American ambassador, I can assure you, Mr. President, that this is indeed the policy of the United States government."

On April 25, the American President sent the Iraqi leader a friendly message to commemorate the end of Ramadan, the month-long Islamic religious observance. In it, President Bush said he hoped "the ties between the United States and Iraq would contribute to the peace and stability of the Middle East."

Days later, John Kelly, the former hard-liner and coauthor of the three-point economic sanctions, told a congressional committee, "This administration continues to oppose the imposition of sanctions, which would penalize American exporters and worsen our balance-of-payments deficit [the Commerce Department's objections]. Furthermore, I fail to see how sanctions could increase the possibility of our exercising a moderating influence on the actions of Iraq."

Now you see it, now you don't. John Kelly was swiftly becoming the Dr. Jekyll and Mr. Hyde of the Iraqi affair.

On July 25—with his attack on neighboring Kuwait but days away—Saddam Hussein summoned April Glaspie, the American ambassador, to his office. It was to be her first solo face-to-face official visit with the Arab leader, and she was given but one hour's notice. There was no time to call her State Department superiors in Washington for advice or instructions.

Hussein's demeanor was cordial, but his message blunt and at times belligerent. He all but came right out and told Glaspie that he was going to invade Kuwait. It was obvious that he wanted to know how the United States would react.

"We do not accept threats from anyone," he said. "But we say clearly that we hope the United States will not entertain too many illusions and will seek new friends rather than increase the number of its enemies. . . . We know that you can harm us, but we do not threaten you. But we, too, could harm you. Everyone can cause damage according to his ability and size. We cannot come all the way to you in the United States, but individual Arabs may reach you. . . . We don't want war because we know what war means. But do not push us to consider war as the only means by which we can live proudly and provide our people with a good living.

"We know the United States has nuclear weapons. But we are all determined either to live as proud men or to die. We do not believe that there is a single honest man on earth who would not understand what I mean."

Saddam spoke for a long time, again mentioning the "infamous" Diane Sawyer program. Finally, Ambassador Glaspie got a chance to speak. She thanked him for the opportunity to talk, then said, "I clearly understand your message. We studied history at school. They taught us to say, 'Freedom or death.' " She mentioned that President Bush's message on Iraq's National Day was one of "friendship," and Saddam Hussein agreed, and then she said, "I have a direct instruction from the President to seek better relations with Iraq."

Ambassador Glaspie added, "I saw the Diane Sawyer program on ABC, and what happened on that program was cheap and unjust. And this is a real picture of what happens in the American media—even to American politicians themselves. . . . Mr. President, I want to say that President Bush wants not only better and deeper relations with Iraq but also an Iraqi contribution to peace and prosperity in the Middle East. President Bush is an intelligent man. He is not going to declare an economic war against Iraq. . . . We have no opinion on Arab-Arab conflicts, like your border disagreement with Kuwait."

Over the next several days, Iraq continued to increase the number of its troops already massed on the Kuwaiti border. The United States sent messages to Kuwait, Egypt, and Saudi Arabia, but all three dismissed the idea of an invasion, putting down the show of force to "Iraqi blackmail."

A number of Arab leaders, among them King Hussein of Jordan and Yasir Arafat, tried to intercede with both Kuwait and Iraq, but they got nowhere.

On July 31, Undersecretary of State John Kelly again testified on Capitol Hill, this time before the Middle East subcommittee of the House of Representatives. Thanks to the CIA, Kelly knew that as of the day before, Saddam Hussein had 300 tanks, 300 pieces of heavy artillery, and 100,000 men on the Kuwaiti border. Despite that knowledge, he testified, ". . . I have confidence in the administration's position on this matter. *We don't have any defense treaty with the Gulf States* [italics added]. We support the independence and security of all friendly states in the region. . . . We call for a peaceful solution to all disputes, and we think that the sovereignty of every state in the Gulf must be respected."

Congressman Lee Hamilton (D-IN) asked pointedly, "If Iraq crossed the Kuwaiti . . . if such a thing *should* happen, though, is it correct to say we have no treaty, no commitment, which would oblige us to use American forces?"

"That's exactly right," replied John Kelly.

With war and peace hanging in the balance, the American official— whose words would be heard that night in Baghdad over the BBC's World Service—had just sent Saddam Hussein a clear message. If he attacked Kuwait, the United States would not intervene.

* * *

The world knows what happened next. Among other things, Norman Schwarzkopf became a national (probably also an international) hero, George Bush's popularity went through the roof, and more than twenty thousand people died.

I'm not going to go into all the details of what happened between August 2 and the following January 17 when the United States began to bomb Baghdad. (For anyone interested in those details, I recommend *Secret Dossier: The Hidden Agenda Behind the Gulf War,* which I wrote with the French journalist Eric Laurent. It was published in France by Olivier Orban and in the United States by Penguin Books in 1991.)

I'm going to conclude this portion of my memoirs by offering proof for my firm belief that this was a war that could, and should, have been prevented—by the United States of America.

When Bob Dole and the other U.S. senators visited Saddam Hussein in Baghdad in April 1990, they apologized to him for the harsh anti-Iraq editorial that had been broadcast by the Voice of America the previous February. They even went so far as to tell him that the man who had written the article had been fired.

That man was William Stetson, and not only had he not been fired; he also was the man who, on July 29, four days before the invasion, wrote an editorial that could have prevented the Gulf War. The reason it did not was that it was never broadcast, and the reason it was never broadcast was that it was stopped—by his own government.

Toward the beginning of the editorial that never was, Stetson had written some tough language: "In recent days there has been a new threat to peace in the Persian Gulf region. Iraq has made threats against Kuwait and the United Arab Emirates. Iraq also has massed thousands of troops, as well as tanks and missiles, near its border with Kuwait. The U.S. is concerned about the build-up of military forces along the Iraq-Kuwait border. U.S. officials have stressed that there is no place in a civilized world for coercion and intimidation."

What different sentiments from those expressed to Saddam Hussein by the American ambassador, April Glaspie, just a few days before.

Toward the end of Stetson's editorial, he had written some more tough and unambiguous language. It read: "As a U.S. Defense Department spokesman said this week, the U.S. remains strongly committed to supporting the individual and collective self-defense of its friends in the Persian Gulf, with whom Americans have deep and long-lasting ties. The U.S. also remains determined to ensure the free flow of oil through the Straits of Hormuz, and to defend the principles of freedom of navigation and commerce. The U.S. would take very seriously any threat that put U.S. interests or friends at risk."

At the bottom of the editorial was a line that was also meant to be part of the broadcast: "That was an editorial reflecting the views of the U.S. Government."

Prior to its scheduled broadcast, this editorial was passed around at a meeting at the State Department. As a result, the VOA was told *not* to broadcast it.

Originally, I had this information from a well-placed source within the United States Information Agency (USIA.) Later, after considerable digging, I managed to meet and interview Mr. Stetson himself. I was surprised to learn that he still worked for the Voice of America. He said that when he was informed his editorial would not be broadcast, he was told, "There is too much up in the air." He also told me he believes that the man who made the decision to scuttle the editorial was John Kelly.

In my opinion, the failure to air the VOA editorial was a significant sign to Saddam Hussein that George Bush would do nothing to stop him from invading Kuwait. What's more, the message the American President had sent Hussein via Ambassador Glaspie had convinced Hussein that Bush would not intervene. And, though Bush knew Hussein had 100,000 troops massed along the border, he never sent any kind of "You better not invade" message. Nor, as far as I have been able to tell, did he ever even consider doing so.

The Gulf War was not necessary. I checked with many top sources in the Middle East, and all President Bush would have had to do to prevent it would have been to send Saddam Hussein this message: "Dear Mr. President" [not "Mr. Dictator" or "Mr. Butcher"], I am concerned to learn that you have 100,000 troops on the Kuwaiti border. Let me tell you that if you cross that border, there will be a war. And I can tell you that you will lose that war. But I also understand that you are having trouble negotiating with Kuwait on an historic issue, your border problem. So I am sending Secretary of State James Baker to Baghdad tomorrow to discuss the problem with you. And I will send him to Kuwait, and we will act as intermediaries to help solve this problem."

Every top Iraqi official now says that if such a message had been sent, it would have stopped the invasion and prevented all the death and destruction that followed. But President Bush did not send that message because President Bush wanted to go to war.

It is important the people understand that the Gulf War has had terrible consequencs, such as the deep financial crises into which several of the Gulf states have slipped, and the fact that in the next two years a number of royal families will be thrown out of power. The Gulf War is also responsible for the huge and horrifying rise in Islamic terrorism, with its ripplelike increase in acts of terrorism worldwide. It is also significant that while many Arab nations did agree to fight with the United States, the great majority of their citizens did not want to see an Arab nation attacked by a Western power.

As luck (if that's the right word) would have it, one of the last stories I worked on as a journalist turned out to be one of the biggest. Coincidentally, like the Gulf War story, it was yet another example of the United States being less than forthright in its dealings with the Arab world.

On November 13, 1991, in a grandiose ceremony at the Justice Department in Washington, William Barr, the acting attorney general of the United States, announced an indictment in the case that had involved so many of us, police and journalists alike, for almost three full years.

He said, "We charge that two Libyan officials, acting as operatives of the Libyan Intelligence Service along with other co-conspirators, planted and detonated the bomb that destroyed Pan Am Flight 103. At this moment, Lord Fraser, Chief Prosecutor of Scotland, is announcing similar charges."

After praising the two-country investigative team, he said, "This investigation is by no means over. It continues unabated. We will not rest until all those responsible are brought to justice, and we have no higher priority. The defendants we indict today are Abdel Basset Ali Al-Megrahi and Lamen Khalifa Fhimah, officers and operatives of the Libyan Intelligence Agency. These defendants are fugitives from justice."

The acting attorney general went on to provide details of the crime, and I paid particular interest to his description of the instrument of death: "The defendants and co-conspirators made a bomb of plastic explosive and a sophisticated timing device and placed it into a Toshiba portable radio cassette player. The radio was put into a Samsonite suitcase."

I was equally interested in the indictment's claim that one of the defendants had flown from Libya to Malta, "where [both] of them had recently worked for Libyan Airlines and had access to the baggage tags of another airline, Air Malta. By using stolen Air Malta baggage tags, the defendants and their co-conspirators were able to route the bomb-rigged suitcase as unaccompanied luggage. The suitcase was put aboard an Air Malta flight that went to Frankfurt, Germany. At Frankfurt the suitcase was transferred to Pan Am Flight 103-A to Heathrow Airport in London. At Heathrow, the suitcase containing the bomb was placed aboard Pan Am 103. It exploded approximately 38 minutes after flight 103 departed for New York. . . ."

I had a problem with this indictment. I was very skeptical about it—just as skeptical as I had been in 1988 when the Germans had arrested Marwan Kreesat, a Jordanian national, and charged him with the very same crime, only to release him three weeks later.

Over the years, I'd investigated a lot of crimes, for both newspapers and magazines (as well as a congressional committee), before turning to television, and to me the cases against these three men—Al-Megrahi and Fhimah, the two Libyans, and Marwan Kreesat, the Jordanian—had not been proven. The main reason I say this is that I happen to be the only Western journalist who interviewed all three of these suspects.

For almost five years, from 1988 to 1993, I headed a marvelous team of ABC investigative journalists. As a result of our work, plus the information I gathered from my interviews with all three suspects, I have come to the conclusion that the United States shifted the focus of world suspicion away from Syria and Iran and toward Colonel Gadhafi of Libya. Why? Among other reasons, because Syria and Iran were helpful to the United States in the Gulf War, the former actively and the latter passively. It is important to remember that the United States wanted Syria to negotiate a peace accord with Israel, which would be difficult, to say the least, if Syria was still charged with the Pan Am 103 bombing. This is not to say that Libya played no role whatsoever, but that there is solid, mounting information that the bomb was not put on Pan Am 103 in Malta, but in Frankfurt.

And I know who did it.

After moving to Paris in 1968, I traveled to North Africa so often that I developed an expertise regarding that region of the world. I visited Morocco, Tunisia, and Algeria frequently, but, for one reason or another, I had spent little time in Libya. Still, I did my homework.

I knew from my reading that following the overthrow of the royal family in 1972, Col. Muammar Gadhafi had seized power. I also knew that his record had both positive and negative aspects.

On the positive side, Gadhafi had efficiently restructured the nation, a feat made a great deal easier by the fact that Libya was one of the world's greatest producers of oil. I was impressed not just by the fact that Gadhafi had struck very good deals for his country with the American oil companies but especially by the fact that he used the proceeds to raise the Libyan standard of living far above that of most other Arab nations.

On the negative side, however, it was clear that Colonel Gadhafi had transformed Libya into one of the premier terrorist nations of the entire world. Not only did he strongly support such important Mideast terrorist organizations as Achmed Jibril's Popular Front for the Liberation of Palestine–General Command (PFLP-GC) and the Abu Nidal movement but he also sent critical aid in the form of terrorist materials to the IRA, the Red Brigade in Italy, and a number of other terrorist groups in France, Germany, and Spain. Information indicated that he had allowed some of the worst terrorist groups in the world, such as Abu Nidal and his people, to set up training camps in Libya for their terrorist activities.

In 1988, when I put together my crackerjack team of Middle East experts and investigators following the bombing of Pan Am 103, we soon learned that the prime suspects were the government of Iran and the PFLP-GC, led by a man named Achmed Jibril.

At first, it appeared that the governments of the United States and Scotland, which were both pursuing active investigations, were coming to the same conclusion. But in the spring of 1991, after the Gulf War, I began to see newspaper articles and television and radio news accounts to the effect that new evidence linked the government of Libya with the crash of Pan Am 103. Similarly, investigators working on the 1989 bombing of a French airliner over central Africa had also found evidence of a Syria-Iran connection and were suddenly leaning toward Libya as the culprit.

One of the reasons why I was skeptical of this late-blooming Libyan connection was that I had interviewed Marwan Kreesat, the Jordanian national the Germans had arrested and charged with making bombs, only to release him not long after. My November 1989 interview with Kreesat—which took place before the FBI or the Scots had talked to him—convinced me that they had the wrong man. The man they had was a most interesting man, and may in fact have been a terrorist bomber some years earlier, but he was not the bomber of Pan Am Flight 103.

Marwan Kreesat was in his early thirties when he'd started working for Achmed Jibril in 1967, after the Arab-Israeli war. He took orders only from Jibril himself. He told me he built bombs that were put on two flights to Tel Aviv—one that exploded and one that did not. Those, he swore, were his only two terrorist acts.

After the 1973 war between Israel and the Arab states, the PFLP-GC fell on hard times. Kreesat had bad relations with some of the leaders of the movement, and, seeing as Jibril had disappeared, so did he. He went back to Amman and started his own business repairing radios and fixing recorders and organs.

Twelve years later, in 1985, he made his first trip back to Damascus. It was a private visit with his wife, who was Syrian, and their children to see her relatives. He had barely arrived when he ran into one of the Jibril people he had known a long time ago. They talked about life in general, and his old PFLP-GC friend asked him if he wanted to see Jibril. He tried to say no, but he was soon summoned to Jibril's secret camp, where the terrorist leader welcomed him back with open arms—and plans for more airplane bombings.

As soon he got back home, Marwan Kreesat, who much preferred his new life to his old one, contacted Jordanian intelligence. They worked out a deal whereby Kreesat would appear to help Jibril, although he would actually be working to help capture him.

Back in 1989, I didn't know how much of this to believe when I heard it directly from Marwan Kreesat, so I absorbed everything I could. I also took copious notes. Almost buried in the pages of one of my notebooks is some information that turned out to be important. He told me that in 1986 and 1987, he went on shopping trips—at Jibril's direction—to buy the necessary equipment with which to build the size and type of bomb that would bring down a huge airliner.

Among other things, that equipment included a Sanyo TV monitor and a Toshiba portable radio cassette player.

Following the directions of Jibril's trusted lieutenant, Marwan Kreesat built bombs in both Japanese instruments. However, he said, following the instructions of his Jordanian intelligence contacts, he had purposely miswired the devices.

In October of 1988, Kreesat was sent to Frankfurt, and then driven to Neuss, where he started building the bombs. Several days later, he and the trusted lieutenant (a man named Delkamouni) were arrested in Düsseldorf. In their car, the police found the Toshiba recorder and a pile of explosives wrapped in brown tape that were intended to be used in the bombing of a nightclub in Frankfurt.

Delkamouni was led away to a cell, but Kreesat was taken upstairs to a room, where he was soon joined by a high-level German police officer in civilian clothes.

"Don't say anything," said the German officer. "You will get a call from your case officer in Jordan." He did, and several weeks later, with the repeated thanks of the German police, Marwan Kreesat was freed. He returned to Jordan.

Near the end of our long interview, Kreesat told me he did not believe the Toshiba cassette recorder brought to Germany by Delkamouni downed Pan Am 103. All four of the bombs that he built were found in Germany. His point is that Achmed Jibril favored the Toshiba cassette recorder.

My reasoned conclusion, then and now, is that Marwan Kreesat is not responsible for the bombing of Pan Am 103.

Early in September of 1991, thanks to the excellent Middle East contacts of one particular member of my ABC investigative team, I found myself meeting with the foreign minister of Libya, Ibrahim Beshari (who surprised me with the effusiveness of his compliments about the accuracy of my book on the Gulf War).

Beshari said he was very concerned about all the information that was coming out suggesting Libya's involvement in the crash of Pan Am 103.

"Totally false," he said, then went on to say that making matters worse was the indictment, just a month before, by a French judge of four Libyans (one of them Colonel Gadhafi's brother) for "complicity in the bombing" of a UTA [French transport] plane over central Africa in 1989.

His greatest concern, he told me, was the failure of the West to see that Libya had made a dramatic change in its policies, resulting in the fact that it no longer had any ties with terrorists. Nor, said Beshari, was Libya involved in chemical weapons or nuclear power, the substance of several recent charges.

Clearly, it was hard to find a Western country with much discernible sympathy for Libya. On the same day that Scotland and the United States announced their indictment, the U.S. Department of Defense and the CIA sent representatives across Europe to meet with defense and intelligence officials in EEC countries to try to convince them to join in with the United States in a military attack on Libya (an idea for which they found little enthusiasm).

At the end of our meeting, Beshari told me, "You have an open invitation to come to Libya and see for yourself. We will provide you access to everything. We will restrict nothing."

As I left the Grand Hotel, I realized that I had a rare journalistic opportunity, especially if the result of the U.S.-Scottish investigation into the Pan Am crash came down the way I now feared it would. And, less than a month later, with their joint indictment, it did. I immediately contacted ABC and suggested that I go to Tripoli right away—Beshari's invitation was still fresh in my mind—to look into the case. They agreed immediately. Then I called my contact and told him to get in touch with Ibrahim Beshari. The call back came almost immediately: "Welcome."

On the way to the Middle East, however, I made a quick stop in Paris to see one of my best sources, a top intelligence officer of the French government. He laid out his information for a full hour, and it completely contradicted the findings of the French judge who'd handed down the indictment of the four Libyans in the UTA attack. On the contrary, he said, French intelligence was of the opinion that the UTA bomb had been made by Abu Ibrahim, the head of the Tripoli-based May 15 movement.

My French contact also confirmed some information I'd gotten earlier, that Ibrahim had sold five suitcase bombs to the Achmed Jibril movement. I'd been told that in January of 1989, a month after the Lockerbie crash, Jibril had gone to Tripoli and met with Abu Nidal, the terrorist. At that meeting, Jibril had complimented himself for putting together the bombing of Pan Am 103.

Because I trusted this source completely, his information backed up my growing belief that something strange was going on in the United States, Great Britain, and France. It seemed that these countries had made a decision to clear Syria and Iran of charges of terrorism by blaming specific Libyans as being responsible for all these crashes. This underscored my need to go to Libya and see what facts I could develop on my own.

On November 23, I left Paris for Libya on a Libyan Arab Airlines jet, and after a most arduous trip—by way of Malta—I arrived at my hotel in Tripoli just before midnight.

The El Mehari was new and sumptuously appointed, which helped to improve my mood, as did the fact that the Libyans obviously wanted to be cooperative. They put me in a presidential suite that overlooked the Mediterranean, and because the Libyan telephone system is so problematic, they had installed a special direct line that enabled me to remain in contact with my bureau in London.

My mood improved even more the next day, a Sunday, for despite the continuing strong wind, the sun was shining. At midday the foreign minister, Ibrahim Beshari, dropped by my room to say hello. We talked briefly, and I spelled out my main objective, which was the chance to interview the two Libyans whom the United States and Scotland had charged with blowing up Pan Am 103.

Beshari said yes, and then, to my surprise, he suggested I also check out the story, promulgated chiefly by the American media, that Libya had both a chemical weapons plant and a terrorist camp.

I told the minister that I had not brought a camera crew with me but that I could get one on very short notice, as it would be good to film my interviews with the two accused men so we could broadcast their information back to the United States.

He agreed immediately, saying that his government would give me access to everything I wanted because it was very unhappy about the indictments and felt it was in a position to prove that they were not true. As soon as he left, I called London and made the arrangements for a producer, a cameraman, and a soundman to come to Libya the next day.

Following a most informative luncheon meeting with Jacques Rouquette, the new French ambassador to Libya, I spent the rest of the day talking with a variety of people, most of whom were top Libyan sources (whom, for the moment, I cannot identify).

I was told a number of interesting things, among them that in January

1989, Achmed Jibril told a top Libyan intelligence official that he was responsible for the bombing of Pan Am 103 (after which conversation he was ejected from Libya); in October 1991, a couple of weeks before the U.S.-Scotland indictment of the two Libyans, the CIA had circulated a document across Europe that charged Libya with being the number-one terrorist nation in the world (its specific charges were that Libya continued to build chemical weapons, continued to host the Abu Nidal movement and to expand his training camp, and that in 1990 Gadhafi had contributed $10 million to terrorist groups); Iran had paid the Jibril movement for the Pan Am bombing, and the money had been deposited in a BCCI account in Abu Dhabi; and, in the past three months there had been three attempts by the Syrians to push the terrorist Carlos the Jackal into Libya (including one time when he arrived loaded down with bags of explosives and weapons). They even showed me the fake Yemeni passport they'd confiscated from the Jackal. I was told that each time, the Libyans refused to let him enter their country.

That evening, Minister Beshari returned to my hotel with the news that his government would give me what I wanted, including the right to film the so-called chemical-weapons plant—and the possibility of filming the (alleged) expanded Abu Nidal terrorist training camp. What's more, he said the two men charged by the United States were on standby for my interview. At some point, my crew arrived from London and came up to my room. Before he left, Beshari promised that both he and Colonel Gadhafi would grant me an on-the-record interview.

By the time everyone left, it was after midnight. I was about to turn in when I noticed the message light on the phone blinking at me. I called down to the desk and learned I had a telex from London. It included the news that Air Malta had issued a statement saying that no unaccompanied bag had been put on the Air Malta flight in question on the night of December 21, 1988, and that Scottish police had confirmed that all the passengers and all the baggage on that flight had been identified.

Over the next five days, my crew and I accomplished a great deal. We also covered a considerable amount of ground.

On the way to interview Al-Megrahi (who, along with Lamen Fhimah, had been described by Acting Attorney General Barr as an "officer and operative of the Libyan Intelligence Agency") we had a little sightseeing, of sorts, to do. We stopped at Gadhafi's former headquarters, which had been bombed in the 1986 U.S. attack on Tripoli. The building was still a shambles, purposely unrepaired, for it now served as a symbol. In fact, a statue had been erected directly in front of the house. It depicted a hand grabbing a plane out of the air, to memorialize Libya's having shot down a United States Air Force plane during the attack.

Inside the house, a huge painting showed bombs—each one marked "USA"—raining down on the streets of Tripoli. So that there would be no possible doubt as to the identity of the attacking force, the painting also included parts of the wings of American planes.

Following our instructions, we went back to the hotel to be ready for an interview with the first of the two indicted Libyans. Once again, it was a case of hurry up and wait. We had to wait for a few hours, but finally we were on our way to the home of Abdel Basset Ali Al-Megrahi.

One of my first questions to Mr. Al-Megrahi produced a surprising answer. I'd asked him if he'd ever worked for Libyan intelligence, and he quickly replied, "No. I was surprised when they told me that. I was surprised because, even in our society here, you have to feel ashamed to work with the intelligence. It's not acceptable to work in this field, you see. So I was actually surprised when they said that."

Mr. Al-Megrahi, who'd worked for Libyan Airlines for almost twenty years, denied all the charges in the indictment and said he could prove that he was in Tripoli on the day the United States and the Scots said he was in Malta planting the bomb. During the course of the two-hour interview, the man never shied away from any of my questions or seemed at all evasive. Nor did he object to the presence of my TV crew. At the end, it was my belief that the man sitting across from me was telling the simple truth. What's more, he said he would *welcome* American and Scottish investigators if they would like to come to Libya and interrogate him.

At six that evening, we left Tripoli for the country, where Beshari was taking us to meet with Colonel Gadhafi. After roughly an hour's drive, we pulled into an area where three commodious tents stood, all with large fires in front of them. Gadhafi, who was dressed in traditional Bedouin clothing, greeted us warmly, and he and I sat down to talk.

Denying all of the charges against his country, the Libyan leader said, "Our feeling is that our country has become the *victim* of terror, particularly from the United States. We are starting to feel a strong persecution complex from America. Libya is becoming a bottle of Pepsi-Cola—they shake it, shake it, until it explodes."

He went on to say that his country had never been a danger to the United States, and, in fact, that they had refused to accept communism, for which the United States should have been grateful. He went on and on, rambling in what was actually a fascinating manner, but then suddenly he returned to the subject at hand.

"On the present crisis, I am angry about the accusations against Libya, but I'm satisfied that things are moving according to law," he said. "I am satisfied that there is a legal way to deal with this. As long as there is life, there is possibility of error, but this must be solved in a civilized way."

I have to say that I was impressed with Gadhafi's moderate tone, which, for the most part, he maintained throughout the entire interview.

"What is happening now is a complete violation of the United Nations. We can go back to the language of reason and dialogue, and that's also explained by the differences between Bush and Reagan. It's not important if we have difference[s] with Bush, it's how we deal [with them]. We are satisfied now that we are dealing with this matter in accordance with international law.

"There were differences between Baker and Schultz. Schultz was irresponsible and insignificant. Baker is [to the] contrary. He is a balanced person, reasonable and responsible. I think we can reach understanding with him and with Bush. As far as the comparison between the attack on Libya by Reagan and Bush's involvement in the Gulf War, there was a difference. Bush went to the world. He got UN resolutions. He got allies. Reagan didn't say he was going to make his own decision. . . ."

The next day, Wednesday, November 27, 1991, we were under the gun. *World News Tonight* wanted a piece for that same evening, so it became essential that we interviw Lamen Khalifa Fhimah, the second indicted Libyan. Unfortunately, we once again got off to a slow start, not leaving the hotel until 3:30 P.M.

At Fhimah's, we were afforded a view of a different slice of Libyan life. Al-Megrahi, our first interviewee, resided in a splendid house, but Fhimah clearly was from a poorer class. He lived in his father's house— not having one of his own—with his wife and five children, all of whom spilled about as we got set up for the interview (to which, for the record, he offered no objection). We sat on cushions, Arab-style, in the living room. A man from the foreign minister's office sat across the room, listening to the interview.

Fhimah denied playing any role whatsoever in the Pan Am case. When I asked him ". . . the most important question first—[were you] involved with placing the suitcase and the bomb on the Air Malta flight?" he answered simply, "Of course not."

His reaction to the indictment? "Surprised. I was surprised to see news about myself, my picture appearing in the media. I don't deserve this, but my name has been mentioned for sure."

Again, the interview went on for several hours, and again, I had the distinct feeling I was hearing the truth.

On our way back to the hotel, we stopped in front of Gadhafi's bombed-out former headquarters for a stand-up shot, with the building and the statue as background. While we were waiting for Foreign Minister Beshari to show up, we heard the news that the United States and the United Kingdom had put out a statement calling on Libya—which had no extradition treaty with either of those Western countries—to send the two suspects out of the country, to pay compensation to the families of the victims, and to stop terrorism.

Thus primed, Foreign Minister Beshari gave me a spirited interview. He made it quite clear that he did not accept the warning of the United States and Great Britain and said that it was unfair to accuse a country of a crime without a trial and before the investigation had been concluded.

It was a good interview, and we worked long into the night to get it edited and ready for New York. We almost failed to get it on the satellite because of some technical foul-ups, but finally we made it—with ten minutes to go before airtime.

It was a good solid piece, one that raised hackles in just the places I thought it would.

The next two days were spent in checking out and filming the so-called chemical-warfare plant and terrorist training camp. The former turned out to be a plant that may have had some connection with chemicals, but not, apparently, chemical weapons. (It lacked a couple of specific items I'd been coached to look for, a decontamination section and a glass-enclosed area.) We had some trouble doing the interview with the men who ran the plant because our soundman's equipment wouldn't work. We finally figured out it was because of the radar that surrounded the plant; the Libyans were convinced that if the American planes ever returned, that plant would be a prime target.

That night, back in my hotel in Tripoli, I read the Libyans' response to the communiqué of the day before from Great Britain and the United States. It stated that Libya was opposed to all types of terrorism, but especially to those aimed at innocent civilians. Describing the document as "not amicable," it added that the government had finally received the text of the indictment against the two Libyan citizens and would deal with it in "a positive and constructive" manner. It promised a serious and thorough investigation.

On Friday, November 29, we left the hotel in the early afternoon for a two-hour drive that brought us to a good-sized camp in the mountains.

Instead of a bunch of fledgling terrorists, however, we saw a refugee camp—for Palestinians coming from Lebanon. There appeared to be about 60 families, with perhaps 150 children. A spirited volleyball game was taking place in a square. There were quite a few houses, and we could make out a medical clinic and a kindergarten. Through the doorway of one building, we could see row upon row of sewing machines. Another building housed a mini-supermarket. After we'd been fed a nice lunch, we were encouraged to walk around and look at anything we wanted to. With no objections from our hosts, we hooked up our special longitude-latitude measuring machine, which would prove this was the same village or camp that the CIA had insisted was a terrorist training site.

After almost three hours, we'd seen what we needed to see, and so we headed back to Tripoli. In the van, we all agreed we had just had a travel experience that was probably unique.

That night, the foreign minister came by to say farewell. He, too, was leaving the next morning. His destination was China. I didn't come right out and ask him, but I figured he was going to try to convince the Chinese—who are permanent members of the UN Security Council—to block a Security Council vote sanctioning Libya for its alleged participation in the Pan Am 103 disaster.

The next morning, Saturday, we left Libya, and as the plane lifted off the tarmac, I could not help but breathe a quiet sigh of relief.

During the Q and A session at the November 1991 press conference in Washington at which the United States and the United Kingdom announced the indictment of the two Libyans, Assistant U.S. Attorney General Robert Mueller was asked if there was any evidence linking Syria and Iran to the bombing. He replied, "We have no evidence linking Syria to this bombing [and] no evidence linking the PFLP-GC to this bombing."

Clearly, both the United States and the United Kingdom were putting all their eggs in the Libyan basket.

As a result, I suspected they weren't going to be too happy when ABC's *World News Tonight* with Peter Jennings used part of my interview with one of the Libyans on November 27, 1991. It took a while for them to decide just how to react, but when they did, it was clear I was right. They were *definitely* not happy.

On March 7, 1992, the *New York Times* ran this headline: BRITAIN TELLS ABC TO GIVE UP TAPES, then, in smaller type: "Seeks Material on 2 Libyans Accused in Pan Am Blast." The first paragraph read: "British anti-terrorist police officers investigating the 1988 bombing of a Pan American World Airways jumbo jet over Lockerbie, Scotland have demanded that ABC News and its senior European editor, Pierre Salinger, hand over tapes and notes of interviews with two prime Libyan suspects. . . . ABC and Mr. Salinger said they would resist the demand [which came in the form of a subpoena]. . . ."

Undoubtedly well aware of how it looked for a British court to be subpoenaing the work product of an American journalist, the British inspector who handed me the document told the reporter it was "called a 'production order.' " Well, they could call it whatever they pleased, but I knew what it was. It was a shortcut to extradition of the two Libyans, whom neither the United States nor the United Kingdom had bothered to interview, despite having been invited to do so by the Libyan government. My point in resisting the subpoena was that if I had interviewed the two suspects, why couldn't they?

It took me only a few days to discover that the CIA and other U.S. authorities had asked the British government to do this. The Americans knew that if they'd tried to get these files by bringing suit in the United States, they'd have been blocked. However, knowing there was no First Amendment in the United Kingdom, they got the Brits to do the job for them. Hardly cricket, in my opinion.

We resisted, legally, and, in fact, the case went all the way up to the British high court before we lost. I was very frustrated by this development, but I could see there was no way we could win this case.

After we had turned over the tapes, Roone Arledge released the following statement:

> While we regret that the court has ordered ABC News to turn over the interview tapes to the British government, we are pleased the Court has upheld our position in principle and has required the government to justify such orders in the future. Because the order does not require ABC News to reveal any confidential sources, we have decided not to appeal the court decision. ABC will comply with the order and turn over the interview tapes out of respect for the court. Since we are compelled to make the tapes public by releasing them to the government, we believe it appropriate to make the entirety of both interviews available to news organizations.

I felt, and still do, that a poor decision had been reached. It is not proper journalistic practice to give the police any film footage that hasn't been shown to the public. The final decision, however, was not mine. When other journalists called for my reaction, I said only that I was "disappointed." In truth, I was mad as hell. That was no way to end what had been a great story.

Oops, I spoke too soon. While that was—perhaps—the end of my participation in the story, it turns out not to have been the end of the story itself. In late March 1995, as my editor was threatening to rip these final pages out of my computer so he could send the manuscript to production, the FBI announced a $4 million reward for the capture and arrest of Ali-Megrahi and Fhimah, whom it continues to identify as "two Libyan intelligence officers."

The FBI, which says the reward is the highest ever offered in a terrorism case, also took the step of placing the two men on its Ten Most Wanted list. And, in a sign of the times, it placed information on the pair on the Internet: "heroes@clark. net."

Clearly, the United States is worried about the possibility of Libya getting a seat on the United Nations Security Council, which it is set to do next year under the regular rotation system among Arab and African countries. If this happens, it would be the first time a country was seated on the council while under UN sanctions. Hence the new U.S. campaign, of which this reward is a significant part.

Nonetheless, as the French would say, the more things change, the more they stay the same. Colonel Gadhafi continues to offer that the two men (who are apparently still in Libya) go before an international tribunal at The Hague. The United States and Scotland, however, still insist that the pair be tried in one of those two countries.

Who knows, maybe I'm not finished with this story yet. Stay tuned.

EPILOGUE

MY DECISION TO leave ABC was based on frustration, not anger. By the end of 1992, the amount of time I was being given to cover important international stories had declined. There had been years when I'd be on the air eighty times on different ABC shows, but by the early 1990s, those numbers had declined all the way to the twenties. At that point, I'd been in London for four years, and I was getting antsy. I may have been sixty-seven, but I had not slowed down. (Thanks to my wife, Poppy, I finally had a wonderful marriage, which is my prescription for a happy life.)

Despite my growing frustration with the network, I wanted to cap my career as a television journalist by returning to the United States as Washington bureau chief of ABC News. When Bill Clinton was elected President, I thought such a move would make almost perfect sense.

Even though I had never met President Clinton, my Democratic contacts were strong, and I felt I could be very helpful to ABC in that post. Top ABC people in Washington, such as Ted Koppel and Sam Donaldson, strongly supported the idea that I take over the Washington bureau. But the ABC leadership in New York opposed the plan—even though I'd offered to reduce my salary in order to get the post—and I began to sense some none-too-subtle nudges toward retirement.

Early in 1993, I had lunch in London with Kirby Jones, an old friend from various Democratic wars, and especially the McGovern campaign in 1972. For years, Kirby had worked for the World Bank, but just six months before, he had left them to go with Burson-Marsteller, the world's largest public-relations company. He said that if I had any notions about switching careers, he would strongly suggest I join his firm, which, he said, had a "serious need" for a Democrat in their leadership. Kirby said he'd be happy to set up a meeting.

Somewhat to my own surprise, I found the idea fascinating. A couple of weeks later, I flew to New York, where B-M has its headquarters, to talk with company executives. We came to an immediate accord, and I agreed to begin working for Burson-Marsteller at the beginning of September 1993. The B-M people wanted me to work out of New York City, but I felt it would be better for everyone concerned if I made Washington my base. They finally agreed.

When the Air France jet touched down at Dulles airport on August 5, 1993, I knew it was an historic day. Waiting to meet Poppy and me were my daughter, Suzanne, and her nine-year-old boys, my twin grandsons, Justin and Joshua. While the boys and their mother had made a number of trips to visit us in Europe—my daughter worked for Air France—it was a wonderful feeling to know that we would now see them often and easily. Another big plus was that I would be much closer to my mother, happily still with us at age ninety-seven, out in California. At the time of my return, I hadn't seen her in four years, the longest period of separation since my service in World War II!

Our first major decision was where to live. We settled into the St. James. Less than a mile from the White House, it's an excellent small hotel that leases suites. That was the base from which we began our search for a house to buy. It took Nicole—excuse me, Poppy—and me but five days to find a wonderful house in Georgetown that just happened to be on O Street, only a few blocks from where I'd lived in 1957.

One of the many pluses of this convenient location was that a number of friends lived nearby. In fact, right across the street was Lloyd Cutler, a founding partner of Wilmer, Cutler and Pickering, one of Washington's finest law firms, and at that time President Clinton's in–White House legal adviser. Lloyd was married to another old friend, Polly Kraft, the widow of the famous correspondent Joseph Kraft. Also across O Street were Rowland and Kay Evans (Rowland having been the Evans in Evans and Novak), and a few blocks away on 29th Street lived two rather newer friends, Smith and Elizabeth Frawley Bagley. On visits back to the United States in recent years, we'd been guests in their homes in both Washington and Nantucket. Smith had been a major contributor to the Democratic party for many years. (In 1993, President Clinton acknowledged this by naming Elizabeth, who'd worked in the State Department during the Carter years and later became a lawyer, U.S. ambassador to Portugal.)

We'd been back but two weeks when Barbara Gamarekian, who'd worked for me at the White House, gave us a garden party. She invited scores of friends from the old days, one of whom was Sue Voegelsinger, another staff person from the office of the White House press secretary. It definitely felt like old home week in Washington.

Not having lived here since 1965—when I lost my briefly held Senate seat—I of course noticed many changes. Perhaps most noticeable, on the physical side, was the great number of new buildings—especially the look-alike office buildings—that lined the K, L, and M Street corridors. Two of my favorite restaurants were still in business, the Jockey Club and Duke Ziebert's (but the latter would close in 1994) and new places like Sam and Harry's served wonderful food. On the one hand, I found it easier to get good cigars, but on the other had to shop around a bit before discovering the best places to buy my beloved Bordeaux wines (to be on the safe side, I kept up my membership in a wine-buying club in London).

One huge change had to do with the safety of the streets in Washington, and even in Georgetown. We were constantly being warned about the vast increase in violent crime. Another very visible change from the 1960s was the large number of homeless people wandering the streets and stooped in doorways, begging for spare change. That situation simply did not exist when I used to live in Washington.

Fortunately, while the streets of Georgetown may not have been as safe as they once were, they were still the streets of Georgetown. And they had changed very little, if at all. What made them, and life in general, so enjoyable was that we had brought our dogs back with us from Europe! Champ and Hillary (a female born just after President Clinton's election) are Cavalier King Charles spaniels, that marvelous combination of spaniel and Pekingese that features the best traits of both breeds.

As I walk the picturesque streets of Georgetown, I can sense Champ's exhilaration. When we first moved to London, the poor dog had to spend six months in what I called prison—the British call it quarantine, claiming it is a precaution against rabies. In fact, since it only takes two weeks to find out if a dog has rabies, this quarantine business is in reality a huge moneymaking operation (the word *scam* comes to mind). The dogs like Washington, but the place they absolutely love is Nantucket, where we have spent our vacations for the better part of the past decade (my wife wisely suggested this idea as a kind of preview for a possible move back to the States; as a result, we have a whole group of friends we see up there every summer).

On the professional level, the biggest and most obvious change in Washington in the years since I'd last lived here is in the relationship between the government and the media in general and between the media and the White House in particular. In the Kennedy years, there was—and I know this is going to sound odd in 1995—something very close to *respect* between the media and the White House. Today, the first word that comes to my mind, and, I would wager, to the minds of most people, is *confrontation*. Just to pick one example out of many, the way the media pounded the White House over the Whitewater scandal would never have happened in the early 1960s.

I found it disconcerting to see how rapidly the power of American political leaders was crumbling away. Clearly, there is a rising frustration in this country regarding politics and politicians. One of the results of this frustration is the sharp increase in the number of politicians who are thrown out of office at each new election—and there's a concomitant rise in the number of officeholders who resign rather than face these angry voters in a reelection bid.

Finally, there's the considerable number of competent, capable, and highly intelligent nationally known politicians who have decided not to run for the highest office in the land because they do not want to be forced to run the professional and personal gauntlet the system now requires them to run. As I write this, three such men—Republicans Richard Cheney, Jack Kemp, and former Vice President Dan Quayle—have announced their *dis*intention to run for the presidency in 1996.

I shudder to think how we would have handled such no-holds-barred inquiries in the 1960 campaign. Consider this letter, which I wrote four years ago.

Mr. Jacques Lesourne
Director, Le Monde
15 Rue Falguiere
75001 Paris cedex 15
FRANCE

6/11/91

Dear Mr. Lesourne,
I have just returned to London and discovered Le Monde of Friday 25th October 1991. I was profoundly shocked when I read your page 1 article on John Kennedy. For a newspaper of the calibre of Le Monde, for a journalist with the reputation of Jacques Amalric, to publish such an article means that Le Monde has joined the rubbish press.
First, the word myth is wrong. This is a word that has been developed by the press, not by those who worked with President

Kennedy. Kennedy's presidency should be measured by what he accomplished not by his private activities. He is a man who saved the world from nuclear war. He is a man who launched the West into space. He is a man who started to break down the racial barriers in the United States. He is a man who was trusted by the American people and created a climate of national feeling about the government and its responsibilities that has disappeared twenty years later. That is not to say that he did not commit errors. It was obviously a mistake to accept a covert operation handed to him by the previous administration to try to overcome Fidel Castro, which resulted in the disastrous Bay of Pigs.

As to his private life, he may very well have had some extra women friends (although I have no personal knowledge of this) but this does not affect his presidential career. To print information put out by Judith Exner is the most disastrous mistake. A number of journalists I know have met Judith Exner and investigated her allegations and come to the conclusion that most of them are false. Judith Exner's policy is the following: when she runs out of money she finds another newspaper which is willing to pay her substantially for more information about John Kennedy. She has been carrying on this activity since the mid-1970's. . . .

I know that French journalism has not been married to investigative journalism. If it was they would make their own investigations of charges against world leaders and not print someone else's unverified information, even claiming that the FBI statements back up none of Judith Exner's charges. Do not forget that the head of the FBI during the Kennedy administration was J. Edgar Hoover, who made substantial false efforts to destroy the presidential image. I have personal proof of this since Mr. Hoover leaked information about me which was totally false.

I have always admired Le Monde and I read it daily even though I no longer live in France. I never believed that I would read something like this in Le Monde with its historic reputation of honest journalism.

Sincerely yours, Pierre Salinger

I include this letter in these memoirs for two reasons. One is to make the point that even though it was written relatively recently, it already sounds almost quaint, so greatly and so quickly have things changed. The second reason is so I might address, and answer, what is probably the question I get asked most often about John F. Kennedy, the man.

That letter to *Le Monde* is one of the few times I have addressed the issue of JFK's marital infidelities in a public venue. I chose not to do so for a number of reasons, not the least of which was that his wife and his mother were still alive.

My answer to *the* question—"Did you know while you were in the White House that the President was having affairs?"—has always been a qualified no. The only difference between my answer through the years and my answer now is that I have never before explained the qualification. I'm not trying to be cute. What I mean is this: I never knew of a single specific incident of the President having sex with a specific woman while I worked in the White House.

That does not mean I happened to believe that JFK was a totally faithful husband. I knew, in general, that before his marriage to Jackie he had been what used to be called "a ladies' man." (And it should be remembered that he did not get married until he was thirty-six years old.) I also knew there were rumors making the rounds in the White House, just as they do in any other office, especially one in which great power is concentrated. I simply did not consider it any of my business, and, unlike today's press secretaries, I did not have to deal with direct questions on the subject. (The one time I did, as I may have already mentioned, I was able to deflect the query by telling the reporter that I didn't see where President Kennedy would have had the *time*—a dodge one would never get away with today. As for the possibility of being asked about "Bimbo eruptions," that is simply beyond my ken.)

Another part of the equation is that it had been a long time since I had been an altar boy myself. (It can generally be assumed that a man who has married four times has had his share of affairs.) I remember one weekend during the Kennedy years when JFK walked into my office while a lady friend was visiting me. I introduced her to the President, and he was his usual charming self. Several hours later, aboard *Air Force One* on the way to Hyannis Port for a working weekend, he said, "Where's that girl you were with?" I said she was back in Washington, to which he replied, "Call her and have her come up." I did. She flew up on a commercial airline, and we spent the weekend (when I was not with the President) in a hotel on the Cape.

My friend Al Bayer reminded me recently of the time when we were all in Los Angeles with the President, who had to address a fund-raising dinner. Bayer and I, along with Peter Lawford, JFK's brother-in-law, were having a drink with the President in his hotel suite prior to going out for a night on the town. I can still see the look of longing (almost to the point of envy) that crossed the President's face when we said our good-byes. As I have said thousands and thousands of times, John Kennedy was *real.* We do neither him nor his memory any favor by remembering him as some kind of plaster saint.

That said, let me make a few observations about JFK and the current occupant of the White House, William Jefferson Clinton. Much has been made of Clinton's "resemblance" to Kennedy. Certainly Bill Clinton as a young man and as an adult was and is a great admirer of the late President. Many people saw him as a new Kennedy. Certainly they were both new-generation Presidents, and certainly they were both charismatic individuals, but there are also many differences, some of which are extremely important and meaningful.

For one thing, Kennedy and Clinton inherited different Americas. The nation JFK took charge of was not in economic hot water—no big budget deficit, no strong feeling about the need to restructure health care, to pick but two examples. Bill Clinton inherited an America just emerging from the Cold War, and thus he had to operate, perhaps sooner than he would have liked, in serious foreign policy areas. (He'd have been better off with some of these situations, such as Bosnia, if his predecessor had handled things more intelligently.)

And then, in 1994, came the November revolution and the takeover of congressional power by the opposition party.

My point is simply that there is not much to be gained by comparing the two administrations on an evaluative basis. That does not mean that the Clinton administration could not improve its image and its effectiveness by studying how we did things in the Kennedy era. The Clintons would do well to recapture the sense of Washington as a giant social city, with the White House as its base, as it was not just with the Kennedys but with *all* the presidencies since then—Johnson, Nixon, Ford, Carter, Reagan, and Bush. It is time for the people in the White House to understand the Washington mentality.

There is one more thing I want to talk about before ending this book. I've been involved in global work for decades, and I am stunned at how badly all nations are dealing with the world today. The central point is the disintegration of history. Whole generations have forgotten history. Even many of today's world leaders have forgotten history. And believe me, as one who has seen a number of international crises firsthand, they cannot be handled without an understanding of history.

After the Gulf War, President Bush put out a statement proclaiming that we had moved to what he called a "new world order." How wrong he was. We are in a new world *dis*order, and a lot of that disorder is linked to the fact that leaders lack an understanding—or even a sense—of history in dealing with significant problems.

Probably the most important example of these mistakes was the Western world's reaction to the end of the Cold War. Everybody cheered! "We have gotten rid of communism!" I can understand that reaction. But those same people should also have understood and spoken out on other issues. They should have understood that so many things had been frozen in time in these Communist dictatorships that when they became unfrozen, they would lead to bloody wars among ethnic groups.

As I wrote earlier in this book, when Marshal Tito died in Yugoslavia, I knew that the nation was going to fall apart, and it did. But the current war in the former Yugoslavia could have been averted if the West had known and remembered its history.

The decision on the part of the European community and the United States to go forward and recognize so rapidly the sovereignty of Croatia, Slovenia, and Bosnia-Herzegovina was a desperate mistake. I am not arguing against their sovereignty, but it was clear that when a nation with that many different ethnic groups breaks up, it is important to have a dialogue with all the different groups before sovereignty is recognized.

What we are now seeing in Russia is of similar importance. When the Soviet Union broke up, it lost its central control of all the different republics and of all the different ethnic groups, as well. There have already been wars—bloody, violent wars—in Azerbaijan, Armenia, Georgia, and Chechnya. In addition, there are growing struggles in the southern Muslim republics, as well as the infiltration of Iranian Islamic fundamentalists. We are likely to see more wars in that part of the world.

The fact is that despite all this violence, we still haven't gotten rid of communism, as was the prediction when the Cold War ended. While Communists are changing their party names to other names, they are still dominant all throughout the Eastern bloc countries and the former Soviet Union. And, of course, we are still seeing communism continuing in countries such as North Korea, China, and Cuba.

More than that, the end of the Cold War had an important impact on the relationship between the European community and the United States. When we got to the end of World War II, the United States acted with great intelligence, creating the Marshall Plan, the Atlantic Alliance, and NATO. During the Cold War, the United States became the backbone of European security as the danger of attacks into Western Europe from the East continued. Because the United States was the backbone, the relationship between it and Europe was strong. But when the Cold War came to an end, many people reacted in a wrong and dangerous way. Many Europeans said, "We have no enemy in the East anymore. So we no longer need the United States." And many people in the United States said, "With the collapse of communism in the Eastern bloc and in the former Soviet Union, why do we have to keep troops in Europe?" The way the United States reacted to the start of the war in Bosnia-Herzegovina was an important example of this mistake.

As we look around the world, there are, of course, many other disorders. The EEC is weakening, and the chances of the Maastricht agreement coming into its plan in the twentieth century appears less and less possible. There is a disintegration of political parties in Europe, a continuing high unemployment rate that deeply frustrates the populations, and the difficult problem of immigration, which has created neo-Nazi parties throughout Europe.

The Middle East is fragile, with the rise of Islamic fundamentalism spurred by the Gulf War. The breakdown of peace talks between Israel and its Arab neighbors, including the Palestinians, could also have dramatic consequences.

China has to be looked at seriously, particularly politically. An intelligent transition from communism to democracy might keep the country together. But the breakup of the central Communist government (something the whole world would like to see happen) could move China into the same situation as the former Soviet Union and the former Yugoslavia. There are many areas of China today that would like to become independent republics. It is important to see the reintegration of North and South Korea, to mention another potential danger.

In South Africa, there has been a move toward a real democracy, but there is still a volatile problem to solve. The dominant black community is poor, and their lives must be changed as rapidly as possible in order to avoid the kind of frustration that would lead to violence.

I am not writing this as a pessimist, but these are the facts. The world needs to look at these problems in the context of history if we are going to have stability in the twenty-first century. And stabilizing the world should be at the top of every leader's agenda. Economically, we are doing much better—the free-trade agreements arrived at in the last few years are having an enormous impact—but economics alone cannot shape the world that is to be.

By the time this book appears, I will have been back in the United States and back in Washington for more than two years. Of course, there is some frustration about how politics and the media are operating in this country. Still, personally, I am extremely happy—I am happy with my wife and my grown children and their children (and my wife's grown children and their children) and I am happy with my work, which gives me the opportunity to travel around the world and try to convince our clients—both corporations and countries—to take a serious look at how this new world disorder can affect them.

I am also happy about being able to see so many old friends and to make new ones. Best of all, in 1994, at a party in California I gave for my mother, I reconciled with my brother George. Over the years, we'd had so many bad moments that I had written him off. But George, once he saw that I was probably back in the United States for good, refused to accept the status quo and called me. His offering, an olive branch, was what I needed. Today, we are back in contact, as brothers should be, especially brothers with so much shared history.

I've had at least my share of tragedy, but I feel I have had far more than my share of happiness. And Lord knows, at the very least I can say that I've seen a lot. Perhaps those people were right years ago when they nicknamed me Lucky Pierre.

INDEX